Contemporary Political Theory

Series Editor
Ian Shapiro

Editorial Board
Russell Hardin   Stephen Holmes   Jeffrey Isaac
John Keane   Elizabeth Kiss   Susan Okin
Phillipe Van Parijs   Philip Pettit

As the twenty-first century begins, major new political challenges have arisen at the same time as some of the most enduring dilemmas of political association remain unresolved. The collapse of communism and the end of the Cold War reflect a victory for democratic and liberal values, yet in many of the Western countries that nurtured those values there are severe problems of urban decay, class and racial conflict, and failing political legitimacy. Enduring global injustice and inequality seem compounded by environmental problems, disease, the oppression of women, racial, ethnic, and religious minorities, and the relentless growth of the world's population. In such circumstances, the need for creative thinking about the fundamentals of human political association is manifest. This new series in contemporary political theory is needed to foster such systematic normative reflection.

The series proceeds in the belief that the time is ripe for a reassertion of the importance of problem-driven political theory. It is concerned, that is, with works that are motivated by the impulse to understand, think critically about, and address the problems in the world, rather than issues that are thrown up primarily in academic debate. Books in the series may be interdisciplinary in character, ranging over issues conventionally dealt with in philosophy, law, history, and the human sciences. The range of materials and the methods of proceeding should be dictated by the problem at hand, not the conventional debates or disciplinary divisions of academia.

Other books in the series

Ian Shapiro and Casiano Hacker-Cordón (eds.)
Democracy's Value

Ian Shapiro and Casiano Hacker-Cordón (eds.)
Democracy's Edges

Brooke A. Ackerly
Political Theory and Feminist Social Criticism

Clarissa Rile Hayward
De-Facing Power

John Kane
The Politics of Moral Capital

Multicultural Jurisdictions
Cultural Differences and Women's Rights

Is it possible for the state simultaneously to respect deep cultural differences and to protect the hard-won citizenship rights of vulnerable group members, in particular women? This book argues that this is not only theoretically needed, but also institutionally feasible. Shachar's fresh approach proceeds from an acknowledgment of the potentially negative effects of well-intentioned multicultural accommodation, which often forces the most vulnerable constituents of cultural groups into an impossible choice: either an allegiance to their culture, or an exercise of their rights. Rejecting prevalent normative and legal solutions to this "paradox of multicultural vulnerability," *Multicultural Jurisdictions* develops a powerful argument for enhancing the jurisdictional autonomy of religious and cultural minorities while at the same time providing viable legal-institutional solutions to the problem of sanctioned intra-group rights violation. This new "joint governance" approach is guided by an ambitiously innovative principle: one that strives for the reduction of injustice between minority groups and the wider society, together with the enhancement of justice within them. Shachar applies this new approach to contested social arenas, such as family law, immigration policy, and criminal justice. She shows how individuals who view themselves as simultaneously belonging to more than one membership community and subject to more than one legal authority can be empowered by their multiple affiliations. Unique in its interdisciplinary and comparative approach, this book makes a timely intervention in current multiculturalist and feminist debates by offering an in-depth exploration of practical legal-institutional solutions to vital normative dilemmas that beset diverse societies around the globe. It will interest students of political and social theory, law, religion, institutional design, as well as cultural and gender studies.

AYELET SHACHAR is Assistant Professor of Law in the Faculty of Law, University of Toronto. She is also currently a Member at the Institute for Advanced Study, Princeton. She has written extensively on issues of contemporary political theory, group rights, and gender equality. Her most recent publications appear in the *Journal of Political Philosophy*, *Political Theory*, and the *Harvard Civil Rights–Civil Liberties Law Review*. She has also contributed to several edited volumes, including *Multicultural Questions* (1999); *Citizenship in Diverse Societies* (2000); and *From Migrants to Citizens* (2000).

Multicultural Jurisdictions

Cultural Differences and Women's Rights

Ayelet Shachar

CAMBRIDGE
UNIVERSITY PRESS

PUBLISHED BY THE PRESS SYNDICATE OF THE UNIVERSITY OF CAMBRIDGE
The Pitt Building, Trumpington Street, Cambridge, United Kingdom

CAMBRIDGE UNIVERSITY PRESS
The Edinburgh Building, Cambridge CB2 2RU, UK
40 West 20th Street, New York, NY 10011-4211, USA
10 Stamford Road, Oakleigh, VIC 3166, Australia
Ruiz de Alarcón 13, 28014 Madrid, Spain
Dock House, The Waterfront, Cape Town 8001, South Africa

http://www.cambridge.org

First published 2001

Printed in the United Kingdom at the University Press, Cambridge

Typeface Plantin MT 10/13 pt   *System* QuarkXPress™ [SE]

A catalogue record for this book is available from the British Library

Library of Congress Cataloguing in Publication data

Shachar, Ayelet, 1966–
    Multicultural jurisdictions: cultural differences and women's rights / Ayelet Shachar.
        p. cm. – (Contemporary political theory)
    Includes bibliographical references and index.
    ISBN 0 521 77209 5 (hardback) – ISBN 0 521 77674 0 (paperback)
    1. Women – Legal status, laws, etc.   2. Multiculturalism – Law and legislation.   I. Title.
II. Series.
K644.S53   2001
346'.01'34–dc21   00-054715   CIP

ISBN 0 521 77209 5 hardback
ISBN 0 521 77674 0 paperback

Two roads diverged in a yellow wood,
And sorry I could not travel both
And be one traveler, long I stood
And looked down one as far as I could
To where it bent in the undergrowth;
Then took the other, as just as fair,
And having perhaps the better claim,
Because it was grassy and wanted wear;
Though as for that the passing there
Had worn them really about the same,

And both that morning equally lay
In leaves no step had trodden black.
On, I kept the first for another day!
Yet knowing how way leads on to way,
I doubted if I should ever come back.

I shall be telling this with a sigh
Somewhere ages and ages hence:
Two roads diverged in a wood, and I –
I took the one less traveled by,
And that has made all the difference.

Robert Frost, "The Road Not Taken"

Contents

Preface

Over the past few years while this book was taking shape, I have been living, studying, teaching, and moving between two countries: the United States and Canada. However, the true origins of this book date back to my childhood in Israel, particularly in the city of Jerusalem. For anyone skeptical about the value of cultural and religious diversity, or the need for the protection of individual rights, a quick visit to this multi-faith, multi-ethnic, and multi-national city soon dispels all grounds for such doubt. Schoolgirls wearing the hijab, the Muezzin's calls for prayer in the mosque, the bells of the Church of the Holy Sepulchre, the personal law tribunals of various Christian sects, the ancient ruins of the City of David, and debates over women's prayers at the Western Wall – these disparate sounds and images combine to form the richly complex cultural mosaic known as Jerusalem. Gender tensions and collective identity markers are part of everyday life here, but they are prevalent in many other parts of the world as well.

The first half of this study explores these complex relationships and critically assesses the potentially negative internal effects of well-meaning policies of multicultural accommodation. It is my belief that we cannot comprehend the ways to resolve these tensions (let alone begin to imagine them), if we do not step back and re-evaluate the inevitable interaction that has taken place between minority groups and the state ever since the inception of modern citizenship. With a view to explaining the dynamic, I address three types of group responses to assimilation pressures, with special attention to the third or "reactive culturalist" pattern of response.

I then examine how different countries have attempted to face the challenge of respecting cultural diversity and protecting individual rights. Since all current legal and theoretical models fall somewhat short of this challenge, the second half of the book offers an analysis of different institutional designs which seek a new and better way of accommodating difference: a reduction of inequality *between* minority groups and the wider society, as well as an enhancement of equality *within* them. In the final chapters of the book, I translate this normative commitment into a concrete set of principles underlying a new approach towards dividing and sharing authority in diverse societies, which I call *joint governance*. This approach takes as its starting point the assumption that some individuals belong to more than one community, and are loyal to more than one source of legal authority. Joint governance thus applies to the specific problem of sanctioned and systemic intra-group violations of group members' rights. But it also speaks to a broader set of contemporary theoretical and institutional challenges concerning the changing role and authority of the state, its relation to competing sources of jursidiction from "above" and "below" the national level, and the emergence of new modes of governance.

Many people have contributed to the development of the ideas expressed in this work. Several of the arguments were developed through the process of writing my Yale doctoral dissertion. I was fortunate at that time to have benefited from the guidance and advice of Jack Balkin, Bruce Ackerman, and Reva Siegel, at Yale Law School. I am thankful for the opportunity that they gave me to think through these issues, and for their confidence all through the earliest and most tentative stages of that project. I also want to single out two of my teachers, Menachem Mautner and Joseph Weiler, in thanks for their enduring faith and uncompromising expectations.

Several individuals deserve special mention because they have influenced and inspired both my thinking and my writing. I am indebted to Ian Shapiro for his encouragement and trust. He believed in this project and gave it a chance long before it deserved such confidence. Rainer Bauböck provided detailed and insightful comments on an earlier version of this manuscript, which culminated in many improvements to the fifth and sixth chapters of this book. Bob Goodin engaged in a lively dialogue with me on several of the issues defined here when they were still evolving out of embryo; I am grateful for his ongoing support and advice. Finally, I wish to express my special thanks to Will Kymlicka. His inimitably articulate and elegant defense of multicultural accommodation first piqued my interest in this subject, and his pertinent and always graceful critiques have continued to enrich my engagement with the complex dilemmas addressed here.

But most of all, I owe my greatest debt of gratitude to Ran Hirschl, whose intellectual and critical acumen can be read like a fingerprint across the face of this text. Literally every idea in this book has grown out of our many hours of discussion together.

Other friends and colleagues who have provided helpful commentary on the manuscript (or earlier versions of some of its chapters) include Rosalie Abella, Seyla Benhabib, Joe Carens, Bruce Chapman, Nancy Cott, Rob Howse, Jay Katz, Karen Knop, Candran Kukathas, Patrick

Macklem, Martha Minow, Mayo Moran, Ed Morgan, Jenny Nedelsky, Wayne Norman, Anne Phillips, Robert Post, Carol Rose, Vicky Schulz, Yuli Tamir, Philippe Van Parijs, Michael Walzer, Lorraine Weinrib, Melissa Williams, Steve Wizner, and Iris Young. I was fortunate to receive comments on this manuscript (just before it went into print) from Brian Barry, Jacob Levy, and Bhikhu Parekh, my co-participants in a panel entitled "Authors as Critics: Multiculturalism in Political Theory," which was held at the American Political Science Association Meeting in Washington DC in summer 2000.

I also want to thank John Haslam at Cambridge University Press for his enthusiastic support of this project; Catherine Frost for judiciously assisting me in the decision of what to keep and what to drop from the manuscript based on her careful reading of several versions of this work; Samina Uddin for meticulously verifying the accuracy of each and every source in the bibliography; Dan Friedman for contributing his good judgment and sense of humor to the process of preparing this book for submission; and Maya Johnson for putting the final touches to the text, which lent some music to my voice.

While writing this book, I have been supported by a Fulbright Scholarship, the Lillian Goldman Scholarship for the Study of Women's Rights at Yale Law School, the W. M. Keck Fellowship in Legal Ethics and Professional Culture, the Cecil A. Wright Foundation for Legal Scholarship at the University of Toronto Faculty of Law, and a Member-in-Residence Fellowship at the Institute for Advanced Study, Princeton.

My work is inevitably influenced by the fact of my own personal history, which includes several simultaneous affiliations and movements between different cultural, national, and territorial borderlines. I owe this special range of experiences to my mother and father, Tmima and Arie Shachar, whose passion for wisdom and openness to adventure have spurred so many of my own inter-cultural travels. I thank them, as well as Naomi Ernst-Hirschl, Erez Shachar, and Tamar Shachar, for all their love and support.

I dedicate this book to the memory of my grandmothers, Esther-Etka Stock and Leah Schwartz. Unlike myself, they were forced to migrate from their home countries. Neither of them tended to talk much about the terrors that they had known while fleeing Europe, and only rarely did they permit any reminiscences of those whom they had lost there to become an aching, living memory. But their pain was often too heavy to conceal. We may now live in a new world order, but the dignity of individuals and of cultural minorities which were more than once brutally violated in the past may yet again stand to become perilously erased. It is with a view towards protecting the fragile structures of peaceful coexistence and establishing a just apportionment of the costs associated with preserving distinct cultural and religious identities, while still allowing women and other historically vulnerable persons a fair and full entitlement to certain basic freedoms, that I have written this book.

I am grateful to the following journals and publishers for permission to print in modified form several of the themes presented here: "Group Identity and Women's Rights in Family Law: the Perils of Multicultural Accommodation," *Journal of Political Philosophy*, vol. 6, no. 3, 1998, pp. 285–305, copyright by Blackwell Publishers; "On Citizenship and Multicultural Vulnerability," *Political Theory*, vol. 28, no. 1, 2000, pp. 64–89, copyright by Sage Publications; "The Puzzle of Interlocking Power Hierarchies: Sharing the Pieces of Jurisdictional Authority," *Harvard Civil Rights–Civil Liberties Law Review*, vol. 35, no. 2, 2000, pp. 385–426, copyright by the President and Fellows of Harvard College; "Should Church and State be Joined at the Altar? Women's Rights and the Multicultural Dilemma," *Citizenship in Diverse Societies*, edited by Will Kymlicka and Wayne Norman, Oxford University Press, 2000, pp. 199–233. Robert Frost's poem "The Road Not Taken" is reprinted from *The Poetry of Robert Frost*, edited by Edward Connery Lathem, copyright and permission by Henry Holt and Company.

1 Introduction

From Canada to India, from Israel to the United States, the problem of multicultural accommodation is high on the global political agenda. In recognition of the importance of cultural diversity, various countries have begun to revisit their public policies, trying to find a more fitting system of accommodation for their varied communities. The hope is that since "we are all multiculturalists now,"[1] we can explore ways in which state law can be rendered sufficiently pluralistic, allowing different communities to be governed by their own institutions and traditions. This trend toward group-based accommodation raises fundamental questions about the distribution of rights and authority in the multicultural state. These questions in turn focus our attention on the legal-institutional mechanisms of multiculturalism, and how they might affect not only the distribution of rights and authority, but also the distribution of social costs.

Both advocates and critics of multiculturalism have given much attention to the potential for accommodation to erode the social unity of already diverse polities. They are quite reasonably concerned that such societies will lose whatever "social glue" holds their citizens together. Yet relatively little thought is given to the effects that the distribution of differentiated rights can have upon the accommodated group members themselves. One of the aims of this book is to right this omission. Yet my inquiry does not stop there. If the state is to take identity groups seriously, we must re-examine yet another fundamental question of political life: that of institutional design and the division of authority. The basic dilemma here is how to divide authority in the multicultural state in a fair and just manner, in order to strike a balance between the accommodation of minority group traditions, on the one hand, and the protection of individuals' citizenship rights, on the other. The dispute over the nature of this balance has important philosophical dimensions. However, its political and legal-institutional dimensions are even more pressing given the realities outside our own study doors. An urgent need to

[1] See Glazer 1997.

1

resolve the problematics of striking such a balance has intensified in recent years, since an increasing number of minority cultures have demanded ever wider autonomy over areas previously regulated by the state.[2]

Many political and legal theorists have come to argue with enthusiasm in favor of accommodating distinctive identity groups by granting them special rights and exemptions, or by offering them some measure of autonomy in matters crucial to their self-definition.[3] Such accommodations, or "differentiated citizenship rights," in Will Kymlicka's terminology,[4] generally aim to ensure that minority groups have an option to maintain what Robert Cover calls their *nomos*: the normative universe in which law and cultural narrative are inseparably related.[5] Multicultural accommodation presents a problem, however, when pro-identity group policies aimed at leveling the playing field between minority communities and the wider society unwittingly allow systematic maltreatment of individuals within the accommodated group – an impact which in certain cases is so severe that it can nullify these individuals' citizenship rights.

[2] The upsurge in interest in multiculturalism is closely tied to the fact that many countries in the world today are already confronted with increased demands for accommodation in matters as different as linguistic and education policy, family law and immigration regulation, national symbols, and public holidays. The rise in demands for group-based accommodation is itself connected to changes in the way modern democracies operate, such as the adoption of race-blind immigration policies, universal suffrage (regardless of gender or race), the rise in the politics of identity, and the moral and legal recognition that equality in practice, or in society, sometimes requires differentiated treatment under the law.

[3] These scholars focus on assessing the justice claims of minority groups, and argue in favor of respecting group-based cultural differences under a new multicultural (or "differentiated") citizenship regime. Among those who have advanced this argument, Will Kymlicka has probably been the most influential (see Kymlicka 1995). While the literature on multiculturalism is too vast to cite comprehensively, the following texts are helpful as an introduction to the field: Bauböck 1999; Carens 2000; Galston 1995; Kymlicka and Norman 2000; Levy 1997; Margalit and Halbertal 1994; Minow 1997; Parekh 2000; Taylor 1991; Taylor 1994; Tully 1995b; Van Dyke 1977; Young 1989; Young 1990.

[4] Kymlicka 1995, p. 26.

[5] Many associate Robert Cover with the use of the Greek term *nomos* to refer to minority communities that generate sets of group-sanctioned norms of behavior that differ from those encoded in state law. See Cover 1983. I use the terms "*nomoi* communities" or "identity groups" in a related manner, to refer primarily to religiously defined groups of people that "share a comprehensive world view that extends to creating a law for the community." See Greene 1996, p. 4. This definition can also apply to other types of minority groups, such as those organized primarily along ethnic, racial, tribal, or national-origin lines, as long as their members share a comprehensive and distinguishable worldview that extends to creating a law for the community. However, all of these definitions of identity groups remain fraught with controversy. For the purposes of this discussion, such groups will be said to share a unique history and collective memory, a distinct culture, a set of social norms, customs, and traditions, or perhaps an experience of maltreatment by mainstream society or oppression by the state, all of which may give rise to a set of group-specific rules or practices. My analysis will focus only on identity groups bent on maintaining their *nomos* as an alternative to full assimilation.

Under such conditions, well-meaning accommodation by the state may leave members of minority groups vulnerable to severe injustice within the group, and may, in effect, work to reinforce some of the most hierarchical elements of a culture. I call this phenomenon the *paradox of multicultural vulnerability*. By this term I mean to call attention to the ironic fact that individuals inside the group can be injured by the very reforms that are designed to promote their status as group members in the accommodating, multicultural state.

This tension between accommodating differences and protecting the rights and interests of vulnerable group members within communities has been brought to the forefront of various countries' public policies, thanks to the recent global socio-political movement toward a multicultural or "differentiated" concept of citizenship. According to this new model, the basic building blocks of a just society continue to rely on the protection of basic citizenship rights and the nourishment of individuals' capacities. However, in certain cases justice also requires the recognition of traditions and unique ways of life for members of non-dominant cultural minorities.[6] Such a model entitles traditionally marginalized cultural communities to seek group-based protections, including the acquisition of jurisdictional autonomy over controversial legal domains, primarily in family law and education. While these multicultural schemes ensure the decentralization of state power and provide for potentially greater diversity in the public sphere, they do not necessarily promote the interests of *all* group members. Indeed, the same policy that seems attractive when evaluated from an *inter-group* perspective can systematically work to the disadvantage of certain group members from an *intra-group* perspective.

Multiculturalism, then, may create serious moral and legal hazards which must be addressed by defenders of differentiated citizenship. Unfortunately, proponents of state accommodation have left unresolved many of the complex questions associated with this new model. For example, if accommodation involves certain identity groups being vested with legal authority over their members, how do we protect group members from routine violations of their citizenship rights, when those violations arise from the traditional practices of the group which we have already sanctioned through accommodation? What entity has the responsibility for intervening when respect for groups becomes a pretext for the systematic maltreatment of certain group members? And how precisely are we to balance the twin goals of accommodating differences and respecting rights? These are the questions I mean to explore in this book.

---

[6] See, for example, Kymlicka 1995; Taylor 1994; Young 1990. Note, however, that several scholars do not agree with the view that formal recognition contributes significantly to the promotion of "human well-being" or a just social order. See, for example, Barry 1999.

Accommodating differences and respecting rights:[7] an unattainable marriage?

I believe the main question we are faced with in the present age of diversity is not whether the accommodation of different cultures can conflict with the protection of certain members' citizenship rights. Undeniably, it often does.[8] The mere recognition of this fact represents, however, only the initial stage in any serious rethinking of the tangled dynamics inhering between the group, the state, and the individual. It tells us very little about how we can best redress the troubling fact that well-meaning accommodations aimed at mitigating power inequalities between groups may end up reinforcing power hierarchies within them. Some scholars have suggested that this tension should lead us to abandon any attempt to enhance the autonomy of minority cultures or to respect their distinct ways of life.[9] But I take the paradox of multicultural vulnerability to raise a different, and more complicated, challenge. We need to develop a conception of differentiated citizenship which is guided by an ambitiously innovative principle: one that strives for the reduction of injustice *between* groups, together with the enhancement of justice *within* them.[10]

In an ideal world, enhancing the autonomy of *nomoi* groups would also always improve the status of at-risk individuals inside the group, or at least would never serve to legitimize the maltreatment of certain group

---

[7] My usage of the term "respecting rights" or interchangeably "individual citizenship rights" is not meant to convey a dyadic conception of rights. Nor do I view rights-bearers as separate and distanced from each other. While it is true that the concept of rights has traditionally implied a moral absolutism in which the self exists in glorious isolation, unencumbered by obligations and relations to others, feminist insights have rejected this narrow understanding of rights. Instead, they have infused this legal category with new meanings, stressing, for example, the relationships and connections that rights construct and enforce, but also the value inherent in the boundary-marking feature of rights (a feature which is of special importance for vulnerable categories of persons, including women). As Martha Minow explains, the whole concept of boundary depends on relationship: relationship between the two sides drawn by the boundary, and relationships among the people who recognize and affirm the boundary. As Minow puts it, "[t]he choice is not between boundaries and connections; it is a question of what kinds of boundaries and connections to construct and enforce." See Minow 1990, p. 11. For a concise overview of these debates, see Kiss 1997; Nedelsky 1993.

[8] I have discussed this tension in Shachar 1998; Shachar 2000a.

[9] One of the scholars who has explicitly suggested that we should abandon multiculturalism is Brian Barry. See, for example, Barry 2001.

[10] My definition of "justice" here draws from Iris Young's "enabling conception of justice," i.e. a conception of justice that refers not only to the distribution of rights but also to the institutional conditions necessary for the development and exercise of individual capacities and collective communication and cooperation. Under this conception of justice, "injustice refers primarily to two forms of disabling constraints: oppression and domination." See Young 1990, p. 39. This conception of justice also shares certain attributes with Philip Pettit's definition of "freedom as non-domination." See Pettit 1997.

members. In such a world, the paradox of multicultural vulnerability would not arise. Unfortunately, the ideal continues to elude us and thus the paradox of multicultural vulnerability continues to persist. In practice, the multiculturalism paradox presents real and troubling problems which require vigilance if we wish to both engage in accommodation and uphold rights. It may be that when the ideal is out of reach, we need to turn to something very different indeed.[11]

In the context of this discussion, that "something different" means switching our focus from the usual multicultural concerns about relations between the group and the state, and drawing back to take in a broader view. This view enables us to see the highly dynamic set of interactions that prevail between the *three* parties to the multicultural triad: the group, the state, and the individual who is situated so as to have interests and rights that derive from *concurrent* membership in both group and state. It is my belief that we cannot comprehend (let alone redress) the plight of the individual caught in the paradox of multicultural vulnerability, if we remain blind to the web of complex and overlapping affiliations that exist between these competing entities.[12]

With this more complete picture in view, we can redirect our thoughts to the kind of institutional design that will get us closer to our goal, which is to accommodate cultural difference within the multicultural state, while simultaneously attending to the interests and protecting the rights of individuals who are put at risk at the hands of their own culture. A new approach to multicultural accommodation must break away from the prevailing yet misleading "either your culture or your rights" ultimatum that underpins existing solutions to the paradox of multicultural vulnerability – solutions which I critically evaluate in this book. Admittedly, we still need a way of determining how much accommodation we should extend, over what matters, and to which groups, depending upon the particularities of each minority society or community. While there are no magic formulas that can neatly resolve the paradox whole, I believe that we can, and should, articulate a new way of practicing multiculturalism.

In this book, I present a new approach to accommodating differences and respecting rights in the multicultural age, known as *joint governance*. This new paradigm proposes the possibility for expanding the jurisdic-

---

[11] Robert Goodin makes this very same point in "Designing Constitutions: the Political Constitution of a Mixed Commonwealth." See Goodin 1996b, p. 229.

[12] My use of the term "individual" does not refer to an atomistic and isolated self. Nor does it assume that the individual lacks agency, or is fully "constituted" by her community. Rather, I use the word to refer to the locus of potential for individual selfhood and freedom, while acknowledging that people operate within manifold social contexts, networks of affiliation, and structures of power. For related accounts, see, for example, Nedelsky 1989; Shapiro 1999; Walzer 1990; Young 1997.

tional autonomy of religious and cultural minorities. But it also offers hardnosed and practical legal-institutional solutions to the problem of sanctioned in-group rights violations. Drawing on many fields of study – including political theory, law, institutional design, sociology, history, and gender and cultural studies – my discussion proceeds in two major steps.

First, I outline the paradox of multicultural vulnerability and how it relates to justifications for the accommodation of cultural differences in the public sphere, via a redefinition of group–state relations. I then review pioneering works by theorists such as Will Kymlicka, Charles Taylor, and Iris Young, who ushered in the current age of multicultural debate. These scholars focused on assessing the justice claims of minority groups, and argued in favor of respecting group-based cultural differences. While I accept much of their shared critique of standard difference-blind citizenship models, I find that what remains missing in their analysis is an awareness of how changes in the division of authority in the multicultural state can impact on the individual. The earliest proponents of multiculturalism too often forget the position of the citizen-insider, who simultaneously belongs to, and is affected by, both the group and the state authority.

Next, I embark on an exploration of the process whereby women have been subject to systemic violations of their citizenship rights under the auspices of state accommodation policies in the family law arena. Understanding this process requires that we appreciate the complex relations between cultural preservation, multicultural accommodation, and the in-group subordination of women. What we need is a theoretical framework that captures both the centrality of family law in the preservation of collective identities and, at the same time, an appreciation of its tendency to perpetuate an unequal distribution of rights, duties, and (ultimately) powers between men and women within the community. By specifically examining the situation of women living in orthodox religious communities, I explore how and why certain kinds of multicultural policies can put these particular women in an impossible bind, so that remaining loyal to their *nomos* means, in practice, forfeiting their citizenship rights. Multicultural policies which invest the group with full authority in the name of accommodation only blind themselves to this problem since they provide little help to women and other at-risk group members. Even more disturbingly, such policies' "respect for difference" often encourages group leaders to exert that much more "sanctioned" internal pressure against its most vulnerable members.

Further, I distinguish and critically evaluate two theoretical responses to the multiculturalism paradox. These two approaches, which I call the "re-universalized citizenship" option and the "unavoidable costs" response, do not merely evaluate the justice claims of minority groups: they cogently discuss the complexities and challenges associated with the

adoption of a differentiated citizenship model. The first and more familiar "re-universalized citizenship" position is effectively articulated by the
recent writings of Susan Okin, while the second and lesser known
"unavoidable costs" argument is well represented by the recent work of
Chandran Kukathas. These two responses may appear to be diametrically
opposed but they effectively function as mirror images of one another,
since both are underpinned by the same basic logic.

Following from this analysis, I proceed to map out the two dominant
legal responses to the challenge of accommodation, which have already
been adopted by numerous democratic countries around the globe. I once
again more specifically examine the accommodation policies related to
religiously defined *nomoi* communities. In modern liberal theory and contemporary constitutional law these communities are considered prime
candidates for acquiring a certain degree of autonomy in arenas crucial
for their self-definition, such as family law and education. But the existing
legal models pertaining to these communities are once again flawed, for
many of the same reasons that plague the "unavoidable costs" and "re-
universalized citizenship" approaches. I thus turn toward the task of envisioning an alternative way of practicing multiculturalism, one which seeks
to enhance the autonomy of distinct *nomoi* communities, while at the
same time providing at-risk individuals with viable legal-institutional
tools to enhance their leverage within the group, as well as the potential to
better control their personal circumstances and communal destinies.

This task begins with a rethinking of the existing responses to the multiculturalism paradox, by remembering to pay special attention to the position of the individual who has affiliations to, and rights derived from, both
the state and the group. The way out of the paradox of multicultural vulnerability lies in a fresh approach: one that rests on a sober acknowledgment of
the potentially negative in-group effects of well-meaning multicultural
accommodations, while also seeking to implement a new institutional
design. This brave new blueprint should be capable of aligning and balancing the benefits of enhanced external protections between groups with the
benefits of reduced internal restrictions. My proposed model of joint
governance describes a repertoire of accommodation designs which can be
combined and applied in creative ways according to different social needs
and arenas. The capacity of joint governance to assume different guises
depends on its establishing structures of authority which require the state
and the group to coordinate their exercise of power, while at the same time
ensuring that no group member is left without fundamental legal rights and
social resources. I am not suggesting, however, that any mere legal formula,
or even the best of institutional designs, can ever single-handedly resolve all
the immensely complex philosophical problems and near-inexorable moral

and ethical tensions that arise out of encounters between different cultural communities in shared political spaces. These tensions seem to be the inevitable predicament of contemporary multicultural societies consisting of members who share equal citizenship but who may adhere to very different normative systems and codes of behavior.[13]

Yet we can, and should, tackle the multiculturalism paradox head on, and seek a better way of addressing the plight of vulnerable group members/citizens. It is my hope that the joint governance approach can make a contribution in this respect, since unlike any of the existing normative and legal models explored in this book, it ties the mechanisms for reducing sanctioned in-group rights violations to the very same accommodation structure that enhances the jurisdictional autonomy of *nomoi* groups in the first place. In this way, joint governance seeks to positively align the benefits of *enhanced* external protections between groups with the benefits of *reduced* internal restrictions.

An exploration of the institutional issues surrounding multicultural accommodation

General principles and theoretical formulations may seem attractive on paper, but we cannot fully appreciate them until we see them interpreted and applied in a variety of specific contexts.[14] Social actions, whether individual or collective, always take place in an institutional context. The spectrum of available choices for different agents is thus shaped and affected by the institutional context in which they are set.[15] Relations between majority and minority communities (as well as within accommodated communities) are always shaped by the unique structures of authority under which they operate. This book therefore makes frequent reference to real-life examples of multiculturalism, as it is practically experienced in the world today. These legal examples include recent multicultural experiments from Canada, the United States, and Britain, as well as from other countries which have adopted expansive accommodation policies in various social arenas such as India, Kenya, and Israel. Such a comparative perspective can provide us with considerable insights

---

[13] In fact, I doubt if any meta-solution to this extremely complex set of issues is theoretically plausible, or practically feasible.

[14] My approach here fits comfortably with that adopted by "contextualist" political theorists. Indeed, it has been largely shaped by their work. See, for example, Carens 2000; Shapiro 1999; Walzer 1983.

[15] The power of institutions lies precisely in their ability to render transparent, perhaps sometimes even invisible, the legal conventions and coercive authority structures that hold any society together, even as these structures actively shape the options, payoffs and expectations of the different players.

into both the potential promises and pitfalls of multiculturalism. Although circumstances may differ substantially from country to country, important lessons can be learned by looking at familiar dilemmas as they appear in less familiar contexts.

Surprisingly, proponents of multiculturalism have given little consideration to a thorough exploration of the legal-institutional dimension of accommodation. Significantly more attention in the ongoing debate has been devoted to the theoretical question of differentiated citizenship. Yet relatively little thought has been given to the key issue of authority: how it might be differently divided in the multicultural state, and what the implications of this change might be for those who experience this new system of authority. Unfortunately, this lack of comprehensive discussion inevitably limits our ability to evaluate the attractiveness of the move toward multiculturalism. For without such a larger understanding of both the practical and the theoretical ramifications, we can only fumble toward implementing specific accommodation measures in different social arenas – and it becomes that much harder to distinguish who stands to gain and who stands to lose under each new approach.[16]

This dearth of discussion is especially puzzling given the unprecedented boom in the contemporary political theory and public policy literature which aggressively re-examines long-standing propositions about the role of the state in relation to competing forces from the sub-state and supra-state levels. In today's world, state-centered perceptions of law and sovereignty are under increasing scrutiny.[17] As a consequence, many functions traditionally invested in the state are presently being re-allocated away from it, in both a downward and upward direction. At the same time, the pressure to retain, or even strengthen, the core social, economic, and political functions of the state has scarcely dissipated.[18] Instead of linking up with these important policy debates, most of the scholarship in the

---

[16] Of the existing literature, Will Kymlicka's *Multicultural Citizenship* offers the most comprehensive discussion of how we might envision the new multicultural state. While Kymlicka's work is path breaking and has, to a significant extent, shaped the debate over multiculturalism in recent years, he does not seek to explore institutional models. Kymlicka's chief concern is to establish that group-differentiated rights can be justified within liberal theory. Yet Kymlicka's typology of group-differentiated rights does provide a useful starting point for such work, by assigning different degrees of accommodation to different types of groups. See Kymlicka 1995, pp. 26–33.

[17] It is common parlance today to describe the contemporary state as caught between several contradictory trends, including increasing globalism, the rise of localism and group-based demands, the solidification of supranational regimes, heightened migration and cross-border intermingling of peoples from different backgrounds, and rising decentralization pressures.

[18] For example, Young 1999 still confines important distributive functions to the state. On the economic argument for a proactive state in a global world, see, for example, Rodrik 1997.

English-speaking world has chosen to respond to this critical impasse by retreating into a rather detached discussion about the philosophical merits of multiculturalism. There is nothing wrong with this pursuit of theory, as long as it is tempered with some consideration of the constraints and logistics of institutional applications. Yet these theories often boil down to a recurring deliberation between autonomy and toleration, as two competing normative justifications for respecting cultural differences.[19] These debates ask *which* of our public values should guide us as members of diverse societies in finding a way to live together peacefully and with mutual respect and equal dignity. However, they provide very limited guidance about *how* we are supposed to structure that multicultural state.[20] They completely neglect to address questions about the institutional dimensions of power and the limits of authority, which are fundamental to political philosophy and inextricably linked to claims about justice. The time for enlarging the scope of the multiculturalist debate is thus highly overdue. It is only by tackling the rougher business of structural design head on – with an eye to redressing power inequalities both *between nomoi* groups and the wider society and *within* those same groups – that we can hope to at last embark on this long-neglected task.

Outline of the book

Proponents of multiculturalism aim to expand the traditional understanding of citizenship. In a realm previously occupied only by the individual and the state, they wish to carve out a public space for identity groups. The first part of chapter 2 offers a brief discussion of the standard models of citizenship and summarizes why we need to move toward a new model based on multicultural citizenship. With this innovation comes new problems, however – problems concerning the appropriate relations between group and state authorities, particularly with regard to jurisdiction over individuals living in accommodated minority cultures. Attempts to come to grips with these problems have given us strong and weak versions of multiculturalism. I outline these different approaches and evaluate them in the light of a conceptual perspective which cautions against the often unseen costs of accommodation. Thus I challenge Will Kymlicka's all-too-easy distinction between "external" and "internal" aspects of accommodation, and to illustrate this point I turn to an exploration of the interrelations between the group and the state. I argue that

---

[19] On autonomy-based arguments see, for example, Levey 1997. On toleration-based arguments see, for example, Kukathas 1997.
[20] My concern for advancing the debate over multiculturalism in this direction is shared by others. See, for example, Bauböck 2000; Van Parijs 2000.

there are three ways in which group members may respond to state assimilation pressures, all of which raise challenges for the multicultural state. The third, "reactive culturalism," is a response aimed at group self-preservation which takes as its goal the maintenance of a separate and distinct ethos. It may in the process, however, enforce hierarchical and rigid interpretations of group traditions which can, once multiculturalism is introduced into the equation, exacerbate the disproportionate costs imposed upon traditionally less powerful group members. In the final section of chapter 2 I critique two common responses to the problem of unfair in-group distribution of costs: first, the argument that says it is not our place to intervene, and second, the argument that says that those at risk are adequately protected by the right of exit. Both, I contend, prove highly inadequate in practice.

Chapter 3 takes the observations developed in chapter 2 and applies them in relation to a specific social arena where the multiculturalism paradox often hits hardest: that of family law. Family law is a hard test case for proponents of the weak version of multiculturalism. Practices and traditions pertaining to the family are central to the self-conception of many minority groups that seek to preserve their differences under a common citizenship regime. However, these very same practices and traditions often impose disproportionate costs on women to such an extent that when group practices are accommodated by the state, their rights as citizens are systematically put at risk. This intimate connection between external and internal aspects of family law is most evident in those groups which have followed the path of the third response to state assimilation pressures – that of reactive culturalism. Thus well-meaning policies designed to accommodate the practices of different minority cultures in the family law arena can actually serve to *sanction* the maltreatment of women according to the rules of their own *nomos*.

Chapter 3 ends with an exposition of the complex relations between cultural preservation, multicultural accommodation, and women's in-group status, and argues that this relationship need not always work to women's disadvantage. For example, women's powerful position in preserving and reproducing collective identities could, in theory, earn them a powerful position within their respective groups. In practice, however, it has often done exactly the opposite: women's indispensable contribution to the intergenerational transmission of group identity has become a main source of in-group subordination, creating a situation that can take an extremely high toll on women under the cover of multiculturalism.

In chapter 4 my discussion shifts from formulating and illustrating the paradox of multicultural vulnerability to asking what attempts have already been made to address it. I identify and map out the leading normative and legal approaches currently offered, and ask how well each fares in terms of alleviating the multiculturalism paradox. My investigation begins with a critical evaluation of two dominant theoretical responses that have emerged in the political theory literature, and which are concerned with the tensions between respecting culture and protecting rights. The first and more traditional response, "re-universalized citizenship," holds that in a conflict between an individual and a minority group, the state should put its weight behind the individual, even if in doing so the state helps to alienate the individual from her group. The second position, the "unavoidable costs" response, claims that although tensions can arise between the goals of accommodating differences and protecting rights, a genuinely tolerant state will very rarely intervene in minority group affairs – even if that minority group systematically violates certain of its members' citizenship rights and imposes disproportionate costs upon specific categories of group member. Such situations, so the argument goes, are the price one pays for upholding a multicultural system. I believe that these two theoretical responses are based on a common error: an oversimplified "either/or"-type understanding of legal authority which is not tailored to respect individuals' manifold identities. As a consequence, neither the "re-universalized citizenship" nor the "unavoidable costs" response offers much hope to at-risk group members who may legitimately wish to preserve their cultural identity, while at the same time exercising their hard-won citizenship rights in an effort to transform power hierarchies from within their different communities. In other words, neither of these responses actually resolves the paradox. Both opt instead to satisfy one or the other of its sides.

In the second part of chapter 4 I move from the realm of theory to practice, and turn to an evaluation of the two most influential current legal approaches for dividing authority over individuals who hold both group and state affiliations. I call these two paradigms the *secular absolutist* model and the *religious particularist* model. For the sake of analytical clarity, I represent each model in its pure ideal type form. This representation is not intended to fully correlate with any specific country's implementation of either of the two models. Rather, it draws on observations of real-life practices of accommodation in various democratic countries, observations which in turn serve as the basis for extrapolating the basic principles of each model.[21] In order to more systematically integrate practical legal experience with accommodation into the normative debate over differentiated citizenship, and to make sense of the vast range of experience with

---

[21] In exploring these two models, I have confined my analysis to mapping the scope and degree of authority that each model would grant to religious communities in the family law arena.

these models, it is helpful to think of the secular absolutist and the religious particularist models as two poles of a continuum. If one imagines a point of conflict arising over the exercise of authority within a given legal arena, one can visualize a line stretching between two extreme choices: the decision to grant full jurisdictional powers to *either* the state (the secular absolutist model) *or* the group (the religious particularist model). It appears that while the secular absolutist model is better at protecting the rights of at-risk group members, it does so at the expense of relegating their cultural identities to the private realm, thereby failing to publicly accommodate their *nomos*. Conversely, the religious particularist model protects cultural diversity, but at the cost of enabling the systematic maltreatment of specific categories of group members at the hands of their accommodated traditions. I evaluate the relative merits and pitfalls of each model in the light of the following two questions. First, how well does the division of legal authority established by this model preserve the cultural uniqueness of minority groups? Second, how does the division of legal powers established by this model affect the in-group status of vulnerable group members? As a result of these key points of inquiry, it seems that neither model provides an adequate balance between the protection of at-risk group members' citizenship rights and the preservation of their group's *nomos*.

In chapter 5, I turn toward exploring some creative innovations with multiculturalism which reformulate the relationship between the group, the state, and the individual. I argue that a truly comprehensive differentiated citizenship model must identify and defend only those group-based accommodations which coherently coalesce with the improvement of the status of traditionally subordinated classes of individuals within minority group cultures. I develop the outline of a new approach to multicultural accommodation and then sketch four accommodation schemes which represent different variants of the new approach in action. I call this new proposed model the *joint governance* approach, because it rests on the recognition that some persons will jointly belong to more than one community, and will accordingly bear rights and obligations that derive from more than one source of legal authority. Instead of having *either* the state *or* the group control the full range of issues affecting their members, joint-governance inspired accommodations open up a new separation of powers fostering ongoing interactions between different sources of authority, as a means of eventually improving the situation of traditionally vulnerable insiders, without forcing them into an "either/or" choice between their culture and their rights.

Joint governance thus envisions a new architecture for dividing and sharing authority in the multicultural state. Governance is now organized along a horizontal rather than vertical axis; it is composed of dialogue between different non-monopolist power centers, rather than a hierarchical imposition by either state or group officials. As such it promises to open up a new field of choices.

Chapter 6 introduces the most optimistically practical variant of joint governance, which I call *transformative accommodation*. This approach aims to enhance the jurisdiction of *nomoi* groups over matters crucial for their self-definition, *and* to ameliorate the disproportionate injury that certain categories of group members can suffer at the hands of their own cultures. This style of accommodation is "transformative" because it is designed to encourage group authorities themselves to *reduce* discriminatory internal restrictions. And it succeeds by persuading them to enact three cumulative principles: the "sub-matter" allocation of authority, the "no monopoly" rule, and the establishment of clearly delineated choice options. All of these principles define how authority can be usefully divided, how transformative accommodation can maintain the separation of powers, as well as how members of groups are able to exercise their agency once jurisdiction has been shared. Since transformative accommodation is designed to alleviate, or at least significantly mitigate, the paradox of multicultural vulnerability by equipping members with means of combating unjust internal restrictions, it also works to preserve and even enhance the accommodation of group traditions through state-backed external protections. So rather than accepting with resignation the potentially injurious effects of well-meaning accommodation, transformative accommodation accepts this problem as its litmus test.

Finally, I evaluate the practical potential of this latest new approach by revisiting some of the most intractable problems encountered in the family law arena. (An exploration of how transformative accommodation works in three other social domains – immigration, education, and criminal justice – is offered in a separate appendix.) By explicitly utilizing a "political" understanding of power and identity, which assumes an interaction between internal and external aspects of accommodation, I demonstrate how this variant of joint governance nevertheless persists in permitting once-vulnerable group members the opportunity to remain full participants in their *nomos* while transforming the conditions of their membership.[22]

---

[22] Taken together, these examples from different social arenas reveal how transformative accommodation provides us with the tools and the justifications for expanding the jurisdictional autonomy for cultural communities, while at the same time creating a dynamic incentive structure that encourages accommodated communities to internally rework their practices.

The road ahead

By accommodating cultural differences and by recognizing certain group-based traditions as legally binding, the multicultural state inevitably finds itself involved, to some degree, in shaping in-group relations. Indeed, even where the multicultural state formally refrains from intervening in *nomoi* groups' traditions, it still participates in the solidification of the power relations encoded in these traditions. Instead of overlooking the *Catch-22* situation by which power hierarchies within groups are propagated through the very accommodationist policies which seek to mitigate cultural biases between groups, we would do better to directly acknowledge it.

We can begin this process by abandoning the kind of thinking that has enmeshed us in an oversimplified and misguided "either/or" fixation, already all too characteristic of current normative and legal approaches. We next need to re-acquaint ourselves with the complex and multi-layered nature of multicultural identity.[23] From there, we can start to think about multiculturalism in ways appropriate to that complexity and multiplicity. Any attempt to seriously address the multiculturalism paradox must begin with the acknowledgment that in today's day and age, no single authority can expect to be the sole source of legal norms and institutions affecting its members. At the same time, well-meaning accommodation by the state, or the distribution of multicultural benefits and costs, does not necessarily affect all group members in the same way. Truly new thinking on multiculturalism requires that we recognize that we are dealing with a highly dynamic system of inter-related interactions occurring between the group, the state, and the individual. Instead of traditionally entrusting either the state or the group with *full* responsibility for improving the status of traditionally subordinated categories of members, we are better off heeding an old truism: the more diffuse the power, and the more entry points to affect the jurisdictions that bind them, the better it will be for the individual. A devolution of state authority to the group can truly serve the interests of women and other traditionally vulnerable group members only if it is accompanied by an institutional design which equips them to dismantle the power hierarchies that put them at risk in the first place. It is possible to envision institutions

---

[23] As Pierre Birnbaum observes, in contemporary multicultural theory "individuals . . . are [mistakenly] understood as the bearers of a single oppressive and quasi-essentialist idealized cultural identity from which no escape is possible. Such an immutable collective identity is not compatible with the expression of other identities (sexual, religious, etc.) in which some might wish to recognize themselves at certain moments of their existence." See Birnbaum 1996, p. 41.

which meet these requirements, and it is through such a creative rethinking – with the complexities of identity held fully before us in view – that we will make our strongest headway against the paradox of multicultural vulnerability.

2   The perils of multicultural accommodation

In recent years debates have raged over how best to combat cultural and religious repression, about whether and how to legally accommodate difference, and about what causes ethnocultural conflict in the first place. Little attention has been paid, however, to the actual effects that multicultural policies are leaving on the lives of members of accommodated groups. Still less consideration has been given to the complex, subtle, and often injurious impact that state accommodation policies can exert on individuals within minority groups – an impact which can be so severe as to nullify some individuals' basic citizenship rights. This represents a serious omission in the multicultural debate. The present chapter aims to address this gap in the critical discussion by exposing (and elaborating) the often unrecognized costs of multicultural accommodation.

In the multicultural context, "accommodation" refers to a wide range of state measures designed to facilitate identity groups' practices and norms. For example, group members might be exempted from certain laws, or the group's leadership might be awarded some degree of autonomous jurisdiction over the group's members. Multicultural accommodation in its various legal manifestations generally aims to provide identity groups with the option to maintain their unique cultural and legal understanding of the world, or their *nomos*. However, multiculturalism begins to present a problem whenever state accommodation policies intended to mitigate the power differential between groups end up reinforcing power hierarchies within them. This phenomenon creates the paradox of multicultural vulnerability, and it points to the troubling fact that as matters now stand, some categories of at-risk group members are being asked to shoulder a disproportionate share of the costs of multiculturalism.

To overcome this problem, a distinction has been drawn by Will Kymlicka between two kinds of multicultural accommodation: those that promote justice between groups, which he calls "external protections," and those that restrict the ability of individuals within the group to revise

17

or abandon traditional cultural practices, which he calls "internal restrictions."[1] Yet this distinction between external and internal aspects of accommodation fails to provide a workable solution in practice for certain real-life situations involving accommodated groups. Worse, it may even tend to reinforce injurious in-group practices in cases where the external protections that promote justice between groups uphold the very cultural traditions that sanction the routine in-group maltreatment of certain categories of historically vulnerable members, such as women. To illustrate this last point, consider the case of *Santa Clara Pueblo v. Martinez*.[2]

In 1941 Julia Martinez, a full-blooded member of the Santa Clara Pueblo tribe and a citizen of the United States, married an individual from outside the tribe. Their several subsequent children together included a daughter named Audrey. This daughter was raised on the Pueblo reservation, so she learned to speak the Tewa language as well as to participate in the life of the tribe. She was, for all practical purposes, a Santa Claran Indian. Yet according to Pueblo family law rules she could not be accepted by the tribe as a Santa Claran. Membership in the tribe was granted only to children whose parents were both Pueblo members or to children of male members who married outside the tribe. Membership was denied to children of *female* members who married outside the tribe. After attempts to persuade the tribe to change its gender-discriminatory membership rules proved unsuccessful, Julia and Audrey Martinez filed a lawsuit in the early 1970s, seeking declaratory and injunctive relief to grant Audrey and similarly situated children full status as tribal members.

For the Martinez family, the importance of obtaining recognition was both symbolic and pragmatic. As Julia Martinez's lawyers explained in their Supreme Court brief:

Denial of membership has caused hardship to the Martinez family, especially in obtaining medical care available to Indians. In 1968 Julia Martinez's now-deceased daughter Natalie, suffering from strokes associated with her terminal illness, was refused emergency medical treatment by the Indian Health Services. This was solely because her mother had previously been unable to obtain tribal recognition for her.[3]

---

[1] See Kymlicka 1995, pp. 34–44.

[2] *Santa Clara Pueblo v. Martinez*, 436 US 49 (1978). For a thorough exploration of the *Martinez* case, see Resnik 1989.

[3] Respondents' brief, pp. 2–3, cited in Resnik 1989, p. 721. Another important related aspect was that the Martinez children were facing denial of education and housing-related monetary assistance, which the United States' federal policy only extends to those Pueblo members recognized by internal tribal law. See Christofferson 1991, p. 170.

However, the US Supreme Court chose not to discuss these dire consequences of denial in terms of their distributive effect. Instead, it focused on the *demarcating* function of the Pueblo membership rules, which were deemed "no more or less than the mechanism of social . . . self-definition," and, as such, basic to the tribe's cultural survival.[4]

In 1978, after an initial defeat in a US District Court, which was then reversed by the Court of Appeals (which held that "the tribe's interest in the [membership rules] ordinance was not substantial enough to justify its discriminatory effect"), the Martinez family finally lost their legal battle to obtain recognition of their children as members of the Pueblo tribe. The ruling meant that the Martinez children (and all similarly situated children) had no right to enjoy the rights, services, and benefits that were automatically granted to children of Pueblo fathers (regardless of their mothers' membership/non-membership status), who, according to the tribe's gender-biased rules, were still considered group members. The Martinez children were thus barred from access to federal services such as health care, education, and housing assistance,[5] just as they were forced to forfeit their right to remain on the reservation in the event of their mother's death – simply because their mother broke the Pueblo's punitive code against women by marrying a non-tribe husband.[6] In a controversial decision, the US Supreme Court upheld this situation by refusing to strike down the tribe's membership rules (and refusing to face their distributive consequences).[7] It rejected the legal claim raised by Martinez on the basis of a "non-intervention" rationale, which lends precedence to the tribe's own criteria for satisfying membership rules as a means of ensuring the tribe's cultural preservation.

The *Martinez* case served to strengthen the autonomy of the Pueblo *vis-à-vis* the state, by granting the tribe autonomy to fully determine its membership boundaries. But the US Supreme Court decision also effectively gave legal sanction to the deprivation of benefits and the systematic maltreatment of a particular category of group member – some Pueblo mothers (and their children) – so long as it was in accordance with the group's traditions.

In this situation, the group's collective interest in preserving its *nomos* is achieved, in part, through the imposition of severe and disproportionate burdens upon a particular class of group member. The *Martinez* case

---

[4] See *Martinez*, p. 54 (citing the opinion of the US District Court of New Mexico, which ruled in favor of the tribe).

[5] For further discussion, see Resnick 1989, pp. 720–722; Christofferson 1991, pp. 183–184.   [6] See *Martinez*, pp. 52–53.

[7] Scores of articles and commentaries were written on the *Martinez* case. Some experts in federal Indian law praised it as a victory to tribal sovereignty, whereas most defenders of women's rights found the case to be difficult because it insulated from review tribal powers related to equal protection and due process provisions.

provides just one example of the tendency in multicultural accommodation toward legitimizing in-group power inequalities. Whenever certain categories of individual are systematically put at risk under the auspices of state-backed accommodation policies such as here, the paradox of multicultural vulnerability is bound to emerge.[8]

Standard citizenship models

"Citizenship," as Justice Warren famously put it, "is nothing less than the right to have rights."[9] It secures rights for the individual by linking her to a state. Individuals are also guaranteed certain basic rights through various international law treaties and supranational instruments, as well as regional intergovernmental agreements aimed at protecting human rights. Yet the state-centered definition of citizenship, entailing a particular legal status based on membership in a specific political community, still remains extremely important.[10] It defines who belongs to a state, and who is entitled to the benefits associated with full and equal membership in that state. A state bears duties to protect the rights of its citizens and residents, irrespective of their group affinity, and is held accountable if such rights are violated under its sovereignty – in certain cases, even if it has not actively participated in such violations.[11]

---

[8] The *Martinez* case, and related Canadian cases, concern the complex set of interactions between an historically oppressed group and the colonizing state which affect the status of citizen insiders. For a comprehensive discussion of the American federal government's involvement in the process by which the Pueblo's membership rules were defined and codified, see Resnik 1989, pp. 702–719. In Canada, the federal government had been directly implicated in the preservation of gender-biased membership rules through the infamous section 12 (1)(b) of the Indian Act. This section held that a female tribe member who married a non-Indian husband lost her status as a tribe member, and could not henceforth register as an Indian and a band member. The Indian Act was unsuccessfully challenged in 1974 in the case of *Canada (Attorney General) v. Lavell*, [1974] SCR 1349. The Indian Act was eventually changed in 1985, but only after the enactment of the Canadian Charter of Rights and Freedoms. See Bill C-31 (An Act to Amend the Indian Act), RSC 1985, c. 32 (1st Supp.). Prior to this change in law, the United Nations Human Rights Committee (UNHRC) ruled against Canada in the 1981 *Lovelace* case. In that case, the UNHRC held in favor of Mrs. Lovelace, who lost her status as an Indian in accordance with the Indian Act after marrying a non-Indian. However, the Committee's reasonings were not based on gender discrimination. Rather, it held that Mrs. Lovelace had a right of access to her native culture and language "in community with other members" of her group, according to section 27 of the International Covenant on Civil and Political Rights. See *Lovelace v. Canada*, UN GAOR, Human Rights Committee, 36th session, Supp. 17, UN Doc. A/36/40 (1981).

[9] See *Perez v. Brownell*, 356 US 44 (1958), p. 46.   [10] See Kymlicka and Norman 1994.

[11] I focus my remarks on citizens and residents as the prime beneficiaries of the rights and protections of the modern state. Under this category I include all persons who permanently reside in a given territorial unit. This definition is broader than a strict immigration law definition, since it can encompass the claims of illegal immigrants, so long as they are *de facto* permanent members of a given polity.

In practice, however, few governments have a perfect record when it comes to protecting the citizenship rights of their members.[12] An emerging body of regional and supranational institutions now permits individuals (rather than state actors) to bring rights claims against national governments.[13] This supranational-regulation regime is still in its embryonic stages. While it may in the future supersede national jurisdictions, this regime is more often conceived as *complementing* state-centered citizenship, rather than replacing it.[14] This means that we need to more closely investigate the legal status which defines citizenship – a unique relationship which grants the individual a stake in the state, and entitles her to the protection of its laws.

Citizenship: the bond between the individual and the state

Since antiquity, citizenship has defined the legal status of membership in a political community. Under Roman jurisprudence, "citizen came to mean someone free to act by law, free to ask and expect the law's protection."[15] This legal status signified a special attachment between the individual and the political community. In general, it entitled the citizen to "whatever prerogatives and . . . whatever responsibilities that [we]re attached to membership."[16] With the creation of the modern state, citizenship came to signify a certain equality with regard to the rights and duties of membership in the community. The modern state began to administer citizenship, and it now determines who secures citizenship, how it is conferred on individuals, what the associated benefits may be, and what rights and privileges it may entail. As a legal status, citizenship has come to imply a unique, reciprocal, and unmediated relationship between the individual on the one hand, and the political community or the state on the other.[17]

---

[12] One need only consult the annual Amnesty International or Human Rights Watch Reports to confirm this observation.

[13] Perhaps the most familiar supranational institution of this kind is the UNHRC. Although this was established as a committee of experts rather than a court, its recent practice reveals an increasingly "court-like trend." For a detailed analysis of this emerging supranational-regulation regime, see Helfer and Slaughter 1997.

[14] Even the new concept of European Citizenship introduced in the 1992 Treaty of European Union (the Maastricht Treaty) and modified in the 1997 Treaty of Amsterdam is explicitly based on state-centered citizenship. European citizenship can only be acquired through one's preexisting affiliation to a Member State. As it currently stands, this new supranational membership therefore *complements* rather than replaces state-based citizenship. Article 8 of the 1997 Treaty of Amsterdam explicitly states that: "Citizenship of the Union is hereby established. Every person holding the nationality of a Member State shall be a citizen of the Union. Citizenship of the Union shall complement and not replace national citizenship."   [15] See Pocock 1995, p. 36.

[16] See Walzer 1989, p. 211.   [17] See Brubaker 1992, pp. 35–49.

The missing third component

Proponents of multiculturalism aim to expand the traditional under-standing of citizenship. In a realm previously occupied only by the individual and the state, they wish to carve out a new conceptual space for identity groups.[18] Standard citizenship models prioritize either individual rights, as in the classic liberal citizenship model, or both individual rights and a strong sense of membership in the political community, as in the civic-republican model. Thus these models, almost by definition, exclude the recognition or accommodation of minority cultures from standard citizenship theory. In the United States, for example, even religiously defined *nomoi* groups – ostensibly protected by the Free Exercise clause of the First Amendment – are often denied accommodation by state authorities as a result of the entrenched existence of the standard citizenship model.[19] At the same time, a certain hard line against identity groups has been rationalized under equal protection jurisprudence as "blindness to differences."[20] This constitutional approach reflects, to a great extent, standard citizenship theory's conceptualization of the identity group as something that should operate *outside* the public sphere. In short, this view dictates that "differences" should be confined to the domain of the private. Identity group affiliations, according to this view, have no salience in the realm of the public, and consequently do not merit any recognized legal status.[21]

Why we need a multicultural conception of citizenship

Proponents of the multicultural citizenship model condemn "blindness to differences" constitutionalism. They call instead for a new vision. Citizenship, they claim, must be re-imagined as "a heterogeneous public in which persons stand forth with their differences acknowledged and respected."[22] A fresher and more nuanced understanding of citizenship begins with the view that group-based distinctiveness, ignored in the past in favor of assimilation to a dominant or majority identity, should now be recognized, respected, and even nourished by the contemporary state.[23]

At the heart of many contemporary justifications for multicultural

---

[18] For a definition of "identity groups," see note 5 in ch. 1.
[19] See, for example, Monsma and Soper 1998.
[20] See, for example, Gotanda 1991; Natapoff 1995.
[21] For a critical evaluation of "the two domains thesis," or the liberal formula for relegating identity groups to the realm of the private, see Spinner 1994.
[22] See Young 1990, p. 119.   [23] See Taylor 1994, p. 38.

citizenship lies a deep concern about power, particularly about the power of the state and dominant social groups to erode minority cultures. The pioneering works of theorists like Will Kymlicka, Charles Taylor, and Iris Young, whose writings in the early 1990s mark the beginnings of the current multiculturalism debate, clearly illustrate this concern. These scholars focus on assessing the justice claims of minority groups, and argue in favor of respecting group-based cultural differences, in addition to the protection of basic citizenship rights, and the nourishment of individuals' capacities.

These authors deploy a variety of arguments to state their case, most of which can be seen as resting on a common strategy: they all agree that difference-blind institutions which "purport to be neutral among different groups . . . are in fact implicitly titled towards the needs, interests, and identities of the majority group; and this creates a range of burdens, barriers, stigmatizations, and exclusions for members of minority groups."[24] Proponents of multiculturalism are thus pointing to the fact that any society, no matter how open and democratic, will always have certain cultural, linguistic, and historical traditions which welcome some of its members more completely than others, because the institutions of that society have been largely shaped in their image.[25]

Part of the problem is that "the state cannot help but give at least partial establishment to a culture,"[26] and that this culture often reflects the norms and preferences of the majority community.[27] The adoption of multicultural accommodations is still said to remedy the disadvantages that members of minority cultures may suffer under other universal or "difference-blind" citizenship models.

Kymlicka builds his scholarly edifice to multiculturalism on a philosophical foundation. He begins by claiming that cultural membership is an important good, which is a relevant criterion for the state to consider

---

[24] See Kymlicka and Norman 2000, p. 4.

[25] This critique shares much in common with feminist arguments about the entrenchment of male standards in the definition of seemingly neutral key societal and legal arrangements. Consider two classic examples: the American case of *Geduldig* v. *Aiello*, 417 US 484 (1974), or the Canadian case of *Bliss* v. *Attorney General of Canada* [1979] 1. SCR 183. In both instances, each country's Supreme Court failed to acknowledge that employment insurance schemes which did *not* include coverage of pregnancy – perhaps the only clear biological distinction between men and women – constituted discrimination against women on the basis of sex. While these cases were later overruled, they are a living testimony to the enduring capacity of law to entrench a particular point of view, and defend it as the point of view from nowhere. Critical race theorists are also engaged in the project of exposing how "facially neutral" laws and policies may in fact codify or create an adverse effect on individuals based on their race.

[26] See Kymlicka 1995, p. 27.

[27] Note that the assumption here is not that a society's standards are necessarily flawed or misguided, but that they are never fully blind to difference.

in distributing benefits, rights, and authority.[28] Kymlicka then proceeds to argue for the justice of taking "differences" into consideration and introducing policies that provide minority cultures with special protections. He chooses not to impute value to ethnocultural communities by virtue of their ethnicity, their specificity, or their vulnerability *qua* communities. Instead, he suggests that minority cultures deserve protection because they provide *individuals* with a secure context of choice, which in turn allows them to make meaningful decisions.[29] Unlike members of the majority, whose cultural context of choice is relatively secure, by virtue of the fact of speaking the majority's language, or their belonging to its dominant ethnic, cultural, racial or religious group, members of non-dominant communities do not enjoy the same guarantees. Minority cultures' traditions, languages, norms, practices, and distinct ways of life may in fact face extinction if no form of group-based accommodation is put into place by the multicultural state in time. Kymlicka thus offers an autonomy-enhancing justification for the adoption of differentiated-citizenship rights within a diverse society.

Young similarly sees group membership as an important social relationship, thanks to its frequently critical ascendance over individual identity.[30] But her argument for respecting cultural differences is even more explicitly political than Kymlicka's. Young insists on transforming extant power hierarchies between groups, by ensuring that previously excluded group members gain meaningful access to the decision-making bodies that govern democratic societies.[31] Like Kymlicka, Young imagines a new heterogeneous public sphere where persons from different groups and with different ways of life can fully participate "without shedding their distinct identities."[32]

Taylor's defense of multiculturalism focuses primarily on the idea that the recognition of persons, in their distinct cultural identities, fulfils a vital human need. Such recognition is essential to our very characteristics as human beings;[33] failure by public institutions to account for our identities as group members can thus inflict harm, particularly on those who belong to non-dominant minority cultures which are denied equal respect. Taylor concludes that we can begin to repair this harm only when different cultural communities gain a presumption of equal worth, which can then translate into certain forms of autonomy and law-making powers.

---

[28] In *Liberalism, Community, and Culture*, for example, Kymlicka criticizes John Rawls's failure to recognize the significance of cultural membership as a "primary good" in Rawls's own terminology. See Kymlicka 1989, pp. 162–166.
[29] See Kymlicka 1989, p. 165.   [30] See Young 1990, p. 45.
[31] See Young 1990, pp. 96–121, 156–191. See also Williams 1998.
[32] See Young 1989, p. 272.   [33] See Taylor 1994.

The emphasis on the links between providing individuals with "an intelligible context of choice, and a secure sense of identity and belonging"[34] thus stands at the core of the quest for a new multicultural model of citizenship.[35] A crucial premise of the quest is the recognition that all cultures do not enjoy an equal chance of survival. Members of the dominant majority possess an institutional advantage which ensures that the capacities and self-respect which make their culture possible are relatively secure.[36] This is not the case with minority cultures, however. Since the birth of the modern state, non-dominant populations have been subjected to extreme assimilationist pressures. Proponents of multiculturalism argue against such coercive practices, claiming that justice requires the state to respect group-based cultural differences.[37] Institutionalized forms of respect are particularly needed where state policies which purport to be neutral mask a bias toward the needs, interests, and inherited particularities of the majority. Such ultimately repressive systems create a range of burdens, barriers and exclusions for members of non-dominant cultural communities.[38]

Potential conflicts: group, state, individual

Unlike the standard thinking on citizenship, which posits a unique, reciprocal and unmediated relationship between the individual and the state, the new multicultural understanding of citizenship also recognizes identity groups as deserving special or differentiated rights.[39] Will Kymlicka, for example, distinguishes between three forms of group-differentiated rights: "self-government rights," which involve the delegation of legal powers to national minorities; "polyethnic rights," which might include financial support and legal protection for certain practices associated with particular ethnic or immigrant groups; and "special representation rights," such as guaranteed seats for designated minority groups within the central institutions of the larger society.[40] Such thinking departs from the perception of citizens as individuals who are uniform in their membership of a larger political community. Instead it views them as having

---

[34] See Kymlicka 1995, p. 105. [35] For further discussion, see Kymlicka 1989.

[36] See Walker 1997, p. 216.

[37] For a comprehensive theory of the role of culture in human life, which in turn serves as the basis for defending multicultural accommodation as an integral part of the principle of full membership in a polity, see Parekh 2000.

[38] For an elegant summary of this critique, see Kymlicka 1999.

[39] As we have seen in the early writings on multiculturalism, theorists like Will Kymlicka, Iris Young, and Charles Taylor all argued in favor of respecting group-based cultural differences, by drawing on a shared view of the shortcomings of the standard citizenship model. I concisely summarize the major claims of this critique in Shachar 2000c.

[40] See Kymlicka 1995, pp. 6–7, 26–33.

equal rights as individuals, while *simultaneously* meriting differentiated rights as members of identity groups.

Surprisingly, Kymlicka pays relatively little attention to religiously defined minority communities. These groups do not occupy a special category in Kymlicka's tripartite typology. Instead, they are lumped together with ethnic and immigrant groups, although their concerns and historical incorporations into the body politic do not necessarily correspond to the *voluntary* criteria for immigration stressed by Kymlicka.[41] Various religious sects such as the Old Order Amish, the Mennonites, the Hutterites, and the Hassidic Jews arrived in North America after fleeing from systemic persecution in their European homelands. In seeking a safe haven in the "new world" they did not intend to break their communal structures or give up their unique ways of life. Rather, they sought a more tolerant political environment in lieu of the often hostile and repressive treatment they had known before. These groups can thus be viewed as possessing a stronger case for demanding accommodation than ethnic immigrants who, according to Kymlicka, have more or less "uprooted themselves" and implicitly surrendered some of their group-specific claims upon their voluntary and individual entry into a new society.[42]

Although they may not seem central to the contemporary debate over multiculturalism, religiously defined minority communities have historically been considered the prime candidates for accommodation, and this notion is prominent in classic liberal theory as well as in the contemporary constitutional codes of most democratic countries in the world. Given this history, the treatment of non-dominant religious minorities offers a relatively rich body of legal experience with different measures of accommodation. As the following chapters will show, this experience can only assist us in thinking more systematically about multiculturalism and citizenship.

Regardless of the specific type of group involved, the multicultural challenge to the standard models of citizenship raises fundamental questions about whether citizens' identities as members of *nomoi* groups should matter publicly, or the extent to which these identities should be politically relevant.[43] If we agree with Kymlicka, Young, and Taylor that

---

[41] See Kymlicka 1995, pp. 20, 63.

[42] According to Kymlicka, the claims of religious groups for accommodation are weaker than those of minority nations (such as the Québécois or First Nations in Canada), because only the latter are entitled to enjoy the most expansive form of differentiated rights: territorial self-government.

[43] These questions are posed by Jürgen Habermas in a short essay entitled "Multiculturalism and the Liberal State." See Habermas 1995.

these identities should matter publicly and should be considered politically relevant, then we must ask how the recognition of identity groups through accommodation should affect what John Rawls calls the "primary subject of justice": that is, "the way in which the major social institutions distribute fundamental rights and duties,"[44] and the division of authority in the modern state. These questions are important because they focus our attention on the legal-institutional mechanisms of differentiated citizenship. They ask us to consider not only the distribution of rights and decision-making authority, but also the distribution of duties and burdens. So the real issue becomes a matter of weighing not only the benefits but the costs of multiculturalism, together with attempting to resolve the problem of their distribution both outside and inside the group.[45]

Schematically, six prototypical legal conflicts can arise under a multicultural citizenship model. Not all are unique to a differentiated citizenship system, but they may take on significant new dimensions under it. They are: (1) individual vs. individual; (2) individual vs. state; (3) identity group vs. identity group; (4) identity group vs. state (the most often discussed legal conflict under multiculturalism); (5) non-member vs. identity group (as, for example, in affirmative action cases); and (6) individual group member vs. identity group. My principal concern is with the final category.

Multicultural accommodation raises complex questions about the appropriate relationships between group and state authorities, particularly with regard to jurisdictions over individuals living within *nomoi* groups. This issue becomes even more pressing when we are faced with systematic violations of citizenship rights which are supposedly endorsed by group traditions. This problem derives from the delicate tripartite balance involved in multiculturalism, which needs to be continually renegotiated between the group, the state, and the individual who belongs to both. We must therefore find a way to enable the multicultural state to allocate jurisdiction to identity groups in certain legal arenas, while

---

[44] See Rawls 1971, p. 7.

[45] My discussion explores the differentiated effects of accommodation on members of minority communities, but the movement toward a multicultural citizenship model may also have significant implications for persons living outside these accommodated communities as well (e.g. by creating more diverse public spaces, and by allocating certain public funds or opportunities based on a combination of personal qualifications and group memberships). In recent years, the reversal of race-based affirmative action programs in the United States illustrates how vicious a response such special rights programs can evoke, regardless of their historical justification. For a comprehensive discussion of the dangers of inter-group conflicts that any theory of multiculturalism must address, see Levy 2000.

simultaneously respecting group members' rights as citizens.[46] Two resolutions are generally offered to this problem, which I have named the strong version and the weak version of the multicultural model.[47] Each has different consequences when evaluated from the perspective of the paradox of multicultural vulnerability.

Strong and weak versions of multiculturalism

The strong version of multiculturalism calls for a fundamental shift in our understanding of citizenship. Identity groups are to be granted extensive formal, legal, and constitutional standing so that they may govern their members in accordance with their *nomos*. In order to free minority communities from the tyrannical imposition of centralized state law – viewed as an "imperial yoke, galling the necks of the culturally diverse citizenry"[48] – the state should introduce at least two accommodation measures. First, it must allow for some degree of self-government for identity groups, and second, it must officially include the voices of identity groups within the constitutional framework and within public discourse.[49]

The strong multicultural model, however, focuses almost exclusively on the problem of injustice between groups. The individual and the state are no longer the central components of citizenship, as they were in the standard citizenship models. Rather, it is the identity group which takes center stage. Yet in its crusade for respect between groups, the strong multicultural model tacitly conceals the phenomenon of in-group oppression. While highlighting the conflicts that exist *between* identity groups or *among* identity groups and the state, the model obscures the power relations *within* identity groups. Also, little consideration is given under this version of multiculturalism to the many problems of group agency (such as the criteria determining who can "speak for a group"), or the political effects of accommodation policies upon the ossification of identity in such minority communities. The strong model therefore oversimplifies the web of relationships that exist between the individual, the group, and the state. It simply replaces the state–individual-centered understanding of standard citizenship theory with a state–identity-group-centered understanding.

---

[46] I am not assuming that citizenship rights are uncontested or crystal clear. They are an outcome of each country's democratic process, besides being codified in the commitments that each polity has taken upon itself by signing and ratifying regional and international human rights conventions.

[47] I have discussed these two versions of multiculturalism in Shachar 1998.

[48] See Tully 1995b, p. 5. See also Tully 1995a.

[49] See Tully 1995b. On other representations of the strong multicultural model, see, for example, McDonald 1991.

Even worse, it does so at the expense of overlooking the potential burdens that these new accommodation measures might impose on the individual who belongs to *both* group and state.

The weak version of the multicultural model more effectively addresses the question of who bears what costs. It acknowledges the potential tensions between the accommodation of identity groups and the protection of citizenship rights. The weak version therefore offers a more compelling model of multicultural citizenship. While proponents of the weak version may disagree about the justifications for specific accommodation policies, they agree on the proposition that a morally adequate treatment of identity groups means providing multicultural accommodation *without* abandoning the protection of individual rights.[50] Will Kymlicka, a prominent representative of the weak version, expresses this goal in the following way:

> I believe it is legitimate, and indeed unavoidable, to supplement traditional human rights with minority rights. A comprehensive theory of justice in a multicultural state will include both universal rights, assigned to individuals regardless of group membership, and certain group-differentiated rights or "special status" for minority cultures.[51]

Moreover, Kymlicka argues that the real test of the multicultural model of citizenship lies in its ability to "explain how minority rights coexist with human rights, and how minority rights are limited by principles of individual liberty, democracy, and social justice."[52] The strong multicultural model fails Kymlicka's test because it emphasizes solely the rights of identity groups. In contrast, the weak version to some degree mediates among the components of the three parties in any multicultural system – the group, the state, and the individual. Unfortunately, the weak multicultural model also contradicts its own central tenet when it advocates accommodation even in cases where putting legal authority in the hands of the identity group means exposing certain group members to routine in-group violations of their individual citizenship rights.

This problem becomes visible when we adopt the perspective of the paradox of multicultural vulnerability: the sober recognition that in reality a well-meaning attempt to empower traditionally marginalized minority communities may just end up re-enforcing power hierarchies within the accommodated community instead. This perennial potential problem raises a serious challenge to Kymlicka's (untested) presumption that multiculturalism is "primarily a matter of external protections."[53] As

---

[50] These justifications range from autonomy-based/valorization of choice arguments, to tolerance/respect for diversity reasoning, to anti-subordination/non-dominance justifications.   [51] Kymlicka 1995, p. 6.   [52] Ibid.   [53] See Kymlicka 1996, p. 160.

the *Martinez* case shows, the external aspects of multicultural accommodation are not so easily distinguished from the policy's internal impact.

This blind spot in the weak version's analysis is partly related to an overly narrow focus on "identity" as singular – as if one's cultural membership were unmediated by other social factors, such as gender, sexual orientation, age, marital status, and the like.[54] This single-axis perception fails to capture the potential multiplicity of a group member's identity-creating affiliations – to her culture, state, family, religion, and the like. Even more troubling, it is blind to the particular vulnerability that traditionally subordinated categories may face in the context of their own cultures, and which may be exacerbated under the auspices of the state's accommodationist policies.

As mentioned earlier, Kymlicka claims that awarding a degree of differentiated rights to *nomoi* groups who seek external protection is a crucial feature of the weak version of multiculturalism, which thus applies a corrective lens to the troubling "blindness to differences" approach of standard citizenship theory. On the other hand, Kymlicka is also committed to the perception that minority cultures which systematically impose internal restrictions upon their members are not equally entitled to accommodation. While this distinction provides a much-needed normative yardstick, two significant problems effectively undercut its viability and feasibility – at least so long as it is not accompanied by a comprehensive legal-institutional mechanism for combating intra-group rights violations.

First, the distinction between "external" and "internal" aspects of multiculturalism tends to collapse when put into practice. Often the jurisdictional powers that are important for the group to ensure its external protection *vis-à-vis* the larger society are the same powers which can be used to perpetuate internal restriction on certain categories of group member. Second, in discussing the limits of toleration in *Multicultural Citizenship*, Kymlicka powerfully argues that "a liberal conception of minority rights will not justify (except under extreme circumstances) 'internal restrictions' – that is, the demand by a minority culture to restrict the basic civil and political liberties of its members."[55] However, there is a tension between Kymlicka's prohibition on internal restrictions and his tripartite typology detailing which groups merit what sort of recognition for their cultural identity. Kymlicka defines national minorities as deserving the most expansive form of accommodation – territorial self-

---

[54] On the usage of a multiple-axis analysis (or "intersectionality") as a response which challenges exclusive and separate categories, especially in the context of race and gender, see, for example, Crenshaw 1989; Volpp 1996.   [55] See Kymlicka 1995, p. 152.

government rights – whereas members of immigrant, ethnic, or religious groups are entitled to less comprehensive accommodation.

Kymlicka holds that in the case of national minorities it would be a mistake for the state to act as if it had the authority to intervene in their internal affairs, even if such groups routinely violate certain of their members' individual rights.[56] "In cases where the national minority is illiberal," he writes, "this means that the majority will be unable to prevent the violation of individual rights within the minority community."[57] By this formulation, however, Kymlicka is taking for granted that a certain type of group (such as a national minority) merits accommodation by the very *nature* of its group type.[58] Yet this is not a sufficient test even according to his own account. We also need to establish that the group does not impose excessive internal restrictions upon its members. Kymlicka seems to overlook this two-step process while addressing the special case of national minorities. Instead, he upholds their entitlement to the fullest degree of accommodation, even though this is precisely what needs to be established by his own internal–external distinction. For if even groups that systematically impose internal restrictions upon some of their members can have their external protections upheld, what can remain of the inside–outside distinction? Kymlicka apparently prefers to overlook this inconsistency by maintaining that groups such as the Santa Clara Pueblo Indians deserve self-governing rights, *regardless* of discriminatory evidence like that found in the *Martinez* case.[59]

This is where Kymlicka cannot make weak multiculturalism work. We saw earlier that Kymlicka protects the situated individual by putting in a qualification on accommodation, which states that no identity group merits differentiated rights if it uses such jurisdictional powers to impose unjust internal restrictions. By this analysis, national minorities like the Pueblo should not receive autonomous self-governing powers when they compromise the rights of their members. Yet Kymlicka clearly supports their accommodation, insisting that any attempt to act differently will most likely be perceived as a form of aggression or paternalistic colonialism.[60] Here Kymlicka is fully consumed by the state–group dichotomy.

[56] See Kymlicka 1995, p. 166. This is surprising because Kymlicka asserts that liberal outsiders have a duty to support "any efforts the community makes to liberalize their cultures," and because he views the violation of group members' rights by their own group as morally unjust. See Kymlicka 1992, p. 144; Kymlicka 1995, pp. 166–170.

[57] See Kymlicka 1995, p. 168.

[58] Jacob Levy offers a related critique by suggesting that we should focus on the nature of the accommodation claim, rather than on the nature of the group which makes it. See Levy 1997, p. 50.

[59] Kymlicka himself selects this example; see Kymlicka 1995, p. 165.

[60] See Kymlicka 1995, pp. 163–172.

This is inconsistent with the careful balancing act which Kymlicka generally observes in his theoretical defense of weak multiculturalism, which keeps the potentially conflicting interests of the group, the state, and the individual more clearly in view.

The conundrum Kymlicka encounters while advocating accommodation to groups which (by his own standards) should not be granted the strongest form of differentiated rights seems to derive from a certain slippage in his position: from a defense of the weak version of multiculturalism into something more akin to the strong version, at least in relation to national minorities. Since Kymlicka takes for granted what still remains to be established (that national minorities merit accommodation), he can only labor to define the role of the state against the paradox of multicultural vulnerability and its nefarious impingements. He thus corners himself into a position that resembles the strong version of multiculturalism when he suggests that the state, as a third party, has little if any authority to intervene in the group.[61] And this formulation is redolent with assumptions about the proper relationship between these two entities to which the individual simultaneously belongs.

Is the state really just an "outside" third party, which is clearly and neatly detached from the "inside" group realm? Or does this supposition conceal certain circumstances that have historically contributed to frictions between the state and *nomoi* groups? Since the late eighteenth century, identity groups have undergone substantial changes, many of them related to the modern state's campaign to transform "the population, space, and nature under [its] jurisdiction into a closed system without surprises that can . . . be observed and controlled."[62]

Today there is no multicultural solution that can replicate a bygone era, long before the rise of the modern state and its ineradicable alternations of the political landscape. Groups can no longer isolate themselves from the broader society as before.[63] Groups that today petition the state for accommodation have already been touched by the operation of that state and, to a significant degree, have been re-shaped in their encounter with it. Some groups have suffered extreme violence, even genocide, in contact with the state. Others have been subjected to a host of direct and indirect means of state intervention, intended to transform their members into "civilized" or sufficiently assimilable individuals worthy of full citizenship. In the latter case, three patterns of responses to such homogenizing pressures can be seen to generally occur.

[61] See Kymlicka 1995, p. 165.   [62] See Scott 1995, p. 231.
[63] Even prior to the creation of the modern state, *full* seclusion by minority group members was rarely, if ever, possible.

Three types of group response to assimilation pressures

We can distinguish three main types of response to the strain of enforced assimilation, wherein identity group members are pushed to become "like their fellow countrymen." These are:

1. the dissolution of all previous community loyalties, or "full assimilation";
2. political, social and economic integration along with the retention of some aspects of the group's cultural traditions, or "limited particularism"; and
3. the employment of explicit measures to preserve group identity as unquestionably distinct from mainstream society, or "reactive culturalism."

Among these three patterns of response, the third raises the most interesting and complex issues for proponents of the weak version of multiculturalism. In reviewing these three response types, I draw in particular on the historical experiences of different sub-sections of the Jewish community and the assimilation pressures they faced in countries such as France, Germany, and the United States. I do so because members of the Jewish community were traditionally seen (at least in the eyes of the Christian majorities of most Western countries) as representing the "quintessential Other": the Other which must be "emancipated" from the group in order to qualify as a citizen.[64]

Full assimilation

The first major response-type is that of "full assimilation." This response can take the form of religious conversion, intermarriage, or simply a decisive break with the past. In the early nineteenth century, with the conferral of civic rights in France and Germany, significant numbers of Jews chose the latter option. They completely renounced their Jewish identity in the hope of becoming culturally undifferentiated members of the body politic. And in exchange for this renunciation, they were granted civil and political rights as individual citizens. Since only men were initially allowed access to the benefits of citizenship, gender affected the nature and timing of decisions about full assimilation. For example, women were less likely to relinquish their communal identity, and if they did so, it was primarily in order to marry a non-group member. Men, on the other

---

[64] See, for example, Karl Marx, "On the Jewish Question," reprinted in Marx 1994, pp. 28–56. For further discussion, see Brown 1995; Smith 1997.

hand, enjoyed more freedom to choose the route and timing of full assimilation.[65]

Indeed, the values and promises of the Enlightenment era deeply influenced many Jews in both France and Germany.[66] Significant numbers of them chose the path to full assimilation.[67] Yet the fact that these individuals forfeited their group identity, and opted to see themselves first and foremost as members of the political community, did not by any means preclude continued discrimination. Even before the Holocaust made Jewishness an ascriptive rather than a self-defined identity, various legal restrictions were imposed upon those identified as Jewish by "blood." Converted Jews and their descendants were made painfully aware that it was not entirely in their power to change their group identity. Subtle and not-so-subtle discrimination ran deep, and occasionally re-emerged even in post-Enlightenment societies. State and social institutions reminded Jews of their stigma of ancestry, even when they had long abandoned any marker, practice, or belief associated with Judaism.

However, the full assimilation option at least enables group members to decide that they no longer wish to follow a minority cultural tradition – in theory if not in practice. But in order for this option to be viable, members of both the minority and the majority cultures must labor to define and maintain a system where a purely universal or non-sectarian citizenship identity is attainable for all. Some might argue that this ideal is unattainable, and that its hold on our imagination is part of the problem rather than part of the solution.[68] For the purposes of our discussion, however, it is enough to remember that for individuals who consciously forgo their group culture and are comfortable viewing themselves as indistinguishable from other citizens, the paradox of multicultural vulnerability does not tend to arise because they do not generally claim any measure of cultural accommodation from the contemporary state.

Limited particularism

The second major type of response to state assimilation pressures is "limited particularism." Groups which have embraced this option typically amend certain aspects of their traditions in order to close the gap between the minority group's culture and the dominant majority's

---

[65] See Hyman 1995, p. 18.

[66] For further discussion see, for example, Goldscheider and Zuckerman 1984; Endelman 1987.

[67] For an engaging discussion of this transition and its implications for the understanding of communal identity, see Stolzenberg and Myers 1992.

[68] For this line of critique, see Young 1989.

norms. These groups thus adapt themselves to fit the public–private divide that many modern states promote. Jewish reform leaders, for example, were willing to exempt their followers from certain traditional Jewish practices in order to facilitate their social, political, and economic integration into the larger society, while at the same time maintaining their distinct religious affiliation (i.e. they did not endorse full assimilation). In the United States, nineteenth-century Reform Jews chose to forsake Jewish identity markers such as the yarmulke (a skullcap traditionally worn by Jewish men) and so were no longer visibly distinguishable as Jews by their dress.[69] Ritual observance was also modified in ways that made Judaism "dignified and American." English replaced Hebrew as the language of prayer, organ music was introduced into religious services, and men and women began to sit together, the men often with their heads uncovered.[70] These changes did not constitute full assimilation, however. Reform Judaism still retained most of the moral statutes derived from the Jewish tradition, and established religious, educational, and philanthropic institutions in order to inculcate a sense of Jewish particularism among their different communities' members.[71]

Groups that follow the limited particularism path can benefit from multiculturalism, especially when contemporary accommodation by the state takes the form of removing historically entrenched sectarian practices which have dominated the public sphere – such as the familiar example of Sunday closing laws, which once imposed such an unfair burden on members of non-Christian minorities.[72] However, groups that choose "limited particularism" rarely demand external protections which can serve as a guise for maintaining internal restrictions on certain group members.

Reactive culturalism

The real source of problems for the weak version of multiculturalism comes from an altogether different response to assimilation pressures: that of "reactive culturalism." This response entails a strict adherence to a group's traditional laws, norms, and practices as part of an identity group's active resistance to external forces of change, such as secularism or modernity. Reactive culturalism can be expressed in various ways – in a rigid reading of a group's textual sources, for example, or by closely

---

[69] See Auerbach 1990, p. 75.   [70] See Auerbach 1990, p. 76.
[71] See Hyman 1995, pp. 10–17.
[72] In the American context, see *Braunfeld* v. *Brown*, 366 US 599 (1961); *Gowan* v. *Maryland*, 366 US 420 (1961). For a critical evaluation of Sunday closing laws in Canada, see Weinrib forthcoming.

monitoring the behavior of its members and quickly quashing any unorthodox interpretation of the tradition as evidence of decay. In all, these amount to attempts to more clearly demarcate the group's boundaries by walling it off from the outside world.[73]

In instances of reactive culturalism, images of women and of the family frequently become symbols of a *nomoi* group's "authentic" cultural identity, a phenomenon which is manifested, for example, in religious communities from Orthodox Judaism to Islamic traditionalism to Evangelical Protestantism. When a group's assertion of its identity becomes inlaid with elements of reactive culturalism, some of its more hierarchical practices may gain heightened significance as manifestations of the group's difference from mainstream society.

In such instances, the interpretation of the group's tradition may become closed in upon itself, thus precluding various possibilities of reform within the tradition. In other words, the *nomoi* group becomes increasingly unable to adapt its law to new conditions. It often follows this path of heightened rigidity out of a fear that any adaptation might lead to increased assimilation and gradual disintegration of the collective *nomos*. Under such conditions, debates regarding the future of the community and its norms are stifled, and in-group attempts to bring about less hierarchical interpretations of the group's tradition are effectively blocked.

Thus reactive culturalism is not simply the expression of a pure unalloyed culture so much as the result of a cross-cultural interaction that has already occurred, in which the state has also played its role. Today, groups which have embraced this reactive option often seek to govern substantial aspects of their members' everyday lives, and thus petition the state for legal permission to do so.[74]

---

[73] Reactive culturalism may also emerge as a response to segregation, especially when members of minority communities seek to assimilate but are rejected by members of the wider society because they are perceived as "too different." I thank Rainer Bauböck who called my attention to this point in a personal communication. Bauböck suggests, rightly in my view, that religious fundamentalism among immigrants in contemporary European societies can thus be understood as reflecting the phenomenon I label as reactive culturalism.

[74] In the arena of education, for example, a *nomoi* group may wish to withdraw its young members from the public school, as was the landmark case of *Wisconsin v. Yoder*, 406 US 205 (1972). In *Yoder*, the US Supreme Court approved an accommodation measure to exempt children at the age of fourteen from two more years of mandatory schooling, as requested by the Old Amish Order community. For a critical view of this decision, see Arneson and Shapiro 1996. Another type of challenge in the education arena might include a demand by group members to exempt their children from exposure to material that challenges the parents' worldview. Unlike *Yoder*, this accommodation claim was rejected by the US Supreme Court in the case of *Mozert v. Hawkins County Board of Education*, 827 F.2d 1058 (6th Cir. 1987), cert. denied, 484 US 1066 (1988). For a comprehensive commentary on this case, see Stolzenberg 1993.

Groups that follow the reactive path may appear to be the best candidates for differentiated-citizenship rights, because they are "different" and make public demands for explicit and uncompromising accommodation. Yet they are precisely the identity groups which are the most prone to abuse multiculturalism. Such internal restrictions of a "reactivist" group can be perpetuated and in fact exacerbated through well-meaning multicultural accommodation. This problem is further aggravated when the outside–inside dichotomy serves as the rationale for the so-called "non-intervention" policy of the state – even in the face of systemic abuse of certain members' citizenship rights.

The inevitable inside–outside interaction

Multiculturalists understandably worry that non-dominant cultures which have reactively asserted their identities will be eradicated by the contemporary state in the name of official neutrality. In the past, the state has vigorously fought expressions of difference that constituted either an outrage against, or merely an affront to, the finer sensitivities of a dominant group.[75] Therefore, certain scholars reacted by championing the view that the state, under a multicultural citizenship model, should both grant greater autonomy to *nomoi* groups, and uphold a policy of "non-intervention" into identity groups' affairs.

The term "non-intervention" refers to a legal policy traditionally associated with two different arenas: *laissez-faire* economics and family privacy.[76] In the multicultural context, a non-intervention policy would defer to the group's traditions, even in instances where the paradox of multicultural vulnerability is at work, that is, where a group's practices are systematically exposing certain categories of members to sanctioned in-group violations in the name of protecting the group's collective *nomos*.[77]

Against "non-intervention"

"Non-intervention" is a misleading term. It re-enforces the myth that, left to their own devices, identity groups could exist as autonomous entities bearing little relation to the state.[78] Of course, if this were the case, then there would be no need to envision a multicultural model of citizenship –

---

[75] See Shaskolsky-Sheleff 1993, p. 194.
[76] For a detailed discussion, see Olsen 1983, p. 1504.   [77] See Kukathas 1992, p. 127.
[78] The "walls" of identity groups are never absolutely sealed. Even under a liberal non-interventionist policy, the state may (and even should) indirectly intervene in identity groups through measures such as tax exemptions. See, for example, Barry 2001, pp. 52–53.

for the very logic of this project requires the state to change the background rules affecting the status of identity groups. And after all, under both the strong and the weak versions of multiculturalism, some entity must define the criteria by which groups will be recognized, accommodated, and awarded group-differentiated rights. Significantly, the state itself plays a crucial role in determining which groups are allowed a degree of binding legal authority over their members, and who in the group is permitted to hold such state-backed legal power.

That identity groups might benefit from having their members bound by the group's traditions rather than by state law is, as I have noted, a perfectly sensible suggestion. But who should define which group's established traditions merit accommodation? And which voices from within an identity group should be recognized by the state as representative of the "integrity of a group's culture?" These questions have yet to be addressed in the multicultural literature, even though they critically concern the muddiest of anthropological, sociological, and ethnographic waters of debate. The paucity of available scholarship on these questions contributes to a prevalent murkiness in the multicultural debate, obscuring the ways in which the state operates among *nomoi* groups.[79]

In the family law arena, for example, multicultural accommodation policies which recognize the authority of religious communities to perform legally binding marriage and divorce ceremonies (in lieu of civil registration procedures) also set standards that define *who* in the group has the legal power to solemnize marriage and divorce.[80] The accommodation of identity groups in the context of a larger political community, therefore, is never just an act of "recognition." Given the interaction between inside and outside forces, as well as the diversity within identity

---

[79] *Nomoi* groups are not the fixed and unchanging essences that they are often portrayed to be. In asserting that identity groups are not to be conceived as non-conflictual or ahistorical entities, I do not intend to imply that identity groups are fictional entities or that they are not at least partly constitutive of their members' identities as encumbered selves. However, I also do not conceive of identity as something which is "virtually burnt into the genes of people." See Vertovec 1996, p. 51. For a critique of biologically or naturally based conceptions of race encoded in law, see Lopez 1994. See also Liu 1991. Liu describes the study of "intercultural relations" as based on the rejection of the perception that "the boundaries of group identity are fixed or at least readily apparent. Such an arrangement makes it difficult to conceptualize the relations between groups or how identities are mutually constructed in moments of contact."

[80] Since marital status has significant consequences not only for the parties involved but also for various third parties, the state sometimes requires a group to establish a register indicating the marital status of their members. When "inside" officials control such tasks for the state, they may be subject to some "outside" regulation. In Israel, for example, where matters of marriage and divorce fall under the exclusive jurisdiction of religious officials, state law regulates the terms of appointment of Jewish, Muslim, and Druze judges serving in religious courts.

groups, the state inevitably affects in-group power relations and legitimizes certain interpretations of an identity group's culture over other possible competing interpretations, regardless of however well meaning the state's accommodation policies might be.

The state-sanctioned delegation of jurisdiction to authorities within an identity group, when accompanied by a "non-interventionist" policy, thus plays right into the hands of power-holders in the group. It allows these leaders to define any potential change in the group's (now state-sanctioned) practices as corruptions of the *nomos*. Members who attempt to bring about in-group changes, by suggesting a less gender-biased reading of its family law practices, for example, are consequently open to accusations of cultural betrayal.[81]

Moreover, the so-called "traditional" treatment of women sometimes becomes a cultural emblem symbolizing a group's authentic identity. Not surprisingly, this phenomenon – a manifestation of reactive culturalism – further complicates the relationship between the group, the state, and the individual. In such instances of reactive culturalism, any state intervention in issues related to family law can be seen by the entire group as a threat to their *nomos*. Enormous pressure is thus put on women insiders to relinquish their individual citizenship rights and to demonstrate group loyalty by accepting the standard interpretation of group doctrine as the only correct reading of their group's tradition.

One argument against state intervention (even when the intervention is to protect the rights of individuals within the group) pleads for the sanctity of cultural tradition. Any state protection of disproportionately burdened insiders is thus seen as a form of interference which threatens the survival of the group and violates its autonomy. This argument seems especially powerful when the arena of intervention is the family, because many *nomoi* groups depend on the family for their continued reproduction and their sense of identity. Yet it is equally and immediately true that *nomoi* groups have already become part of the state in the modern world. The emphasis on insulating a group's tradition is, at least in part, connected to other inevitable pressures that are imposed on the group from the wider society surrounding it. In fact, one of the predictable consequences of this ongoing interaction with the state is that some more

---

[81] For a description of such accusations against women by certain (more conservative) sections of Islamic communities in the Arab world, see Haddad 1998, p. 20: "[certain] Islamists fault the Arab women for appropriating the concepts of equality and liberation from the West. In this she has become an importer, they say, an imitator rather than a creative originator. Her body dwells in her country, while her mind is in the West." Clearly, however, there are various other views on women's role in Islam, as well as a plurality of Muslim positions on the relationship between the traditional *shar'ia* and the idea of equal rights regardless of gender. See, for example, An-Na'im 1990; Bielefeldt 1995.

"reactive" groups will actually ossify and reify their once-living doctrine out of the fear of cultural assimilation.[82]

The choice then is not between "intervention" and "non-intervention," because *nomoi* groups are always reacting to the effects of state power, even when they claim to be most isolated from them. Rather, the question is what kind of accommodation the state should engage in, and with what legal-institutional mechanisms. If we accept the proposition that power relations, hierarchies, and subordination may exist not only *between* groups but also *within* groups, and that in-group dynamics are influenced by the relationship between the state and identity groups, then we should be aware that multicultural accommodation may do more than merely "recognize" a group's identity. In many ways, it indirectly participates in the ongoing process of redefining the essential traditions that constitute a group's *nomos*.[83]

Given that a group's established traditions are more fluid than we sometimes acknowledge, it is theoretically possible to re-interpret those traditions that impose systemic risks and costs on certain insiders without endangering the group's identity. Admittedly, changes are difficult to bring about in any established system. Moreover, a group's hierarchical traditions sometimes become cultural flags that distinguish the group's own culture from the world outside. In such situations, group members who disproportionately bear the costs of accommodation often wind up being punished when they call for changes in the group's "essential" practices, since their actions are taken as a betrayal of the group. Under such conditions, focusing solely on the external effects of accommodation enables power-holders to twist the language of respect for groups into a license to internally subordinate certain group members.

The "domestic impunity" fallacy

Artificially compartmentalizing the relationship between the group and the state into a fixed inside–outside division thus conceals the extent to which both are in fact interdependent.[84] It also permits identity groups to surround themselves with barriers so inviolable that whatever happens *inside* those groups happens *outside* the jurisdiction of state law. In other words, if a violation of individual rights occurs within an identity group,

---

[82] In a different context, John Borrows eloquently phrases the dilemma that reactive culturalism raises for identity groups themselves: "[T]radition can be the dead faith of living people, or the living faith of dead people." Groups which have taken the "reactive" turn may run the risk of inhering in the former alternative. See Borrows 2000, pp. 332–333.

[83] Even groups that aspire to complete cultural isolation must interact to some degree with outside forces – though that interaction may be centered on their efforts to more clearly demarcate their own boundaries.   [84] See Scott 1988, p. 37.

the violation is categorized as a "private affair." The state, as an outside entity, has no business intervening. This binary opposition leads us astray, however, not only because it ignores the web of relations between inside and outside, as well as the fragility of these categorizations, but also because it obscures the fact that what constitutes a "private affair" is in itself defined by the state's regime of law.[85]

The (re-)establishment of a "privacy zone" in the identity group context is sometimes justified by an appeal to the "right of exit" rationale – the rationale that every individual has a right to leave her group if she so wishes. This rationale suggests that the solution to the problem of systematic sanctioned in-group maltreatment is not to devise less hazardous accommodation policies, nor to envision more creative legal-institutional solutions; it is simply to permit at-risk group insiders to leave if they do not like their group's practices.

In fact, this right of exit solution offers no comprehensive policy approach at all, and instead offers a case-by-case approach, imposing the burden of resolving conflict upon the individual – and relieving the state of any responsibility for the situation, even though as the accommodating entity it still has a fiduciary duty toward all citizens. Specifically, the right of exit argument suggests that an injured insider should be the one to abandon the very center of her life, family, and community. This "solution" never considers that obstacles such as economic hardship, lack of education, skills deficiencies, or emotional distress may make exit all but impossible for some.[86]

It is not at all clear how the accommodating non-intervening multicultural state envisioned by proponents of the "right of exit" option is supposed to ensure that group members who wish to exit their traditional cultures can viably do so. By turning a blind eye to differential power distributions within the group hierarchy, and ignoring women's heightened symbolic role in relation to other group members, the right of exit rationale forces an insider into a cruel choice of penalties: either accept all group practices – including those that violate your fundamental citizenship rights – or (somehow) leave.[87]

According to this logic, once individuals enter (or choose to remain within) minority communities, they are presumed to have relinquished the set of rights and protections granted them by virtue of their citizenship.

---

[85] For a detailed account of the legal construction of the privacy discourse, see Siegel 1996.
[86] In other words, little thought is given under this approach to questions of *enabling* exit (assuming, for the sake of argument, that we accept it as the appropriate solution to addressing the paradox of multicultural vulnerability). For further critiques of the right of exit rationale, see Mahoney 1992; Kymlicka 1992, p. 143.
[87] For a defense of this position, see Kukathas 1992.

But consider this analogy: it could be argued that the state must not intervene in any couple's marital affairs, even in cases of domestic abuse,
because the battered wife's failure to leave a marital relationship into
which she voluntarily entered nullifies the offense. This in fact was the
legal doctrine for much of the nineteenth century in American law, which
favored the policy of state non-intervention in the domestic arena and
interpreted a woman's consent to marriage as implied consent to atrocities
such as rape or battering by her spouse.[88] This doctrine of implied consent
assumes that those who have not used the exit option have implicitly
agreed to their own subordination. Given this historical background, it is
troubling that after abolishing the implied consent doctrine in state law, we
find it resurfacing in the context of the contemporary defense of "non-
interventionist" multiculturalism.

Summary

We saw in this chapter how standard citizenship models fail to carve out a
conceptual space for *nomoi* groups in the public sphere, and instead focus
solely on the bundle of rights and obligations that individuals bear toward
the state. The new multicultural vision of citizenship improves upon the
standard theory by bringing in a third element, alongside the individual
and the state: the identity group. With this significant improvement
comes new problems, however, concerning the appropriate relationship
between group and state authorities, particularly with regard to jurisdiction over individuals living within *nomoi* groups. As illustrated by the
Martinez case, accommodation by the state which is designed to enhance
the autonomy of the group can also play a role in sanctioning in-group
power hierarchies. This is the paradox of multicultural vulnerability, and
it calls attention to the less recognized costs of accommodation, as well as
to the fact that these costs are often disproportionately borne by traditionally less powerful categories of group member.

The benefits of multiculturalism must not be treated in isolation from
the costs of accommodation. Hence, this chapter challenges the real-life
applicability of Kymlicka's too simple distinction between "external" and
"internal" aspects of accommodation. Even Kymlicka, who pays careful
attention to the potential conflict between enhancing cultural diversity
and protecting individual rights, fails to provide a satisfactory answer to
explain why *nomoi* groups, which under the cover of multiculturalism
engage in unfair in-group practices, deserve state accommodation for
such practices in the first place. My conclusion, however, is not that

---

[88] For further discussion, see West 1990.

multiculturalism cannot fulfil the promise of accommodating deep differences in the public sphere, but rather that we must be extremely cautious about what type of multiculturalism we engage in. We must not slide unintentionally from a tripartite framework into a group-versus-state dichotomy. I caution, in short, against equating respect for groups with a license to subordinate at-risk group members.

Paying attention to the often less recognized costs of accommodation leads to a broader re-examination of how we arrived where we are today. Certain contemporary *nomoi* groups assert their identity by systematically violating the citizenship rights of their members for the sake of preserving a distinct *nomos*. Yet the *nomoi* groups claiming accommodation from the state have already been affected by the operation of that state, and their behavior is in some sense a response to that experience. There are three main types of response to assimilation pressures, and each in turn affects the kind of response it elicits from the state. The first response, "full assimilation," involves the rejection of the group's traditional distinct identity by individual members in their hope of becoming culturally undifferentiated citizens. It expects the state to uphold non-discriminatory civil standards. The second response, "limited particularism," occurs when group leaders transform certain aspects of the minority tradition in order to approximate the majority's practices, thus enabling group members to participate fully in the public sphere without losing their unique cultural identity. This compromise assumes that the state will remove culture-specific symbols from the public sphere and from state law. The third and most complex response, "reactive culturalism," describes active resistance from the group to external forces of change, a resistance often manifested through a rigid reading of the group's *nomos* and by strict monitoring of the behavior of group members. It is this response which requires the state to examine ways of publicly and politically accommodating group identity. And it is through this expectation that minority groups might advocate the adoption of a strong version of multiculturalism. Groups that have embarked on this latter path raise serious challenges to the weak version of multiculturalism when they demand public accommodation of their differences and, at the same time, seek immunity from state intervention into their "private affairs."

Yet adopting a policy of "non-intervention" only aggravates in-group restrictions, without solving the multiculturalism paradox. The "right of exit" solution similarly fails to provide a comprehensive answer. Instead, it throws upon the already beleaguered individual the responsibility to either miraculously transform the legal-institutional conditions that keep her vulnerable or to find the resources to leave her whole world behind.

Surely it is troubling when a solution demands that those who are the most vulnerable must pay the highest price, while the abusers remain undisturbed in their home communities. Women, in particular, suffer under these two options. The next chapter more closely examines the effects of well-meaning accommodations upon women in the family law arena, and considers the disproportionate burden that they often bear for the sake of preserving the collective.

3 Family law and the construction of collective identity

No solution to the paradox of multicultural vulnerability can be found unless we have a clearer understanding of where the paradox hits hardest, and family law provides an excellent test case for just such a study. Clearly, when the state awards jurisdictional powers to the group in the family law arena, it enhances the group's autonomy. At the same time, this re-allocation of legal authority from the state to the group may also expose certain individuals within the group to systemic and sanctioned in-group rights violations. This manifestation of the multiculturalism paradox in the family law arena does not cause a problem for the strong version of multiculturalism, since the strong version is primarily concerned with strengthening the *nomoi* group, even at the expense of imposing disproportionate costs upon individuals inside it. But it does raise a serious dilemma for the weak version of multiculturalism.

The dilemma is this. There are good reasons to support accommodation in the family law arena, especially in the case of non-territorial *nomoi* communities that demarcate membership boundaries through personal status and lineage rules. Prime among the reasons offered for supporting accommodation is the fact that in many of these groups the rules encompassed in their system of family law fulfil a task similar to that of citizenship law for a state.[1] A *nomoi* group's membership rules, encoded in family law, thus provide the bonds which connect the past to the future, by identifying who is considered part of the tradition. This is particularly true of rules that define group membership by virtue of birth and marriage, and thereby demarcate a pool of individuals who are collectively responsible for maintaining the group's values, practices, and distinct way of life. Group membership rules, like state citizenship laws, cannot by themselves guarantee that all children born to a *nomoi* group will necessarily

---

[1] They are the mechanisms whereby a society perpetuates itself and achieves continuity over time, retaining its coherence and identity even as members are born and die, join or depart the group. For a discussion of the diachronic dimension of citizenship law, see, for example, Galloway 1999, p. 202.

choose to remain active members of that group, or that they will decide to follow its tradition. But *nomoi* groups, like states, ultimately acquire the majority of their members by birth[2] instead of through adult choice.[3]

Nomoi groups struggling to preserve their differences under the common citizenship regime of most modern *states* often lack the institutional authority to formally determine who belongs to their community. Few can issue formal documents of membership or require members to contribute taxes directly to the collective. Thus many minority communities depend on traditions pertaining specifically to the family in order to preserve their distinct cultural identities.[4]

The gatekeeping function of family law challenges the weak version of multiculturalism because it forces us to face both the "external" and the "internal" aspects (and consequences) of accommodation. Even under standard citizenship models the arena of family law tends to remain troublesome for all of the underlying philosophical questions which it brings to the fore. These include concerns about the degree to which the state may define "the family," as well as public policy issues such as population control, reproductive freedom, and the proper limits of parents' control over their children. However, these and other questions related to the terms and procedures defining families and the legal relationships within them have become particularly acute in the context of multicultural or differentiated citizenship models, as minority communities increasingly demand *legal* recognition of family law traditions as necessary to preserve the group's collective identity.[5] Such recognition strengthens the autonomy of *nomoi* groups – for without the ability to define its own membership boundaries, no community can survive.[6] In the current age of

[2] According to the United States Census Bureau, in 1999 the percentage of the United States population that was foreign born was only roughly 10 percent of the US population – even after one of the largest immigration waves in the United States' history. On average, then, more than 90 percent of the population of a high-immigration country like the USA acquires membership in the polity by birth. For a concise presentation of this empirical data, see Feldblum and Klusmeyer 1999.

[3] For a position which advocates a model of political membership by consent rather than by birthright, see Schuck and Smith 1985. For a qualified defense of birthright, see Eisgruber 1997.

[4] In the context of Muslim communities which have been ruled by Western colonial regimes, this assertion of identity often bears a specifically anti-imperialist tone. For further discussion, see Hélie-Lucas 1994; Shaheed 1994.

[5] One of the lingering effects of colonialism upon indigenous peoples in North America has been the establishment of a connection between a woman's marriage status and her entitlement to tribal membership (where a non-Indian marries an Indian husband), or her exclusion and loss of status (where an Indian woman marries a non-tribal or a non-Indian husband). See my discussion of the *Martinez* case in ch. 2.

[6] Control over the definition of who is and who is not eligible for full membership is recognized as crucial for the preservation of collective identities, and international law explicitly leaves it to each state to lay down the rules governing citizenship. For further discussion,

diversity,[7] the state is relatively receptive to minority cultures' requests for greater degrees of legal control over their own family affairs.[8]

If we focus solely on the group-versus-state relationship, we can reasonably agree that it is almost always in the interest of identity groups to gain greater authority over their affairs. Indeed, this is precisely what distinguishes the new multicultural understanding of citizenship from the standard citizenship theories. But if we add the concerns of the situated individual to this same picture, the issues suddenly become more complicated. This is because accommodation comes to have different meanings for different group members as a result of preexisting power hierarchies.[9] A growing body of research shows that accommodation in the family law arena may impose a systemic, sanctioned, and disproportionate burden upon some categories of group member rather than others: primarily, but not solely, women.[10]

Incidental vs. systemic in-group violation

Not every act of accommodation necessarily leads to the paradox of multicultural vulnerability. Problems culminating in this paradox tend to arise only when the group upholds certain practices that disproportionately

see, for example, Dinstein 1976; Oestreich 1999. However, the right of each state to lay down the rules governing citizenship does not imply that a state is free to ignore the needs and interests of non-members within its territory (be they foreign workers, refugees, or long-term residents). Various regional and international law documents now specify the basic protections of such persons.   [7] To borrow James Tully's phrase (Tully 1995b).

[8] While this trend is still controversial, it nevertheless looms large on the public policy agendas of many multicultural societies. For example, Canada, Australia, New Zealand, England, and the United States have all been revisiting their family law policies in recent years, exploring different ways in which state law can be pluralistic enough to allow different communities to be governed by their own institutions on certain matters of marriage and divorce proceedings. For a concise overview of recent changes in the family law policies of Australia, New Zealand, Canada, England and Wales, see Atkin and Austin 1996; Bainham 1996; Parkinson 1994; Pearl 1995; Poulter 1998; Syrtash1992, pp. 195–236.

[9] However, we need to differentiate between random impositions against particular group members, and those which have been built into a group's cultural system and which routinely burden only a certain category of group member. Certain violations, e.g. most of those against women in the family law arena, are *systemic* rather than *accidental*.

[10] For country case studies that recount the disproportionate burden that women bear when their group's personal status laws and property relations codes are accommodated by the state, see, for example, the collection of essays in Cook 1994; Howland 1999; Moghadam 1994a. Family law accommodation can also, under certain circumstances, impose disproportionate costs upon children, especially in cases where the *nomoi* group receives exclusive jurisdiction over issues such as custody, guardianship, child-support payments, adoption, and education. Children may be better off if the community controls *some* of these issues, but they may become pawns in the power dynamics if the community controls *all* aspects of family law. An illustration of this latter point is found in the Israeli case of CA 3077/90 *Plonit* v. *Ploni*, 49 (2) PD 578, which I discuss in great detail in Shachar 2000c.

expose the citizenship rights of some members to risk.[11] Consider the following hypothetical situations (A and B), which illustrate two different cases where autonomous decision-making power over a specific arena is awarded to the group.[12]

In situation A, as part of its multicultural accommodation policy, the state devolves to the group full discretion over matters that are important to the group but which are not encoded in its *nomos*, such as policy decisions concerning resource development.[13] This allocation of powers strengthens the group's autonomy *vis-à-vis* the state, because important decisions shaping future generations will now be made by the group in accordance with its own decision-making mechanisms, without any need to consult or receive approval from another level of government. If the state so empowers the group, however, there is always the possibility that some individual members of the group will be worse off in comparison with their situation under state law. Let us assume, for instance, that a Native American tribe has been awarded jurisdiction over matters of resource development and that a majority of its members have decided to open a gambling facility on the territory under tribal jurisdiction. Let us also assume that a similar decision could not have been made under state law because state law prohibits gambling activities. The tribe's decision might succeed in developing the tribe's resources, or it might fail. Either way, the justifications for adopting the decision are not dictated by the group's established tradition[14] because the provision of gambling opportunities does not fall under the identity-preserving imperative dictated by the group's *nomos*.

The tribe's decision to open the facility will undoubtedly exert both an economic and a social impact on tribe members. Although a successful casino might accrue a certain financial benefit to members of the tribe, members given to compulsive gambling will certainly pay for the facility in a different coin. Random majority policy decisions can thus potentially injure certain group members. But the infringements on members in

---

[11] Of course, one could argue that no state accommodation measure ever will affect all group members perfectly equally. But this misses the crux of the problem. The multiculturalism paradox does not refer to incidental rights violations. Rather, it is concerned with *systemic* intra-group practices that adversely affect a particular category of group members.   [12] The substance of this discussion is dervied from Shachar 2000a.

[13] This is akin to an example given by Kymlicka, who discusses powers which are gradually being transferred by the United States and Canada to North American tribal/band councils. See Kymlicka 1995, p. 30.

[14] While no identity group's "established tradition" is ever fully fixed or immune to change, a group's authoritative textual interpreters emphasize specific norms or practices as having a dominant status over any given period. Thus an established tradition in religious groups, for example, usually consists of a recognized corpus, which in turn is subject to re-interpretations by a group's recognized leader or inside court.

such cases are not encoded in a group's established traditions so much as incidental.

In situation B, an identity group is awarded jurisdiction over a social arena substantive to its self-definition, such as family law. The group thus has authority to construct its membership boundaries, that is, to decide who by birth or marriage is eligible for group membership, and what kind of legal relations between spouses will prevail within the community. What is granted in this second situation is not a previously undetermined policy issue like gambling, to be determined by the group's decision-making mechanisms. Instead, a well-defined "text" of social practices and legal norms is given authoritative status.[15] The interpretation of the group's established traditions is rarely, if ever, open to public deliberation. In theory, legal powers are thus transferred from the state to the group's members. But in practice, such powers are wielded primarily by the group's authorities because they are recognized by the state as "speaking for the culture," and are therefore entrusted with official clout to implement the group's traditions. And such accommodation might come at the cost of exposing certain group members to systemic, sanctioned intra-group violations of their citizenship rights, all with the unwitting blessing of the multicultural state.

The qualitative difference between situation A and situation B lies not in the state's devolution of powers to the identity group, but in whether or not the multicultural state accommodates a social and legal disadvantage that is *already evident* in the group's established traditions. When restrictions upon a certain category of insider are built into the established traditions of a group, the tension between multiculturalism and citizenship is further aggravated since the infringement of rights is no longer merely incidental but instead is deeply inherent. Under such conditions, the disproportion-ate injury imposed internally upon some (but not all) group members is directly related to the external ways in which the state accommodates the *nomoi* group. Thus in situation B, the external and internal aspects of multicultural accommodation are mistakenly considered separate.

The anatomy of family law

Recently, feminist scholars have begun to seriously investigate the tangled relationship between family law, gender, and the reproduction of collective

---

[15] *Nomoi* groups generally have a recognized corpus of texts by which they govern the group's public life and individuals' behavior. In the case of religiously defined *nomoi* groups, for example, these texts can include holy scripts and their authoritative interpre-tations. Other groups might only have unwritten customary traditions which guide behavior. My reference to "texts" here includes both the written and oral dimensions.

identities. Although this relationship is obviously complex, writers from various disciplines agree that women occupy a special position in constituting collective identities: "[o]n the one hand, they are [full] members of collectives, institutions or groupings . . . On the other hand, they are a special focus of . . . concerns as a social category with a special role (particularly human reproduction)."[16] Yet women's unique position in *nomoi* groups as "cultural conduits" gives rise to an ironic problem: these crucial cultural roles have traditionally been expressed in the realm of the family, through adherence to a set of gender-biased norms and practices which often subordinate women.[17] Traditions pertaining to the family are central to the self-concepts of many *nomoi* groups. However, these very same laws and practices often subordinate women to such an extent that when their groups' practices are accommodated by the state, women living in *nomoi* groups risk losing their basic rights as state citizens.

Scholars have focused on particular case studies which examine how women become emblematic of political positions and of cultural identity in particular local-historical processes.[18] Of particular interest are case studies of religious communities, which show that women are assigned "the role of bearers of cultural values, carriers of traditions, and symbols of the community" primarily because they carry out the tasks of nurturance and reproduction.[19] A group's family law policies thus incorporate women's important and potentially powerful roles as "bearers of the collective" into the group's *nomos*, while simultaneously consolidating a system of unequal power relations between men and women.

There are two perspectives integral to any discussion of family law.[20] One is more outward looking or externally focused. This can be described as family law's "demarcating" function, which maintains a group's membership boundaries *vis-à-vis* the larger society. The other perspective is more interpersonal or inwardly directed. This can be called family law's "distributive" function, which shapes and allocates rights, duties, and

---

[16] See Anthias and Yuval-Davis 1989, p. 6. Note that their analysis of women's unique position is not aimed at essentializing their role as childbearers and care-givers (i.e. as biological and cultural reproducers of collective identities), nor does it express the view that all "human reproduction" experiences of women are similar. Anthias and Yuval-Davis therefore differ from cultural feminists who glorify mothering as the epitome of an ethics of care. Compare with West 1988. For a critique of West's "essential woman," see Harris 1990.

[17] This is the case, for example, when the marital options of a woman are officially determined by a male guardian – a father, husband, brother, or uncle. See Freeman 1990.

[18] Of the rapidly growing body of literature which treats the relationship between gender and the construction of collective identities, see, for example, the following collections of articles: Afshar 1987; Grewal and Kaplan 1994; Kandiyoti 1991; Moghadam 1994a.

[19] See Moghadam 1994b, p. 4.

[20] The discussion in this sub-section is based on Shachar 2000b, pp. 202–208.

ultimately powers between men and women within the group.[21] The distinction between these two functions parallels the distinction between two legal aspects of marriage and divorce: personal status and property relations. Divorce proceedings generally involve both aspects, a change in personal status (the demarcating function) and a determination of property relations between the spouses (the distributive function). While often intermingled in practice, personal status and property relations are legally two distinct subjects. [22]

Family law's demarcating function

The demarcating function of family law – that is, the centrality of family law in defining and regulating a group's membership boundaries – can best be understood in terms of the two basic means through which group identities are maintained. These two means, which are often intertwined, have been generally categorized as "the racial, ethnic, biological and territorial, on the one hand, and the ideological, cultural and spiritual on the other."[23] Anne McClintock stresses the former, emphasizing that collective identities "are frequently figured through the iconography of familial or domestic space."[24] Moreover, she observes that even the term *nation* derives from *nasci* (Latin): "to be born," and that national collective identities are also symbolically figured as domestic genealogies.[25] Benedict Anderson also suggests that communities are best viewed as akin to families and religious orders.[26] Such communities are understood by their members as having "finite, if elastic boundaries, beyond which lie other nations."[27] Defined in this fashion, group membership derives its meaning from a system of "differences,"[28] which must be demarcated by membership boundaries.

Family law demarcates membership boundaries in two related ways:

[21] Being officially accepted as a member may also affect one's eligibility to receive certain distributive benefits designated as available only to group members (as, for example, in the *Martinez* case). Other distributive consequences may include the rate of taxation and the right to dwell in a given country.

[22] For further discussion, see Vestal and Foster 1956, pp. 23–31.

[23] See Ben-Israel 1992, p. 393.   [24] See McClintock 1993, pp. 62–63.

[25] Ibid. The analogy here between identity groups and nations is confined to the mechanisms of biological and cultural reproduction. The focus of this discussion remains concerned with the situation of *nomoi* groups which exist within the framework of a larger political entity (the state), rather than with groups seeking national independence or secession from the larger body politic. The present study is engaged with discovering how *nomoi* groups seek accommodation for their differences *within* the boundaries of a state composed of a heterogeneous citizenry.   [26] Anderson 1991, pp. 143–144.

[27] Ibid., p. 7.

[28] For a discussion about the construction of "difference" as a relational term, see Minow 1990. See also Parker et al. 1992.

first, by developing complex lineage rules which determine who, by virtue of birth, is eligible for acquiring full membership in the group, and secondly, by defining who by way of marriage can become a group member.[29] It is not surprising therefore that *nomoi* groups have developed various social and legal mechanisms for controlling the personal status and the reproductive activity of women – for women have a central and potentially powerful role in perpetuating the collective.[30]

Intra-group policing of women,[31] if encoded in the group's *nomos*, is partially achieved via the implementation of personal status laws and lineage rules which clearly state how, when, and with whom women can give birth to children who will then become full and legitimate members of the community.[32] In *nomoi* groups which stress the "biological descent" of identity, legal marriage is a necessary but not sufficient condition for granting group membership by birth. Therefore, a child may be born in a marriage legally recognized by the *nomoi* group without being considered a "blood" member of the community.[33]

Although there are no *genetic* grounds for distinction between children born of mixed marriages, in many *nomoi* groups the *gender* of the "full blood" parent often becomes the sole determinant of legal and social belonging to a given community.[34] Clearly, personal status laws and lineage

---

[29] Accordingly, a family law tradition loses its opportunity to set the legal terms for membership if a *nomoi* group permits anyone interested in joining the group to become a full member.

[30] See Klug 1989, p. 31. I view reproduction and mothering, like other human relationships and institutions, as constructed by law, history, and society, rather than purely inscribed by biology. For similar views on reproduction and mothering, see e.g. Glenn 1994.

[31] Men, too, are controlled by such laws, but not in a similarly discriminatory and oppressive fashion.

[32] Yet even within this legal paradigm, there is some leeway for defining the specific legal means through which membership boundaries are codified in a *nomoi* group's traditions. Although they may all share the notion that group membership is legally transmitted by birth, different religious traditions have developed different "membership transmission procedures." The Jewish tradition, for example, dictates that membership by birth is transmitted along matrilineal lines, while other religious traditions, such as Islam, dictate that group membership be transmitted along patrilineal lines.

[33] Consider, for example, the Santa Clara Pueblo's membership rules which were upheld by the US Supreme Court decision in the *Martinez* case:
1. All children born of marriages between members of the Santa Clara Pueblo shall be members of the Santa Clara Pueblo.
2. . . . [C]hildren born of marriages between male members of the Santa Clara Pueblo and non-members shall be members of the Santa Clara Pueblo.
3. Children born of marriages between female members of the Santa Clara Pueblo and non-members shall not be members of the Santa Clara Pueblo.
4. Persons shall not be naturalized as members of the Santa Clara Pueblo under any circumstances.

[34] Historically, in virtually all democratic countries the husband's nationality traditionally determined the nationality of the children in a mixed marriage, as well as the wife's nationality. According to this principle, a native-born woman who married a foreign national lost not only her legal personality (as a *femme covert*) but also her own nationality

rules are a product of a particular group's history and established traditions; yet they are nonetheless perceived as reflecting a real "biological" distinction between children worthy of being granted full membership and those excluded from the group. For example, the *Halakhah* (Jewish religious law) constructs "blood" taboos with regard to the status of children born to a Jewish father who marries outside the faith. Since group membership in the Jewish community is transmitted along matrilineal lines, a child born to a Jewish husband and a non-Jewish wife cannot become a member of the Jewish community at birth.[35] In order to acquire full membership (that is, a religious affiliation as a Jew), a child of a Jewish father and a non-Jewish mother would have to go through formal, although simplified, procedures of conversion. As in other religious *nomoi* groups, the act of conversion requires rites of passage which constitute a symbolic "re-birth" into one's new religious affiliation. Of course, the analogy to birth is not accidental. Even in the United States, an "alien" has to go through a "*naturalization*" process in order to become a full member in the political community, i.e. to "fill in" for what has not been acquired "*naturally*" by birth.[36]

Interestingly, under the same Jewish family law, a child born to a Jewish father and a non-Jewish mother *after* she has converted to Judaism becomes a full member of the Jewish community *at birth*. But the distinction between the status of children born to a non-Jewish mother and those born to a non-Jewish mother who has converted to Judaism, simply cannot be explained in terms of "blood." As the authors of *The Myth of the Jewish Race* observe, "the genetic make-up of the children born to such mixed couples [between a Jewish father and a non-Jewish mother who has or has not converted into Judaism] remains the same."[37] Hence, the distinguishing factor is cultural – i.e. the mother's conversion is perceived as an indication that her children will grow up in a Jewish home.

However, even if we accept the argument that many biological categories are socially constructed (as I think we should),[38] we must nonetheless recognize that a group's transmission of membership by birth (as codified in its family law rules) is an important factor in the maintenance of the

and independent citizenship status. This was the official government policy during specific periods of American history. For a detailed discussion, see Bredbenner 1998; Cott 1998; Sapiro 1984. Today, only a minority of nation states continue to uphold gender-biased citizenship laws specifying that the father's nationality alone decides the nationality of children born to a mixed marriage. See Stratton 1992.

[35] The legal situation is different in Israel, where Jewish nationality for the purposes of the national public register is not identical with the Jewish Orthodox definition of religious affiliation. See Akzin 1970; Ginossar 1970.

[36] "Nature" and its cognates also come from *natus*, to be born; thus "nature" and "nation" share an etymological, if not a socio-historical, root.

[37] See Patai and Wing 1975, pp. 91–92.

[38] Of the growing literature on this subject in the context of race, see e.g. Harris 1995; Lopez 1994. More generally, see Crenshaw et al. 1995; Delgado 1995.

group's self-concept. Family law thus assumes a pivotal role in the construction of a shared identity among group members who constitute an "imagined community."[39] Family law's peculiar power lies not so much in its delineation of "blood" membership as in its value as a political expression of the group's power to determine its (non-territorial) membership boundaries, i.e. a self-defined legal procedure for autonomously demarcating who falls inside and outside the collective.[40]

Family law's distributive function

Besides the demarcation of a group's membership boundaries, family law also defines property relations between the spouses and, in the event of death or divorce, determines the economic and parental consequences of this change in personal status. Through the distributive aspect of family law, a group's property rules govern the allocation of resources and obligations between spouses during a marriage, as well as after the marriage ends. Property relations relate to a wide range of issues which need to be settled upon death or divorce, such as a spouse's right to an estate or post-divorce support, control of land, or entitlement to child custody. Granting legal authority to accommodated communities over property relations often exerts a negative economic impact on women. Indeed, in many *nomoi* groups the distributive function of family law only serves to entrench persistent inequalities. It often perpetuates women's dependence on other family members for survival, crippling their ability to gain minimal economic self-sufficiency. For example, a divorcée without a share in matrimonial property has no title to joint property held in the ex-husband's name, and therefore no means of obtaining independent credit toward a livelihood.[41] Unfortunately, women living within accommodated *nomoi* groups may learn at times of marital crisis that they have limited or no legal rights to property, land, or even post-divorce financial support.[42]

---

[39] See Anderson 1994.

[40] In the common law tradition, this sovereignty was recognized under the doctrine of "marriage good where celebrated is good everywhere." That is, as a general principle of conflict of laws, a country should grant the fullest recognition to any marriage valid in the parties' home country (or under the parties' personal laws). The logic behind this principle is aptly summarized by Richard Cleveland: "[f]rom the time of clan and kin communities to the twentieth century, status has been and still is the true expression of the fact that there are different ideas about fundamental relations strong enough to [be of] obvious advantage in wholesale dealings. Status is still a serene monument to the originality of independent political communities." See Cleveland 1925, pp. 1094–1095.

[41] For a detailed discussion of property relations and gender issues as they relate to customarily discriminatory marriage and divorce rules, see Nyamu 2000.

[42] In some Muslim communities, for example, although an ex-wife is entitled to the return of her dowry (or *mehar*), she is not necessarily entitled to alimony payments for more than three months after a divorce (the *iddat* period). For a concise overview of these family law distributive rules, see Nasir 1990.

In other words, women who observe the group's tradition and feel obliged to follow its demarcative and distributive rules may find that they are entitled to little if any compensation for years devoted to the family and the cultural community at large.[43] Thus, although women's agency in reproducing the collective might be expected to establish a dominant position within their respective *nomoi* groups, the emphasis on women's unique role in the task of procreating the group has actually produced the opposite effect. In fact, the legal autonomy granted to *nomoi* groups in the family law arena can be explicitly detrimental to women's basic rights.[44] Precisely because this membership preservation system contributes to the construction of "internal restrictions" within any given group, we cannot risk considering the delegation of legal powers in the family law arena as merely a matter of "external protections."[45]

Cultural preservation, multicultural accommodation, and women's in-group subordination

Although family law is clearly implicated in the formation and perpetuation of in-group power relations, to date there has been no attempt to systematically evaluate how accommodation in the family law arena works to demarcate a group's membership boundaries while also maintaining distributive hierarchies along the gender line. The present study seeks to provide a thorough account of these complex issues by analyzing women's unique capacity to contribute to the collective, their sanctioned in-group vulnerability, and the relationship between a group's reactive manifestation of its cultural identity and its heightened control of women through family law.

Women's heightened responsibility and heightened vulnerability

Nomoi groups often celebrate women's responsibilities as the bearers of legitimate children and as primary socializers of the young. Such a

---

[43] In Kenya, for example, "[d]ivorce under both African customary and Islamic laws can be extrajudicial; one party can unilaterally bring about the divorce without any requirement that a court hear the dispute . . . In the case of divorce, women married under Islamic and African customary laws are almost never entitled to marital property and are rarely provided with a maintenance." See Muli 1995, p. 79. See also Freeman 1990. In other cases, distributive family laws can have dire consequences for a mother's right to custody over her children if they specify that a child's father is his/her natural legal guardian, and that only in the event of his death or disappearance can the mother assume the role of legal guardian. For a concise discussion of this problem in the context of Hindu Guardianship and Minorities Act of 1956 in India, see Singh 1994.

[44] Clearly, however, not all women within a given *nomoi* group suffer intra-group injuries, even if they are subject to the same family law code. This is partly because women in religious or ethnic communities, as elsewhere, differ in social status, wealth, or age.

[45] The reference here is to Will Kymlicka's "external protections/internal restrictions" distinction, as already previously discussed.

narrowly pronounced glorification of women's contribution to the collective can be traced throughout various religiously defined *nomoi* communities, ranging from Orthodox Judaism to Muslim traditionalism to Protestant Evangelism.[46] The typical emphasis on women's cultural and biological role tends to serve as a rationale for severely limiting their choices in terms of educational and employment opportunities, besides maintaining property allocation rules that significantly curtail their access to independent means of livelihood.

Women clearly make an important contribution to the transmission of collective identity. This should be taken as an empirical observation, not as an essentializing statement.[47] The relationship between women and the social construction of group identity may not always assume the same form, but the ways in which women are regulated, especially in *nomoi* groups that have adopted the reactive culturalism response, seems typically fivefold.[48]

Since women reproduce future members of the collective, their reproductive activities are often the first to be closely monitored by their identity groups. Women are generally controlled in terms of the situations in which they are allowed to marry and have children. In other words, they must procreate in ways that will preserve the membership boundaries and autonomous identity of their group. Second, the conditions under which marriages and childbearing are considered legitimate are of special importance. Third, women's function as cultural conduits for the group's unique history and identity imposes a duty to faithfully transmit the group's social norms, customs and traditions, collective memories, and specific expectations to the next generation.[49] Fourth, women can embody the entire symbolic significance of their group, particularly under reactive culturalist conditions. An abstract female image may serve as an

---

[46] See, for example, Meiselman's praise of women's contribution to the Jewish Orthodox collective in Meiselman 1978. For a critical evaluation of the in-group controls imposed on Muslim women, see Hélie-Lucas 1994. For a discussion of gender issues and modern evangelicalism in the United States, see Bendroth 1993. Bendroth's core argument is that "[g]ender issues stood at the heart of [the] fundamentalist desire to be different." Ibid., p. 3. For a comprehensive discussion of religious laws concerning the family, and their potentially negative impact on women through their entrenchment in state policies, see, for example, Howland 1997.

[47] See Yuval-Davis and Anthias 1989. These sociologists focus primarily on the phenomenon of ethnic and national collectives, but the dynamics that they discover in operation are much the same for other kinds of identity groups.

[48] See Yuval-Davis and Anthias 1989, pp. 6–11. For further elaboration, see Yuval-Davis 1997.

[49] Having identified women as conduits for the group's practices and traditions, Anthias and Yuval-Davis do not address the messy problem of women's collusion in their own oppressively rigid gender ascriptions, which also renews itself from generation to generation.

emblem for the group; an abstract female figured as endangered and in need of protection lends still greater resonance. Moreover, differences among groups are often demarcated by women's public manifestation of their group membership, as in the case of wearing the veil.[50] Fifth, women may participate alongside men in political struggles for the enhancement of the group's autonomy *vis-à-vis* the wider society.[51]

Because *nomoi* groups view control over marriage and divorce as crucial to their survival, they tend to urge the state to accommodate their differences by awarding them jurisdiction in matters of membership demarcation, including family law.[52] Such allocation of legal powers can certainly lend assistance to the group's struggle for self-preservation. But accommodated family law traditions do not simply define membership boundaries: they also regulate the distribution of rights, duties, and ultimately power between men and women within the community. The latter distributive aspect of family law becomes especially salient during separation or divorce proceedings. When marriages dissolve in close-knit *nomoi* communities, multicultural accommodation in the family law arena can bring deep tensions and dark inequalities to the surface.

The agunah *test case*

Jewish family law is unblushingly informed by a tradition that praises the contributions women make to the survival of the collective, primarily through their domestic roles as mothers, caregivers, and managers of the home.[53] Yet their heightened responsibility can give them to heightened vulnerability as well. According to Jewish law a husband can "anchor" his wife in a religious marriage – even if the relationship has been formally

---

[50] Much has been written in recent years about the political function of the *chador* and the *hijab* in asserting Muslim identity. For different feminist opinions on the politics of the veil, see Abu-Odeh 1992; Tohidi 1994; Galeotti 1993.

[51] In cases of national collectives the fight might be for full independence. See Yuval-Davis and Anthias 1989, p. 10.

[52] The other major arena where *nomoi* groups seek accommodation for preserving their distinct identity is in education. Deference to minority communities' request to preserve their unique way of life (in this sphere) may lead, *inter alia*, to the restriction of these children's social mobility. Such accommodations in education may result in several inadvertent limitations, including a lack of exposure to more pluralist and diverse aspects of the curriculum, mandatory high school education, or participation in a learning environment that treats all persons as equals, regardless of their race, gender, culture, religion, etc. These issues have arisen in some of the most controversial religious accommodation cases brought before the US Supreme Court in recent years, such as *Mozert, Yoder, Kiryas Joel*, and *Bob Jones University*.

[53] See e.g. Berman 1973. Interviews with women who "returned" to Orthodox Judaism (*baalot teshova*) also reveal that they "appreciate the clear and unambivalent feelings in Judaism toward motherhood." See Kaufman 1985.

terminated by state law – by refusing to consent to the religious divorce decree (the *get*). Such an "anchored" woman (or *agunah*) cannot "acquire herself" or become free to marry another man within the Jewish faith, as long as her husband refuses the *get*.[54] While she can remarry under secular or civil law before a judge even without obtaining the *get* (since in the eyes of state law the first marriage has already been legally terminated), "she must then abandon her convictions and, to some extent, abandon traditional Judaism."[55]

The origins of this divorce practice are found in biblical divorce law, and *Halakhic* authorities have instituted various legal constraints to limit a husband's unequal power at divorce through interpretation of Jewish law. But the *agunah* problem is still a serious cause for concern to Orthodox Jewish communities around the globe.[56] Orthodox leaders clearly do not encourage the "anchoring" of wives by estranged husbands, nor the imposition of barriers to their spouses' religious remarriage. Yet no rabbi or *beth din* (Jewish religious court) can force a spouse to grant the *get*, because under Jewish tradition the act of divorce is a private (contractual) release between two parties. Differently put, divorce according to Jewish tradition is not ordained, nor is it strictly speaking a religious act, although it does take place in a religious context.[57] If both parties agree to the divorce, the *get* procedure can be effortlessly arranged. But if one of the parties refuses to consent (in the majority of cases the husband), then that spouse can use the *get* as a tactic to impede the other party from entering into a new marriage, or as a means of extorting rights to which that (recalcitrant) spouse would not normally be entitled under state law. Most problematically (from the perspective of Jewish law), some recalcitrant husbands abuse the *get* procedure as a means of blackmailing their former spouses.[58] They offer consent to the religious divorce only on the grounds that the other party agrees to relinquish certain property, support, custodial, or access rights, or agrees to

---

[54] The *agunah* problem in Jewish law is rooted in the biblical law of divorce, in the book of Deuteronomy 24:1: "A man takes a wife and possesses her. She fails to please him because he finds some [matter of] indecency (*ervat davar*), and he writes her a bill of divorce (*sefer keritut*), hands it to her, and sends her away from his house." Rachael Biale offers a concise and clear analysis of the interpretive controversies regarding the biblical formation of Jewish divorce law, and a description of the various legal constraints imposed by *Halakhic* authorities in the course of Jewish history to limit a husband's right in divorce. See Biale 1984, pp. 70–101.

[55] See Syrtash 1987, p. 313. The same set of tensions arises in Muslim communities, where the wife is free to remarry according to state law but is still considered married by *shari'a* law. See Pearl and Menski 1998, p. 79.

[56] Despite significant changes in Jewish divorce law which better protect women and grant them some power in divorce proceedings, for the most part the power still remains in the hands of men.   [57] For a detailed discussion, see Bleich 1984.

[58] See Breitowitz 1992.

the modification of these rights.[59] This is an unintended consequence of the interplay between state law and group tradition. But it should not surprise us given the web of mutual influences that constantly binds the group, the state, and the individual.

Although Orthodox Judaism springs from a rich tradition of legal innovation,[60] it has so far failed to offer a viable *Halakhic* solution to the *agunah* problem.[61] Part of the problem lies in the fact that representatives of Orthodox Judaism (the most conservative branch of Judaism) have drifted toward the reactive culturalism path since the late eighteenth century, when members of the Jewish community were for the first time given the opportunity to fully join the larger society as equal citizens – so long as they relegated their religious "differences" to the private sphere. This external change has caused radical internal changes to the organization of the Jewish community, especially since significant numbers of individuals have indeed chosen to either fully assimilate or to embark on the path of limited particularism. Among those who have resisted these two alternatives, state and societal assimilation pressures have in certain cases led to stricter readings of *Halakhic* marriage and divorce law in the name of protecting "authentic" Jewish tradition and ensuring its continued survival.

This strict enforcement of the tradition has generally subjected women to greater pressure in the family law context. For instance, since birthright membership in the Jewish tradition is determined along matrimonial lines, the consequences of an "anchored" woman's intimate relationship with another man can be dire. According to the Orthodox Jewish community, any children produced by such a union are considered "illegitimate" and hence inadmissible as members.[62] This sanction, like other social measures, is intended to impose a heavy cost on those group members who dare to break the marriage and divorce tradition of their community. However, it is women's role in *symbolically* reproducing the collective that serves to provide justification for imposing strict regulation over them – even while no equivalent controls are imposed upon their husbands. Here again we are witnessing how women's crucial contribution to the group's survival often subjects them to strict and subordinating in-group controls, particularly when it comes to the regulation of marriage and procreation.

To further complicate matters, community-based social sanctions traditionally used by fellow members of the Jewish community to force a husband to grant the *get* are in decline. Social measures such as moral

---

[59] See Syrtash 1987, p. 314.   [60] See Elon 1985.   [61] See Washofsky 1981.
[62] These children bear the shameful label of *mamzerim*, and are forbidden from later converting to Judaism.

persuasion and social boycott or ostracism are no longer widely employed; they are even irrelevant if the recalcitrant spouse can acquire a divorce in accordance with state law, but still confine his spouse to a religious marriage.[63] Such sanctions also lose their effectiveness in a setting where an anchoring husband can maintain his group membership while supporting himself financially from outside the community. His wife, on the other hand, rarely has the basic material security or freedom required for the same flexibility. Thus, while the ability of the community to regulate the behavior of men who already have a partial exit is decreasing, the restrictions on women who have no similar access to external sources may, ironically, remain intact if they are not increased. This points to some of the troubling ways in which power inequalities within the group may become exacerbated when we fail to consider the complicated effects of state policy on *nomoi* groups struggling to preserve their distinct identity in what they often perceive to be a hostile "outside" environment.

Reactive culturalism and multicultural accommodation

The inability of Jewish Orthodox leaders to find contemporary solutions to problems such as the anchored woman should be seen as part and parcel of Orthodox Judaism's attempt to "reactively" preserve what they view as the "authentic" tradition of Jewish law. Rigid interpretations of a group's family law system are often upheld through an appeal to the common interest of *all* group members in survival. However, women and other at-risk group members tend to bear most of the costs in this process of cultural self-preservation. Since the policing of women is often encoded in the group's *nomos*, and that *nomos* is often accommodated by the state, women's vulnerability is increased and their ability to seek legal remedy against the group is significantly reduced.

Once a group's self-concept is inlaid with elements of reactive culturalism, a carte blanche devolution of jurisdictional powers from the state to

---

[63] Related problems are also a source of concern for Muslim minority communities in countries like Canada and England. See Pearl and Menski 1998, pp. 59–80. While English law does not recognize Muslim marriage or divorce proceedings, Islamic law operates as an "unofficial" system of law. Attempts to coordinate the marital status of individuals according to English and Muslim law has led members of the Muslim communities in the United Kingdom to establish informal dispute resolution forums and the development of formal bodies such as the Islamic Shari'a Council. The Council provides expert advice to lawyers and courts on matters of Islamic law, and deals with difficult marital disputes, the majority of them concerning divorces where the wife had obtained a civil decree but the husband refused to release her from the Muslim marriage. For a concise description of the Council's work, see Badawi 1995. On Canadian and American attempts to coordinate religious and secular systems of marriage regulation, see Shachar 2000c.

the *nomoi* group proves to be inevitably detrimental. It may legitimize the maltreatment of women in the family law arena, because such maltreatment is encoded in the group's tradition and is sanctioned by the accommodating state. Furthermore, the granting of full jurisdiction to the group over the demarcating and distributive aspects of members' marriage and divorce affairs does nothing to encourage the group to find solutions, from within its own established tradition, that permit a less discriminatory reading of family law.[64] It can become extremely difficult for women to alter the gender-discriminatory traditions inscribed within family law, because even attempts to redefine the distributive aspect of family law (which often is considered secondary to the sub-matter of demarcation) can be perceived as an assault on the group's demarcating function. Instead of an alert arbiter, multicultural accommodation thus becomes an accomplice in silencing group members who criticize the imperatives of the collective *nomos*, by permitting group authorities to construe such criticisms as acts of cultural betrayal.

What makes this situation a truly complex problem is the fact that although they may be subject to such injurious burdens within their communities, women may still find value and meaning in their cultural tradition and in continued group membership. This phenomenon is especially visible in situations where the minority culture as a whole is subject to repressive pressures from the outside society. Under such circumstances, group members feel expectations and often obligations to rally around their cultural membership,[65] rather than any inclinations to struggle for reform from within.[66]

Summary

A delegation of authority to the group in the family law arena may seem in harmonious keeping with the strong version of multiculturalism. Yet this decision acquires a new and more complicated dimension when we examine it from the perspective of the weak version of multiculturalism, especially when we also consider the potentially conflicting interests of all three parties in the multicultural triad – the group, the state, and the

---

[64] Obviously, not all claims for in-group change possess the same merit. However, reactive culturalism can build formidable resistance against seeking innovative and gender-inclusive solutions that remain faithful to the tradition.

[65] This is not to imply that such a "common identity" is ever fixed or uncontested in its meaning. The more relevant question is whether such cultural membership is perceived as worth preserving by group members themselves in the first place.

[66] For an illustration of how this phenomenon actually occurs, see my discussion of the Indian Supreme Court case of *Mohd. Ahmed Khan* v. *Shah Bano Begum and Others*, AIR 1985 SC 945, ch. 4.

individual. Family law thus serves as a concrete example of the deep tensions embedded in the move toward a multicultural citizenship model. It is concerned with a set of rules that allows the group to define its membership boundaries (and regulate internal relationships), the better to preserve its coherence, continuity, and distinct cultural identity over time. But it also illustrates the concrete costs of multicultural accommodation and how they can be disproportionately imposed on some group members when group traditions with built-in discriminations are granted state-backed authority. The *agunah* reality in Jewish divorce law provides a coercive case in point of even-handed multiculturalist policy gone ineffectually awry, leading to ever tighter regulation of women's choices especially in instances of reactive culturalism.

Under circumstances of perceived threat to the collective it is not surprising that minority group members (including women) may seek state accommodation of their group's traditions in different social arenas. Yet in respecting a minority culture's personal status and property rules, contemporary defenders of multiculturalism may unwittingly defer to a set of group-based rules and traditions that have a particular and often detrimental effect on certain (but not all) group members. The family law realm thus vividly illustrates the troubling paradox of multicultural vulnerability, by demonstrating how well-meaning attempts to respect differences often translate into a license for subordination of a particular category of group members – in this instance, primarily women.[67]

To overcome this problem we must recognize that multicultural accommodation can be fraught with deep tensions between the potentially conflicting interests and perspectives of all three parties in the multicultural triad – the group, the state, and the individual. We must balance these competing claims and complexities as we seek to devise new and better legal-institutional mechanisms for resolving the multiculturalism paradox.

---

[67] As mentioned earlier, children too may be unfairly burdened by such a move toward differentiated citizenship.

4   State vs. *nomos*: lessons from contemporary law and normative theory

We have already seen how well-meaning accommodation by the multicultural state can systematically put some individuals at risk, turning respect for group differences into a license to subordinate certain group members. In this chapter, the point of inquiry shifts from a formulation and evaluation of the multiculturalism paradox, to an investigation of how contemporary theoretical responses, as well as established legal models, address this conundrum. This analysis proceeds with a review of various established legal models that attempt to strike a balance between accommodating difference and respecting rights. A surprisingly broad spectrum of legal experience with accommodation is actually available, especially in the specific domain of state and religious communities' relations. We can thus identify two distinctly influential approaches for dividing legal authority between the state and the group which have developed out of the long history of the relationship between church and state. These two approaches are known here as the *secular absolutist* model and the *religious particularist* model.[1]

Each of these legal approaches constitutes a decisive point on the continuum of accommodation. One end of this continuum can be seen in the secular absolutist model, which proposes a "strict separation of church and state" – while the religious particularist model forms the other end of this continuum, with its vision of a more expansive structure of accommodation.[2] Historically, both first arose in response to the concerns of religiously defined *nomoi* groups. Under classic liberal theory and most contemporary constitutional law codes, these groups were perceived as the prime candidates for state accommodation. Today, all kinds of identity groups are

---

[1] For the sake of brevity, these two models are not explicated beyond the purpose of demonstrative argument. However, these two legal models do not represent merely theoretical constructs. They in fact reflect practical experiences in different legal systems. Their specific profiles are derived from an examination of the histories of various countries' divisions of authority and definitions of jurisdictional boundaries between the two major institutional players in the modern history of family law – religion and the state.

[2] The precise scope and level of accommodation advanced by each model is always shaped in a particular context and in relation to a specific set of historical precedents.

making claims for accommodation, and they often do so under legal systems informed by these models. An example of this residual pattern of influence can be found in the much criticized 1990 *Oregon* v. *Smith* case, where the US Supreme Court held that the ceremonial use of peyote by members of the Native American Church does not justify a special free exercise exemption from a generally applicable law.[3] Because many of the crucial questions facing today's decision-makers have for some time now been forced to address religion-based differences, considerable insight can be gained by studying the basic principles encoded in these legal models.[4] But to get there, we must first critically assess emerging theoretical responses to the paradox of multicultural vulnerability which have recently appeared in the literature.

Two theoretical responses to the paradox of multicultural vulnerability

The second wave of political writings on multiculturalism in the late 1990s moves away from merely evaluating the justice claims of minority groups to discussing the complexities and challenges associated with the adoption of a differentiated or multicultural citizenship model. Particular emphasis is placed on the potentially *conflicting* needs and interests of the three major players in any multicultural system: the group, the state, and the individual. Specifically, two seemingly opposed points of view have come to dominate this subsequent wave of scholarship.[5]

The first and more traditional position can be labeled the "re-universalized citizenship" position. This model assumes that the state must throw its weight behind the individual in any conflict between the individual and her minority group, even if the state contributes to the alienation of the individual from her group in so doing. Proponents of this approach include authors such as Amy Gutmann, Brian Barry, Ian Shapiro, Stephen Macedo, and Susan Okin.[6]

The second position can be labeled the "unavoidable costs" argument. It claims that a genuinely multicultural state has little if any justification

---

[3] The *Smith* decision was based on a narrow reading of the free exercise clause, according to which *any* state interest in prohibiting socially harmful conduct, e.g. drug consumption, must outweigh the burden imposed by the government on a given minority group's religious beliefs and practices. Congress sought to overrule *Smith* with the enactment of the 1993 Religious Freedom Restoration Act (RFRA), but this Act itself was later invalidated by the Court in the 1997 *City of Boerne* v. *Flores* decision.

[4] Other scholars have also drawn on the public record of "church–state" relations for their commentaries on the contemporary issues of multiculturalism. Valuable studies of this kind include, for example, Moodod 1996; Bader forthcoming.

[5] I develop the critique of these two approaches in Shachar 2000c.

[6] See e.g. Gutmann 1993; Macedo 1998; Arneson and Shapiro 1996; Barry 2001.

for intervening in a minority group's affairs – even if that minority community systematically violates certain members' basic citizenship rights. This argument is represented in the works of scholars such as Michael McDonald and Chandran Kukathas.[7]

The re-universalized citizenship option

The first and more familiar position is effectively articulated in the recent writings of Susan Okin.[8] Okin argues that the relationship between multiculturalism and feminism amounts to a zero-sum game, in which any *strengthening* of a minority group's rights implies an accompanying *weakening* of rights for that minority group's female group members. Okin concludes that if diverse societies wish to achieve greater gender equality, then they should completely abolish minority group practices which do not adhere to the state's legal norms, or else they should require these practices to "transcend" themselves to such an extent that they practically conform to the norms and perceptions of the majority communities.[9] Okin is particularly concerned about the protection of women's rights in response to the growing tide of opinion in favor of multicultural accommodation policies. She argues especially vehemently against Kymlicka's outline for a differentiated-rights policy, claiming that "group rights are potentially and in many cases actually antifeminist."[10] It may well be that Okin is correct in asserting that a basic tension exists between the traditional practices of many minority groups and the citizenship rights of women who live within those minority groups. However, Okin's argument is problematic for at least two reasons.

First, she claims that "much of most cultures is about controlling women,"[11] based on sweeping generalizations about the majority of the world's different cultures and religions. Okin views this phenomenon as universal and synchronic. Indeed, she states that "virtually all cultures, past and present"[12] are bad for women. Yet Okin fails to recognize that the power dynamics at play within cultural groups are not static. She assumes instead the "innate-ness" of cultural identity, overlooking arguments about the malleability of culture and the various political manifestations

---

[7] See Kukathas 1992; Kukathas 1997; Kukathas 1998. See also McDonald 1991. McDonald argues from a communitarian point of view, while Kukathas upholds a "cultural *laissez-faire*" libertarian position. However, their non-interventionist policy recommendations are closely related, as is their shared concern that proponents of the weak version of multiculturalism will only extend protection to minority groups that are themselves liberal. See McDonald 1991, p. 236; Kukathas 1992, pp. 122–123.

[8] See Okin 1997; Okin 1998. [9] See Okin 1998, p. 680. [10] See Okin 1997, p. 26.

[11] See Okin 1998, p. 667. [12] See Okin 1998, p. 678.

of identity that may dramatically affect the intra-group status of women.[13] She also fails to address the fact that many religious and cultural traditions have been substantially altered over time – as a result, in part, of women's resistance and agency.[14]

Second, women who remain loyal to minority groups' cultures appear as victims without agency in Okin's account.[15] Women who participate in minority group traditions and their politicized expressions are characterized as victims of such extreme socialization that they are said to be no longer even capable of discerning gender inequalities.[16] As Okin puts it, women living in minority cultures are "socialized into inferior roles, resulting in [a] lack of self-esteem [and] a sense of entitlement."[17] But by making such blanket statements, Okin glosses over two important questions: *why* women might support certain aspects of their cultures, even when these cultures systematically impose disproportionate burdens on them; and *how* women might renegotiate their historically disadvantaged position through the infusion of new meanings into their group's *nomos*.[18] Okin seems to ignore such expressions of women's resistance by overstating her case, and by portraying millions of women around the world as powerless victims who are unable to comprehend or resist the injuries they suffer at the hands of their own cultures. Furthermore, Okin fails to recognize that women within non-dominant communities may find their cultural membership a source of value and not only a source of oppression – a site for power, meaning, and resistance (*vis-à-vis* the larger

---

[13] For further discussion, see, for example, al-Hibri 1992; Hijab 1998.

[14] For example, Okin does not acknowledge the various ways in which women try to improve their intra-group status, critique their subordination, and resist the controls imposed on them, without giving up their cultural identity.

[15] This equation of women's cultural loyalty with lack of agency fits into the broader zero-sum pattern of Okin's analysis, which assumes the world can be divided into clear-cut dichotomies: "us" versus "them," "good" versus "bad." Okin discusses "liberals" in comparison to "non-liberals" (mainly referring to communitarian thinkers), feminists vs. multiculturalists, and "those who consider themselves politically progressive" (progress) vs. "those [who] in the present look to the past" (traditionalism). See Okin 1998, pp. 663–666, 678. The thread that unites all these pairs of friends and foes is tellingly revealed in the title of her article "Is Multiculturalism Bad for Women?" (Okin 1997).

[16] See Jeffery 1998, p. 222.

[17] See Okin 1998, p. 675. According to this view, we should consider women who remain loyal to their group cultures as mere puppets, coopted or caught up in a massive "false consciousness" trap regarding their subordinate position within their cultural communities.

[18] Women's attempts to transform their cultures' gender-biased family law norms can often begin through a challenge of the ways in which cherished religious scriptures have traditionally been interpreted. Women have appealed to the rich legacies of their cultures to demand greater gender equality, as in the case of various Muslim feminists bringing reinterpretations to the *Qur'an* and the *shari'a*. See, for example, Mernissi 1996. In the case of Orthodox Judaism, see, for example, Heschel 1995.

society or internally) – which nevertheless remains beset by such harsh realities as heightened vulnerability and strict intra-group controls.[19] Okin consequently draws too oversimplified a picture, where cultural membership and its accommodation is either "good" or "bad" for women. She refuses to consider what it most often is: possibly *both* good *and* bad, simultaneously.

Thus, while Okin points to the very real potential for sanctioned mal-treatment of women in certain social arenas by some cultural traditions, she provides a very unsatisfactory explanation of why so many women participate in traditions that are to their distinct disadvantage (compared to other group members). Her explanation of this extremely complex question is relegated to a passing remark: "older women often become co-opted into reinforcing gender inequality."[20] Even if we accept Okin's assertion that multiculturalism is merely bad for women (ignoring for a moment the important possibility that women may find value in the accommodation of their cultural memberships), perhaps the most crucial consideration Okin ignores is that women will stay in minority groups because they have no real alternatives. We can surmise that this is often the case, especially under legal regimes that both severely restrict women's rights to acquire independent means of livelihood (e.g. through control over property or waged work) or to develop their educational skills, and circumscribe women's ability to seek recourse and remedy against group-sanctioned practices that systematically disadvantage them. Under such constrictive conditions, the main problem may not be that older women have been coopted by community group think.[21] Rather, it seems plausible that the agency of women is at least equally affected by the legal-institutional framework in operation as it is adminis-tered by *both* the group *and* the state.

Okin's views lead her to suggest that women might be "much better off . . . if the culture into which they were born were . . . gradually to become extinct."[22] This conclusion assumes that the best solution to the complex relations between the group, the state, and the individual lies simply in reiterating the lexical priority of state norms over any competing sources

---

[19] Other commentators on Okin's work share this concern for female group members bereft of power and agency, and the implicit "us/them" dichotomy (or "Western majority cul-tures" and the Rest, as Homi Bhabha puts it), which Okin constructs in order to support her reductionist horror-story of immigrant, Asian, Middle Eastern, African, and Latin American "Others." See the responses by Bonnie Honnig, Aziza Y. al-Hibri, Sander L. Gilman, Abdullahi An-Na'im, Bhikhu Parekh, Homi K. Bhabha, and Janet Haley in Cohen et al. 1999.   [20] See Okin 1998, p. 680.

[21] I am in agreement with Carol Rose's observation that "the property-less or entitlement-less person has no alternative game to play." See Rose 1992, p. 453.

[22] See Okin 1998, p. 680.

of authority, such as those arising from group traditions.[23] But this approach has already been attempted by various modern states over the past two centuries, and it has met with only partial success. This approach has failed to suppress the quest of some minority group members (both male and female) to preserve their distinct cultural identities, even when the preservation of these non-dominant traditions and unique ways of life entailed the high costs of direct and indirect measures of suppression. Unfortunately, the "re-universalized citizenship" option solution to the paradox of multicultural vulnerability is guided by an "either your rights or your culture" ultimatum, in which women may *either* enjoy the full spectrum of their state citizenship rights *or* participate in their minority communities. They cannot have both simultaneously.

The "re-universalized citizenship" option thus forces at-risk group members into a stand-off between two vital aspects of their lived experience. It fails to provide room for women (or any other category of group member facing systemic risk of internal maltreatment) to maintain their cultural identity, if they still hope to be able to utilize their state citizenship rights to transform their historically subordinated intra-group status. Instead, this response to the multiculturalism paradox imposes a potentially wrenching decision upon those already left vulnerable, while withholding the legal and institutional resources necessary for improving their positions from within their *nomoi* groups.

The unavoidable costs approach

The unavoidable costs approach suggests that cultural tolerance requires a strictly non-interventionist multicultural policy on the part of the state. "Tolerance" here means that minority cultures are best left alone to practice their own traditions, even if those traditions routinely condone the maltreatment of certain classes of group members. The recent work of Chandran Kukathas illustrates the contours of this argument.

Kukathas claims that because state citizens have the freedom to associate, they should be given the right to preserve their distinct cultures and live by the norms of their cultural associations – even if these norms clearly differ from those of the wider society.[24] Kukathas therefore defends the

---

[23] This conclusion pays too little heed to the fact that group members of minority communities possess manifold affiliations. These affiliations may be to several different communities with which the group member is involved in different ways. Instead of seeking refuge behind such neatly defined and lexically ordered units as "state," "group," and "family," we are better off acknowledging the grittier reality of several different levels and kinds of social and political affiliations at work at one and the same time in a single (female) group member.   [24] See Kukathas 1992, pp. 116–118.

rights of minority cultures to impose as many internal restrictions as they wish upon their members, as long as individuals within these communities are allowed a formal right of exit.[25] According to this view, group members should be denied appeals to the state to intervene on their behalf against the cultural community, even if their citizenship rights are systematically violated in intra-group situations. Similarly, no outside entity should be granted the authority to demand changes in a group's cultural practices because, in Kukathas's view, such a demand would amount to "intolerance and moral dogmatism."[26]

Kukathas's argument is problematic for at least three reasons. First, he considers minority group members' right of exit to be dispositive, without ensuring that group members will actually be able to exercise this right. Kukathas fails to explain how the hands-off state he imagines can ensure that its citizens have the means, capacities, and freedoms to abandon their traditional cultures, when according to his schema such a state should ideally "do nothing."[27] Minority group members such as women who are subject to strict intra-group controls and sanctioned maltreatment are precisely those members who commonly lack the economic stability, cultural "know-how," language skills, connections, and self-confidence needed to successfully exit from their minority communities. This approach thus compounds the "associated costs" for accommodation of minority group members who are rarely in a position to utilize the right of exit option.[28]

Second, because Kukathas promotes a non-interventionist state policy (or a *laissez-faire* position toward minority groups), he must also maintain a rigid conceptual opposition between the "inside," minority group-controlled realm, and the "outside," state-controlled realm. Kukathas over-essentializes the distance between minority-group cultures and the

---

[25] See Kukathas 1992, p. 133.   [26] See Kukathas 1997, p. 78.

[27] See Kukathas 1998, pp. 686–699.

[28] These associated costs of accommodation may include what Brian Barry usefully classifies as intrinsic costs, associative costs, and external costs. Barry argues that only the latter type of costs justify state intervention against the group. At the same time, he is careful to note that the associative costs of exit (which he views as regrettable but nonetheless legitimate) "might be so grave as to undermine the voluntariness of membership." See Barry 2001, p. 152. While Barry's typology is illuminating, it fails to account for the fact that the impact of associative costs can vary depending on the positioning of the individual within the group. The more vulnerable she is, the more likely that these costs (or the mere threat of their imposition) will more severely restrict her choices. Barry also overlooks the fact that the very definition of what count as "legitimate" or "illegitimate" costs may shift over time. Legal history painfully reminds us that acts we now define as clear violations of rights (e.g. marital rape, spousal abuse, racial discrimination, or sexual harassment) were not even recognized as illegitimate or illegal behavior until late in the twentieth century. I thank Jacob Levy for bringing Barry's typology to my attention.

dominant state culture, thereby denying the inevitable interplay between them. Although Kukathas admits that all cultural communities are predominantly social and historical constructions, his non-interventionist policy prescription may nevertheless end up reifying group identity by turning an essentially fluid and mutable cache of customs, beliefs, and practices into a far more fixed and unchanging one.

This, in turn, leads to a third shortcoming. Kukathas's justification for a comprehensive protection of minority group practices from state intervention seems to explicitly rely on the assumption of individual freedom of association. But the main beneficiaries of this non-interventionist policy are most likely to be cultural communities that acquire the bulk of their members by birth, rather than by explicit adult consent.[29] The only way to overcome this potential difficulty is to assume that all adult individuals who are group members have indeed made a conscious choice, and the proof (according to this argument) lies in their continued group membership. To reach this conclusion, Kukathas, like Okin, must downplay the fact that minority group members possess multiple affiliations – to their minority groups, genders, religions, families, states, and so on. These different facets of individual identity may overlap and crisscross in complex ways. None can be said to have absolute priority over all others at all times. Yet Kukathas consistently prefers to ignore this potentially fluid intersection of affiliations, reducing this richness of personal identity into a single opposition instead: minority group member vs. citizen. This rigid framework means that once state citizens enter (or choose to remain within) minority communities, they are regarded solely as group members. And group members are further presumed to have relinquished the set of rights and protections granted to them by virtue of their citizenship. If a certain group member does *not* avail herself of her right of exit, this is because in Kukathas's view she has chosen to accept *all* of her group's practices and policies, including those that violate her basic state-protected rights as citizen. Kukathas's blindness to individual differences of position within cultural community hierarchies thus allows him to condone state inaction with respect to minority groups' affairs, even in the face of group-sanctioned, systemic maltreatment of certain classes of group members.

Transcending the either/or framework

The "re-universalized citizenship" option and the "unavoidable costs" argument present opposing solutions to the paradox of multicultural

---

[29] See McDonald 1991, p. 233. I discuss this problem in greater detail in Shachar forthcoming.

vulnerability. While advocates of the "re-universalized citizenship" option argue that it would be better for at-risk group members if their minority cultures became extinct, proponents of the "unavoidable costs" argument reach the opposite conclusion: minority groups' traditions should be respected by denying others the right to intervene in their practices.[30] The immediately apparent opposition between these two approaches belies a more fundamental continuity. Both approaches offer a misguided "either/or" resolution to the paradox of multicultural vulnerability. Both require that women and other potentially at-risk group members make a choice between their rights as citizens and their group identities. But this amounts to a choice of penalties. *Either* they must accept the violation of their rights as citizens in intra-group situations as the precondition for retaining their group identities, *or* they must forfeit their group identities as the price of state protection of their basic rights. Neither the "re-universalized citizenship" option nor the "unavoidable costs" approach has satisfactory answers to offer women and other members who legitimately wish to preserve *both* their cultural identities *and* to challenge the power relations encoded within their minority groups' traditions.

A critique of current legal approaches

We now turn toward another pairing of ways in which legal authority is currently divided between the state and *nomoi* groups in diverse societies: the secular absolutist and the religious particularist models. Unfortunately, these two approaches prove to be no more practically successful than the "re-universalized citizenship" and "unavoidable costs" theories of accommodation. For although the secular absolutist and the religious particularist approaches both acknowledge that accommodation sometimes threatens group members' citizenship rights, they each fail to offer a model that can facilitate diversity while simultaneously protecting group members disproportionately burdened by state-accommodated traditions. Furthermore, in both cases we see the option to empower at-risk individuals within their *nomoi* groups is denied. While these approaches obviously take slightly different forms in different countries, it remains nonetheless helpful to describe the key features of each, and to refer to its typical style of implementation. My intention here is not, however, to offer a comprehensive comparative analysis of how specific countries have sought to deal with the highly delicate and politically charged subject of accommodation in the family law arena. Such arrangements are influenced by each country's own particular

---

[30] See Kukathas 1992, pp. 117–118.

history, population make-up, "national narrative," social, political, and economic struggles, as well as cultural self-understanding. The present analysis seeks to offer a clarification of the legal alternatives currently available to us.[31]

The assumption that underpins this discussion is the belief that the key to breaking the "either/or" impasse lies in re-examining the question of *jurisdiction* – that is, the methodology for determining which legal forum possesses the authority to resolve a given legal dispute, according to certain legal principles. From an institutional point of view, jurisdiction is essentially an expression of a political arrangement which separates powers between competing entities in a given polity (e.g. federal governments, localities, churches, regional, and international fora). Since these competing entities share a desire to control and shape certain aspects of individuals' lives in various social arenas, conflicts over jurisdiction are a common feature of the contemporary political-legal reality in democratic countries. Thus, a consideration of the paradox of multicultural vulnerability in the context of the broader jurisdictional issues that have partly created it will allow us to develop more effective solutions to dismantle it. Moreover, this attention to a pattern of specific experiences with jurisdiction in different countries provides a much-needed empirical grounding that is too often lacking in the current normative debate over differentiated citizenship models.

The secular absolutist model

The secular absolutist model is based on a strict separation between church and state.[32] Under this model, the state has the ultimate power to define legally what constitutes "the family," and to regulate its creation and dissolution. The secular absolutist approach is practiced, for example, in civil law countries such as France, Germany, and the Netherlands, where a uniform secular state law is imposed upon all citizens in family law matters, regardless of those citizens' group affiliation(s). Under the secular absolutist model, religious officials have no formal role in defining or celebrating marriages. Even if a religious (or

---

[31] The present discussion focuses on the relationship between the state and religious communities, because they represent in some regards the most developed legal-institutional models available. I do not mean to imply that only religious groups are plagued by the multiculturalism paradox, nor that they are necessarily more hostile to women. Our historical experience with church–state relations simply happens to provide a rich source of instructive examples in this specific domain.

[32] The term "church" here does not refer only to Christian religious institutions. Rather, it is a generic name for all institutions pertaining to religious and customary communities.

customary) marriage ceremony takes place, it holds no validity in the eyes of state law. The couple may, of course, decide to perform a religious ceremony because of its symbolic or emotional value.[33] However, the only way to change status formally (e.g. from single to married, or from married to divorced), is under the provisions of state law.

In its ideal form, the secular absolutist model withholds legal recognition for a marriage or divorce performed by a representative of a religious or customary family law tradition. This refusal to grant recognition to cultural or religious authorities thus erodes *nomoi* groups' power to preserve their cultural distinctiveness through formal and autonomous demarcation of their membership boundaries. The secular absolutist model also refuses to acknowledge the distributive aspect of religious or customary family law traditions. In other words, the state does not allocate *any* legal authority to the *nomoi* groups over issues of status or property relations, preserving for itself the *ultimate* regulatory power over the citizenry in matters of marriage and divorce.

In theory, the major apparent advantage of the secularist absolutist model is that it creates a legal regime in which the state equally burdens all churches, or *nomoi* groups. That is, all forms of religious or customary marriage and divorce proceedings, whether of Christian, Muslim, Jewish, Hindu or of any other religious or customary origin, have *no* legal validity under state law. Prima facie, this approach prevents *nomoi* groups from claiming that the state supports only the practices of the majority in the family law arena.

In practice, however, the allocation of legal authority set by the secular absolutist model clearly does not encourage the preservation of *nomoi* groups through the accommodation of their differences, as it fails to address both the demarcating and the distributive aspects of "other" family law traditions. The secular absolutist model is based on the presumption that religious or customary practices are relegated to the "private" realm (having no formal, and in this sense, "public" validity in legal terms). This public–private distinction, as has already been observed by many political theorists, does not put minority groups on equal footing with the dominant culture,[34] since minority cultures often "come to the game after it has already begun," and do not define the governing standards of a society's institutions.[35] In the context of marriage and divorce regulation, this problem is especially salient, given the

---

[33] Thus, even when a state consolidates its exclusive authority over a person's marital status, religious ceremonies are not necessarily abolished.

[34] See Iris Young's now classic argument in Young 1989.

[35] For further discussion on this point, see Spinner 1994.

historical record is such that "in the West [at least], the link between Christianity and state law has long been particularly visible in the area of family law."[36]

Among the conflicting claimants to sovereignty in the history of family law, it is the state rather than the church which is the newcomer.[37] In fact, the very character of marriage as a public, regulated institution evolved with the rise of Christianity in the West. The church used its dominant position during the late Middle Ages to formalize a set of rules regulating marriage. These rules were formally pronounced and expounded by ecclesiastical courts which enforced canon law. Through marriage, church authorities regulated individuals' conduct, with regard to both the requirements for its valid celebration, and the rights and obligations which this change in status entailed for the parties.[38] Under this ecclesiastical family law regime, a marriage could no longer be terminated by the informal, private act of the parties. Rather, a divorce, if at all possible under church rules, required the official cooperation of a functionary of the church. The state did not seize jurisdiction over marriage and divorce from the church until the late eighteenth century, when the vesting of power over family law in secular authorities was seen as a symbol of modern European state-building. As Nancy Cott observes, "for as long as the past millennium in the Christian West, the exercise of formal power over marriage has been a prime means of exerting and manifesting public authority."[39] Since we tend to accept the state's regulation of marriage and the family as something more or less taken for granted, we easily forget how much the state's involvement in governing the creation of dissolution or marriage is in fact a fairly recent phenomenon.

The emerging concept that the family constituted a topic of concern for the regulatory power of the state permitted, at least in principle, the termination of marriage by a civil official. Yet for most of the history of the modern state, unless a serious cause of fault had been established, no individuals could simply choose to terminate even their secular marriage.[40] According to this view, a secular marriage could be terminated only by an official of the state, and only upon proof of wrongdoing (or

---

[36] See Weisbrod 1987–1988, p. 753.   [37] See Weisbrod 1987–1988, p. 746.

[38] In the sixteenth century, it became necessary to institute formal proceedings in an ecclesiastical court, to submit to an official investigation, and to obtain a formal decree in order to terminate a marriage. See Rheinstein 1953, p. 9.   [39] See Cott 1995, p. 108.

[40] Even France, which had in the post-Revolution era adopted a zealous variant of the secular absolutist model, found it hard to maintain the idea that divorce could be based simply upon the free will of the two parties. See Rheinstein 1953, pp. 5–6.

"fault") on the part of one of the parties.[41] But even this secular concept of *fault* divorce (dominant in most Western countries' family law codes until late in the twentieth century) is clearly rooted in the Christian concept of marriage as a sacrament, and "for this reason . . . [is] indissoluble by man."[42] So marriages created by the state still retained features of the dominant majority's conception of marriage as a relationship established for life, even when church and state were already formally divided from one another.

Another stark example of the underlying connection between religious and secular perceptions of marriage is found in the famous 1878 US Supreme Court anti-polygamy decision in *Reynolds* v. *United States*, where the court held that "marriage, while from its very nature a *sacred* obligation, is nevertheless, in most civilized nations, a civil contract, usually regulated by [state] law."[43] In fact, monogamous marriage was conceived by secular authorities as "the most crucial precondition of public order – as a 'pillar of the state.'"[44] This view was generally accepted as the appropriate one for the state to adopt, "in essence, because it was the view of the [prevailing] Christian Churches."[45]

A Christian underpinning has thus influenced the "secular absolutist" notion of family relations since the inception of the modern Western state. This is significant because it shows that rather than being a fully objective standard, this approach often implicitly favors a state regime informed by the historical influence of the dominant majority.[46] New influences may come to gain greater salience with time. For example, family law has not been unaffected by twentieth-century trends of secularization and liberalization. And in almost all countries women have finally achieved nominal, though not always *de facto*, equality in the family law arena. Yet in a world of profound and accelerating change, the public institution of marriage seems to remain stubbornly informed by cultural-specific values, "standing out as a pillar of stability."[47] Although apparently neutral, the defining precepts and principles regulating marriage and divorce under the secular absolutist model still impose a greater

---

[41] This concept of "fault" divorce was abolished only recently in most Western countries, in what has been dubbed the 1970s' "no-fault revolution." For a concise introductory essay on this and other related changes in modern marriage and divorce law, see Glendon 1980.

[42] See Rheinstein 1953, p. 8. Other religious traditions such as Judaism or Islam do not uphold a similar conception of marriage as "indissoluble by man."

[43] 98 US 145 (1878), p. 165 (emphasis added).   [44] See Cott 1995, p. 108.

[45] See Weisbrod 1987–1988, p. 754.

[46] A contemporary reminder of this point can be seen in the current highly charged debate over same-sex marriage.   [47] See Rheinstein 1953, p. 3.

burden on citizens whose family law traditions are not aligned with the prevailing practices of the dominant majority. In short, this model offers a poor record of successfully accommodating *nomoi* groups' traditions.[48]

But the secular asbsolutist model holds a better record as far as citizenship rights are concerned. Because this model provides no accommodation in the family law arena, group members are subject solely to state law (rather than their group's tradition) in matters of status and property relations. This means that while the regulation of marriage and divorce by the secular state is not neutral in its effect upon *nomoi* groups (since it presents greater obstacles for a group seeking to preserve its cultural identity), the formal separation of church and state has the advantage of better protecting the rights of at-risk group members by removing marriage proceedings from the "sacred" realm. So, for example, once family law is governed solely by the secular state, the content, rationale, and definition of marriage and divorce law can be challenged by the citizenry and transformed via regular channels of democratic politics. It seems reasonable to suggest, then, that the secular absolutist approach – even if far from perfectly protecting the rights of women undergoing divorce proceedings, for example – at least ensures their formal entitlement to equal treatment, unlike some *nomoi* group traditions which may uphold marriage and divorce laws that discriminate against women.[49]

However, the absolutist approach, like the "re-universalized citizenship" response, is based on the assumption that in order to enjoy whatever rights they are entitled to as citizens, women and other at-risk group

[48] In practice, with the recent upsurge of religious and cultural diversity in most Western countries, this model is in great need of reform. Otherwise, the state runs the risk of *de facto* losing its jurisdictional authority over group members who are following their own groups' family law traditions in the realm of "unofficial law." This is a problematic situation because group traditions have no legal validity in the eyes of state law, but may have dire consequences on the rights of individuals. As in the previously discussed case of the Jewish *agunah*, the failure to recognize the existence of a subterranean system of unofficial law often works to the disadvantage of women. For discussion of similar hardships affecting Muslim communities in the United Kingdom, see Pearl and Menski 1998, pp. 77–80. On certain attempts to resolve this problem in the context of American and Canadian law, see Hamilton 1995, pp. 113–139; Shachar 2000c, pp. 411–426.

[49] Although state regulation of the family is now based on equal protection jurisprudence, gender-neutral rules may still fail to ensure the needs of the traditionally weaker parties in the family, i.e. women and children. See the classic study by Weitzman 1985. Weitzman shows that following divorce the standard of living for men rises by approximately 42 percent while that of women fall by 73 percent. Recently these figures were challenged by other scholars, who claimed that the relevant figures are not as extreme as Weitzman had initially reported. See Peterson 1996. It is clear, however, that divorce tends to improve the standard of living for men but not for women. Studies conducted in other countries confirm that the economic consequences of divorce in Britain, Australia, and Canada conform to the general patterns found in the United States. See, for example, Eekelaar and Maclean 1986.

members must abandon their group's traditions. Thus under the pure secular absolutist model the jurisdiction of the state is extended into family law, totally overriding the authority of *nomoi* groups to shape and define, in a publicly recognized sense, matters of family law which are of great intimate and political concern to their members. Rather than engaging with its constituent groups on this vexing issue, the state bypasses the complex issue of potential in-group rights violations by categorically refusing to work with citizens in their capacity as group members.[50]

While some countries have preserved the rigid application of the secular absolutist model, other countries such as Canada, Australia, Britain, and the United States have in recent years introduced a modified version of the same model. According to this "less absolutist" variant, the state still retains its *ultimate* authoritative power to regulate citizens' marriage and divorce affairs; however, state family law codes have been reformed to permit greater cultural diversity. For example, civil authorities may invest religious officials with concurrent authority to solemnize marriages. Under the New York Domestic Relations Law, for example, a religious ceremony that takes place in New York State and that is solemnized by an authorized religious official would be recognized as valid in the eyes of the state. Similarly, the draft American Uniform Marriage and Divorce Act (UMDA), to be adopted state by state, suggests that the solemnization of marriage may be accomplished either by a civil authority or "in accordance with any mode of solemnization recognized by any religious denomination, Indian Nation or Tribe, or Native Group."[51]

Though permitting greater legal diversity in marriage proceedings, the state according to this variant of the secular absolutist model reserves for itself all regulatory power in the event of divorce.[52] Ironically, this modified version of the secular absolutist model has only further expanded the power of state law over minority cultures by creating a formal link between the civil proceedings of divorce and the removal of all religious or

---

[50] For example, according to the secular absolutist model the state will not work with a Muslim woman, as a *Muslim* woman, when she turns to the state seeking a fair settlement in divorce proceedings. In order to resolve the situation she must choose between suffering a single but substantial injustice or dismissing her entire *nomos*. In this way the state belittles her investment in the *nomos* as something that can be easily set aside. Furthermore, such lack of recognition can force minority communities to pursue *de facto* their family law customs, though without any formal accommodation. This can further complicate the status of a woman caught in the flux, since her marriage is valid by her own group's traditions but not necessarily by state law. This can mean that she is not entitled to any state rights at divorce, for example, since her marriage is not considered valid in the eyes of state law. For a discussion of these problems in the context of contemporary English law, see Bano 1999.   [51] UMDA §206.

[52] For an analysis of this legal scenario at greater length which utilizes a rich set of examples from contemporary American and Canadian jurisprudence, see Shachar 2000c.

customary barriers to remarriage.[53] Nevertheless, this "less absolutist" variant is important because it provides formal recognition of certain aspects of minority communities' family law traditions. At the same time, it creates a legal route for secular authorities to limit the exploitative power used by religious spouses to gain excessive rights in exchange for religious divorce decrees. While this legal arrangement may well resolve some individual instances of oppression, it does not create any incentive for religious or customary communities to reexamine their internal (discriminatory) norms. The practical result of implementing such a "conciliatory" model thus remains problematic, because it may just incite more reactive culturalist response. Even well-meaning modifications by the state still have the effect of preserving a basic imbalance, since this legal arrangement specifically purports to endow civil authorities with discretionary power to refuse to make a secular divorce decree absolute or to adjourn property proceedings until satisfied that all religious or customary impediments to remarriage had been removed.[54]

In sum, the secular absolutist model is attractive in its different variants because it ensures, at least formally, that at-risk group members have access to all the rights and protections guaranteed to all other citizens at divorce. However, this model fails to address the identity-preserving function of family law, and may also systematically discriminate against minority cultures by tacitly enforcing the norms of the dominant culture in the family law arena. Finally and most significantly, it forces at-risk group members to confront an ultimatum: a choice between their rights or their community.

The religious particularist model

This second legal paradigm better addresses the problem of respecting cultural differences by granting religious and customary communities the authority to pursue their own traditions in the family law arena. According to this model, the state does not intervene in or regulate citizens' marriage and divorce affairs. Instead, recognized religious communities are vested

---

[53] See New York State's Domestic Relations Law section 253, enacted by the Law of 1983, ch. 979 § 1, eff. 8 August 1983. In 1992, section 236B was added to New York's Domestic Relations Law, in order to provide more effective tools for civil authorities to pressure an otherwise recalcitrant husband. In Canada, see Canada Divorce Act, RSC 1985, ch. 3 s. 21(1) (Supp. II 1985), enacted in 1990, ch. 18, s. 2; Family Law Act, RSO ch. F-3 (1990).

[54] Such state-imposed removal of barriers to remarriage may, under certain circumstances, enhance the bargaining power of women who want to preserve their cultural identity but have no legal powers, under their *nomoi* groups' traditions, to force their spouses to follow the "proper" proceedings of a religious divorce. See Washofsky 1981. For further discussion, see Shachar 2000c.

with legal power over matters of personal status and property relations. In extreme versions of this model, there is no uniform state law which governs matters of marriage and divorce. Rather, different *nomoi* groups are recognized by the state, and their autonomous courts are designated as the exclusive fora for the adjudication of certain family law matters.

The religious particularist approach can be attractive from a multiculturalist point of view because it offers a pluralistic legal system in which each community is self-governing in the matter of family law. Unlike the secularist absolutist model, which is exercised in countries where the regulation of family law has already been assumed by the state, the religious particularist model is exercised in countries where the state never directly challenges the power of group-based authorities to regulate citizens' marriage and divorce affairs.

Historically, the religious particularist model was manifested in the practices of the Ottoman empire's *millet* system. It is less often recognized that a related method of particularist accommodation was also practiced by the British colonial administration in certain conquered overseas territories through its practice of "indirect rule."[55] Unlike colonized territories where the *terra nullius* (vacant land) legal fiction permitted the colonizers to ignore existing tribal legal systems (as was the case in the British colonies of North America and Australia, for example), in African and Asian colonized territories British administrations rarely tried to replace Islamic, Hindu, or customary family law practices with the English common law. In these cases, matters of family law were generally left to the autonomous jurisdiction of the relevant religious and customary communities.[56] Today, many countries that were once subject to Britain's "indirect" colonial rule (such as Kenya, Israel, and India) still maintain a pluralistic system of family law that approximates a religious particularist model.

In Kenya, for example, the state has enacted a set of statutes to recognize the diversity of personal laws governing the family relations of different groups of citizens. These include the African Christian Marriage and Divorce Act (ACMDA) (Cap. 151), the Hindu Marriage and Divorce Act (HMDA) (Cap. 157), and the Mohammeddan Marriage and Divorce Act (MMDA) (Cap. 156).[57] Marriages or divorces conducted in accordance

---

[55] For further discussion of the "indirect rule" as a reflection of the colonizers' narrative of a clear and hierarchical divide between Europeans and Africans, marked by separate systems of law which are defined in opposition to one another, see, for example, Mamdani 1996. See also Hooker 1975.

[56] However, the British colonial administration never adopted a carte blanche non-intervention policy. Instead, it formally reserved for itself the power to refuse to recognize specific customary practices, if these practices were perceived to be incompatible with "morality, humanity or natural justice."   [57] See Kabeberi-Macharia 1992.

with these statutes must follow the formalities and procedures set out in Christian, Hindu, or Islamic personal law, or must be in accordance with the uncodified, but widely followed, Kenyan customary law.

In Israel, the legislature has gradually codified the arena of family law with its multiplicity of legal sources, dating back to the Ottoman empire's *millet* system. However, Israel has no uniform state marriage and divorce law. Instead, each religious community has autonomous courts which hold jurisdiction over its respective members' marriage and divorce affairs. A non-religious district court has the authority to dissolve a marriage only if the spouses belong to different religious communities. Therefore, "[i]n matters affecting their families, Israelis must function as Jews, Muslims, Druzes, etc."[58] Past legislative attempts to "divest" religious communities of their legal authority to determine matters of personal status (i.e. marriage or birthright membership) failed after they met formidable resistance both from members of minority groups (Arab Muslims in particular) and from Israeli representatives of Orthodox Jewry.[59]

In India, legal struggles over the scope of religious communities' regulation of personal status matters reflect the bitter dissent between the Hindu majority and the Muslim minority. The complex system of personal laws in India was recognized by the British colonial administration, and was largely preserved at Indian independence in 1947.[60] Today, religious communities in India still govern a broad range of family law issues including marriage, divorce, maintenance, guardianship, adoption, and succession.[61] As in Kenya and Israel, matters of personal status in India are primarily divided along religious lines, permitting each community to demarcate its membership boundaries through birth and marriage.

As explained earlier, *nomoi* groups often use family law as a way to construct their membership boundaries. Under the religious particularist

---

[58] See Edelman 1994, p. 121. The Israeli system grants different groups different degrees of exclusive jurisdiction in matters of family law, a practice that originated with the Ottoman and the British empires. The widest jurisdiction is enjoyed by *shari'a* (Muslim) courts. The variety of Christian denominational courts have more limited mandates, and exercise jurisdiction over matters of marriage, divorce, and maintenance. Rabbinical and Druze courts have exclusive control only over matters of marriage and divorce.

[59] See the debate in the *Knesset* prior to the enactment of the Women's Equal Rights Law, 1951, 5 LSI 171.

[60] For an excellent overview of these different personal laws, see Sagade 1996.

[61] Hindus in India are governed by the Hindu Marriage Act of 1955, the Hindu Succession Act of 1956, the Hindu Guardianship and Minorities Act of 1956, and the Hindu Adoption and Maintenance Act of 1956. Muslims are governed by the *shari'a* Act of 1937, the Muslim Women's Dissolution of Marriage Act of 1939, the Muslim Women's (Protection of Rights on Divorce) Act of 1986, and uncodified Muslim personal laws. Christians are governed by the Christian Marriage Act, the Indian Divorce Act, and the Indian Succession Act. Parsis, too, have codified laws of marriage, divorce, and succession.

model, identity groups' differences are fully recognized and underwritten by state law. Each community is given autonomous powers to demarcate its membership boundaries and to preserve its cultural distinctness. However, these groups can also use these powers to perpetuate a community structure that includes an unequal distribution of rights, duties, and (ultimately) power between men and women within the community, as well as to enforce gender-discriminatory rules that would never have passed constitutional muster outside the protected realm of religious personal law.

Thus, while the religious particularist model maintains the autonomy and sovereignty of different minority cultures (upholding the demarcating function of family law), it is problematic in terms of women's rights, particularly when the jurisdiction it extends to *nomoi* groups reaches beyond pure status issues to include matters of property relations between spouses (the distributive function of family law). These relations can be structured so as to disadvantage or even exploit women. In so doing, they put at risk women's rights to fair and equal treatment and may interfere with their capacities to make and pursue significant life-choices. While in Kenya, Israel, and India women are guaranteed on paper full and equal citizenship rights by state law, in practice their basic rights may be circumscribed with impunity by their groups' family law traditions. Hence, the preservation of *nomoi* groups' cultural distinctness through multicultural accommodation often imposes severe internal costs, which are disproportionately allocated in a way that tends to compromise the citizenship status of certain sub-sections of the group by upholding the structural impediments imposed upon them by a rigid reading of the group's traditions.

A good illustration of the drawbacks of an extreme religious particularist resolution to a group-based family law conflict can be found in the Indian Supreme Court's much-discussed 1985 *Shah Bano* decision.[62] The facts of the case were as follows. Shah Bano, a seventy-three-year-old Muslim Indian woman, was unilaterally divorced by her husband by way of a Muslim *talaq* divorce after forty-three years of marriage. Shah Bano turned to a magistrate court to obtain state-decreed alimony payments from her ex-husband, although under a standard reading of Muslim personal law she was only entitled to alimony for the first three months following the dissolution of marriage (the *iddat* period).[63] When the case reached India's Supreme Court, the court ruled in favor of Shah Bano. It imposed on her ex-husband maintenance payments of 179.20 rupees (approximately $14) per month in accordance with the provisions of a state law, which stated that a divorced woman, so long as she had not

---

[62] *Mohd. Ahmed Khan* v. *Shah Bano Begum and Others*, AIR 1985 SC 945.
[63] For a concise overview of these family law distributive rules, see Nasir 1990.

remarried and was unable to maintain herself, was entitled to minimum maintenance support by her former husband.[64]

The Court ruled that the state-defined statutory right of a neglected wife to maintenance stood regardless of the personal law applicable to the parties. The Court reasoned that this right was enacted specifically in order to provide a quick and summary remedy for a class of persons who were unable to maintain themselves. Therefore, as the Chief Justice put it, "[w]hat difference would it then make as to what is the religion professed by the neglected wife?" The Court thus chose to emphasize the distributive aspect of the dispute between Shah Bano and her former husband, and downplayed the demarcating aspect of family law. It imposed a monetary obligation on the more financially solvent party (the husband) to support at least the basic needs of his former dependent (the wife).

This decision, which dealt with a relatively standard balancing-of-resources dispute between ex-husband and ex-wife, nevertheless unleashed a public furore and ended in a confrontation between the Muslim minority and the Hindu majority. In the political arena, and in contrast to the Court's construction of the legal issue, it was conceived to be all about "external protections" and the demarcation of collective identity. The *Shah Bano* decision was considered by traditionalist representatives of the Muslim minority community as proof of Hindu homogenizing trends that threatened to weaken Muslim identity.[65] In response to this decision, Muslim religious leaders in India launched a massive political campaign. Specifically, these leaders demanded that the government exempt Muslim women from recourse to state law in matters concerning the distributive aspects of divorce.

The response of the more conservative representatives of the Muslim community to the decision can be partly understood as justified offense at the Court's overstepping of its mandate, when it declared that the "true position" of Muslim personal law was similar to the answer the Court itself reached. In other words, the Court suggested that even under Muslim law there are certain conditions where a Muslim husband is under an obliga-

---

[64] Section 125 of the 1973 Code of Criminal Procedure establishes an "order for maintenance of wives, children, and parents," if any person having sufficient means neglects or refuses to maintain his wife, children, or parents in need. A magistrate may impose, upon proof of such neglect or refusal, an order upon such a person to make a monthly allowance for the maintenance.

[65] Since the issue has been rehearsed mostly as a debate over external protections (particularly but not exclusively with reference to the Muslim minority community), women's particular interests and vulnerabilities to internal restrictions by their groups' personal law traditions have been hard to maintain as a separate issue. Precisely because of their multiple identities – as group members, as women, as citizens, and so on – female group members have been severely pressured to emphasize the group aspect of their identity, sometimes at the expense of giving up their claims for improved gender status.

tion to provide maintenance to his wife beyond the *iddat* period. In doing so, the Court meant to suggest that there was no conflict in this case between the state's law and the parties' personal law. Yet the relationship between these two sets of laws – religious and state based – has always been extremely vexed in India, and such conflict cannot be simply willed away.[66]

And so it was not. In 1986, a year after the Supreme Court handed down its controversial decision, the Indian Parliament bowed to the pressure of conservative Muslims. The Parliament overruled the Court's decision in *Shah Bano* by passing the Muslim Women's (Protection of Rights of Divorce) Act. This new Bill, despite the reassuring sound of its name, removed the rights of Muslim women to appeal to state courts for post-divorce maintenance payments. In addition, it also excused Indian Muslim ex-husbands from other post-divorce obligations.[67] As a result, the Muslim Women's Act now deprives Muslim Indian women of benefits that they would receive if they lived in certain Muslim countries, where Muslim family law policies are generally observed by the state.[68]

The Muslim Women's Act was a victory for the religious particularist point of view in that it unequivocally overturned the Supreme Court's decision in *Shah Bano* – a decision that was viewed by members of the minority culture as interfering with the protected realm of internal group affairs. Unfortunately, in the midst of the political debate about the limits of minority groups' jurisdictional autonomy, the interests of insiders like Shah Bano, who fought to relieve some of the disproportionate brunt they were made to bear under this system, were largely ignored. Ultimately, under the pressure of charges that she had betrayed the Muslim community, Shah Bano contacted the press and publicly announced her rejection of the Supreme Court's decision on her behalf. After her long and ultimately futile struggle, she was faced with a tragic "your culture or your rights" choice; frail and tired, she found herself forced to assert her loyalty to the *nomos* at the expense of her citizenship rights.

---

[66] The debate over the Uniform Civil Code, for example, goes back to the 1950 Indian Constitution, which in Article 44 guarantees that "the state shall endeavor to secure for the citizen a uniform civil code throughout the territory of India." The state did endeavor to reform the Muslim personal law in the past, but these legislative proposals were not encoded into state law since they were opposed by the more conservative sectors of the Muslim community. The current political debate in India concerning the Uniform Civil Code has re-emphasized the significance that minority communities attach to autonomously controlling their members' family law affairs. On the contemporary Uniform Civil Code debate in India, see Jayal 1998.

[67] Such as the obligation of a Muslim father to maintain his minor children beyond a period of two years. See section 3(b) of the Act. For a critique of this provision, see Diwan 1987, pp. 155–158.

[68] On this last point, see Everett 1997, p. 89. See also Hijab 1998. More generally, see Mayer 1999.

The complex set of interactions between the group, the state, and the individual can also affect the self-concepts of *nomoi* groups themselves. Particularist accommodation policies may alter groups in fundamental ways by inviting them to defensively articulate their traditions, via the "reactive culturalism" response. They may maintain their distinctiveness, but only at the cost of halted social progress. This approach makes cultural difference a virtue in and of itself, regardless of the consequences for individual members.

Although we might expect that the delegation of jurisdictional powers to the group will allow its representatives to be more flexible in their interpretation of its established traditions, in practice such granting of exclusive legal powers to *nomoi* groups may tacitly encourage group leaders to become even more resistant to alterations or reinterpretations of their existing policies. When the state must choose a particular authority within the accommodated group to which it will delegate authority, preexisting religious or traditional leaders find themselves suddenly transformed into political figures within a definite institutional hierarchy.

Law is a way of codifying contingent relationships between dynamic entities within a polity. The wording of the codification has an effect on those entities and this should be recognized and responsibility taken for the consequences.[69] The state and the groups within it are all complex and dynamic systems that are affected by the way that legislation for multicultural accommodation is introduced and enacted. Because they are smaller systems than the state, *nomoi* groups are affected more profoundly by whichever model of accommodation is adopted. In a state governed according to the religious particularist model, the state allocates jurisdiction to the *nomoi* group because of its "differentness," and the simplest way for a group to assure itself of recognition is to claim that existing differences are central tenets of the *nomos*. If what justifies accommodation is the distinctiveness of the group, then the group has a strong interest in emphasizing its social differences by holding back internal changes. The religious particularist model therefore creates an institutional drive for *nomoi* groups to remain as different as possible. This model effectively rules out the possibility that a tradition, which is distinct from the practices of the surrounding majority, can be both dynamic and highly mutable. Instead, *nomoi* groups are led to valorize difference as a primary principle, not only in matters of self-demarcation but as a general dictum. Consequently, a group member who calls for a change in the group's policies is more likely, under this model, to be treated by her

---

[69] Robert Cover, for example, has written of the "jurispathic" and "jurisgenerative" tendencies of the rule of law as enforced by the state. For further discussion, see Minow et al. 1995.

group as a "traitor" than if her group had never been accommodated at all.[70]

Thus the allocation of full authority to *nomoi* groups in contested social arenas can serve to obstruct organic processes of change in the community. It can result in a kind of interpretive "freeze" in the group's *nomos* because it permits leaders in the group to construe all "alternative" suggestions for reform as signs of cultural decay and corrupting outside infiltration, "enforced by the wider society interfering in [the group's] internal practices."[71] Ultimately, the particularists' refusal to allow any external forces to interfere with a group's internal policies ensures that those who pay the highest price for accommodation are the group members who are least able to protect themselves against entrenched in-group power hierarchies.

In sum, the religious particularist model, like the "unavoidable costs" argument, tends to compromise at-risk group members' citizenship status in order to safeguard a cultural imperative. Still more disturbingly, it creates a political *dis*incentive for religious courts or minority group leaders to lessen the disproportionate burden imposed upon certain subsections of members within these groups, or even to take an interest in these members' rights.

The insufficiency of current theoretical and applied legal models

This chapter has sought to expose the fundamental problems underlying current theoretical and legal paradigms for dividing jurisdiction over individuals with multiple affiliations. They share one basic misguided assumption: that group members cannot be *simultaneously* subject to more than one source of legitimate legal authority. Whether explicitly or implicitly, current legal and theoretical thinking tends to assume that *either* the state *or* the group should exclusively govern group members' affairs.

This "either/or"-type of thinking requires us to make a preliminary determination regarding the membership community to which the individual is primarily affiliated, so that we can decide who should have ultimate authority. Despite all the attention given to the interests of the individual in current legal models, actual individuals are very seldom consulted for their opinions about their own identity. Instead, a once-and-for-all decision as to how identities will be organized and accommodated is reached (by state or group authorities), and this preordained

---

[70] For a discussion of this problem in the context of adherence to Muslim personal status laws, see Hélie-Lucas 1994. [71] See Kukathas 1992, p. 122.

identity system is then used as a basis for allocating jurisdiction over citizens/group members in the multicultural state.

In the secular absolutist model, for example, the assumption is that regardless of an individual's multiple affiliations, she is first and foremost a *citizen*, and hence subject to the state's jurisdiction, whereas in the religious particularist model, it is presumed that in certain spheres of life the faith community is of such importance to the individual that her primary affiliation is that of *group member*, and therefore that the group should prevail. Like the two theoretical responses to the multiculturalism paradox discussed earlier, the secular absolutist and the religious particularist models are in some sense mirror images of one another. Both the theoretical and the legal approaches reduce the complex interplay of beliefs, practices, and loyalties to a simple and exclusive declaration of affiliation, forcing individuals to choose between their culture or their rights. Secular absolutism and religious particularism share a view of the individual as belonging primarily to either the state or the group, but not simultaneously to both. This in turn dictates that full jurisdiction over the individual must either rest in the hands of the state or of the group. This division of legal authority locks the individual into a punishing dilemma: she can either participate in her culture and run the risk that her rights as a citizen will be violated, or else she can choose to keep her individual rights protected by the state and abandon her group identity. We need to overcome this rigid dichotomy, and devise a realistic conception of identity in diverse societies which is more in keeping with the contemporary multicultural age.

A more promising starting point lies in the recognition that each membership community has an interest in overstating its jurisdiction over the individual. However, neither the group nor the state can adequately protect the different subtleties of an individual's identity as *both* a group member and a citizen. Any fresh approach which seeks seriously to address the paradox of multicultural vulnerability must adopt a more refined conception of multicultural identity that better reflects the actual dynamics at work in contemporary diverse societies between individuals, the group, and the state. It should be practically feasible for individuals to function *both* as citizens with state-protected rights, *and* as group members with participatory status in an accommodated minority community.

Resolution of this problem requires acknowledgment that power itself is never static and does not map neatly onto a division between inter-group and intra-group categories. Rather, it is a relational, dynamic concept. Similarly, it is necessary to reject the tendency artificially to compartmentalize individual identity into narrow all-or-nothing allegiances. Instead, we should adopt a wider perspective that permits a more respectful understanding of individuals in their multiple, complex, and potentially conflicting facets of identity.

This problem of understanding identity is compounded by a larger failure: the failure of major normative and legal models to conceive of viable institutional designs that simultaneously preserve the *nomos* and protect the rights and interests of members who face systemic discrimination from accommodated traditions. As we have seen, despite the best of intentions, existing approaches remain caught in a multicultural bind: they can effect a reduction in inter-group cultural domination, but only at the expense of affirming in-group power inequalities – or vice versa. In light of this practical failure in policy, it is imperative that we envision an altogether different way of sharing power between competing jurisdictions in our increasingly diverse societies. A new multicultural paradigm must break away from the binary opposition that underlies all existing solutions to the paradox of multicultural vulnerability. We need to foster more institutional imagination that can appreciate the situational complexity faced by individuals who are culturally and legally tied to both the group and the state. My intention in the following pages is to encourage this kind of rethinking through a new approach to multicultural accommodation: one which strives for the reduction of injustices between groups as well as the enhancement of rights within them. Addressing these complex challenges in critical perspective, while directly tackling the neglected aspects of multicultural institutional design, is the primary task of the remaining chapters in this book.

5   Sharing the pieces of jurisdictional authority: mapping the possibilities

Our legal institutions must recognize the situational uniqueness of our contemporary political-legal reality. This requires a paradigm shift in our thinking: a shift that both encompasses and enables a deeper and wider understanding of situational complexity, as experienced by individuals culturally and jurisdictionally tied to multiple communities. Since none of the presently available normative or legal models provides an adequate balance between respecting cultural difference and protecting individual rights, we must begin imagining possibilities for institutions through a new approach – *joint governance*.

The joint governance approach

Joint governance considers the challenges of multiculturalism by recognizing that some persons will belong to more than one political community, and will bear rights and obligations that derive from more than one source of legal authority. More specifically, joint governance promises to foster ongoing interaction between different sources of authority, as a means of improving the situation of traditionally vulnerable insiders without forcing them to adhere to an either/or choice between their culture and their rights.

This can be done by envisioning a radically new architecture for dividing and sharing authority in the multicultural state, one which encourages a mode of governance composed of dialogue between different non-monopolist power centers, rather than an imposition by "all-knowing" state or group officials.[1] Joint governance thus offers an innovative new

---

[1] Instead of focusing on traditional state-centered and hierarchical governing processes, policy researchers are now increasingly emphasizing the need for cooperation between different levels of governance, as well as between "multiple agencies, institutions, and systems which are both operationally autonomous from one another and structurally coupled through various forms of reciprocal interdependence." See, for example, Hirst 2000; Jessop 1997. These new processes, which have gained center stage in recent years, are increasingly discussed in terms of "governance." Related developments in the legal arena are described as a move toward "trans-governmentalism," where the unitary voice of the

approach to the paradox of multicultural vulnerability by seeking to translate into concrete policy measures a key normative commitment: enhancing justice between groups and reducing injustice within them.

Joint governance is based on a "cultural" understanding of institutions which holds that the action and agency of individuals, groups, and states is *situational*, i.e. it varies in different institutional settings and to some extent is shaped by them.[2] The challenge and promise of this new approach lies in its capacity to create new structures of shared authority (joint governance) which recognize "situationality," by linking the mechanisms for reducing sanctioned in-group maltreatment to the very same accommodation structures that enhance the jurisdictional autonomy of *nomoi* groups in the first place.

Mutually re-enforcing rights and nomos

I use the term "joint governance" to describe a repertoire of accommodation techniques which can be combined in creative ways in different social arenas. Joint governance is based on the awareness that the paradox of multicultural vulnerability arises from three sets of intersecting and conflicting interests: those of the state, those of the group, and those of the individual who belongs to both. This new approach aims to allow the individual to function simultaneously as citizen and as group member, and to be subject to input from both state law and her own group tradition. It rests on the recognition that both the state and minority groups have a legitimate interest in shaping the policies under which their citizens/group members operate. Instead of assuming that all accommodation issues necessarily spring from a conflict between state interests and group interests (the strong version of multiculturalism), or a conflict between the interests individuals have as citizens and those that they have as group members (the "either/or" dichotomy), joint governance encourages us to see a third alternative: the coherent set of interests that individuals invoke

state is eroded by the emergence of direct channels of communication between courts, administrative agencies, and legislatures worldwide. Such horizontal networks decentralize decision-making processes within states, and offer a richer context of influence between communities. On these sub-national, national, and trans-national developments see, for example, Bellamy 2000; Knop 2000; Post forthcoming; Slaughter 1994; Slaughter 1997.

[2] Of the growing body of literature on the relationship between structure and agency, as conceived by new institutionalists that stress the "cultural approach," see March and Olsen 1989. Of particular interest here is Elinor Ostrom's analysis of collective action problems, which shows how a new structure of cooperative decision-making can change individuals' perceptions of their options and their assessment of their self-interest. See Ostrom 1990. On the international level, other scholars advance the claim that state identities and interests must also be viewed as constructed by social and institutional structures, rather than as exogenously given. See Wendt 1994.

in order to maintain their agency within both of the larger communities of which they are a part. The existing literature encourages us to see these interests as oppositional: your culture or your rights. *Either* individuals choose the agency that belongs to them as citizens, *or* they can claim the agency that belongs to them as members of a culture, together with the roles that culture offers or assigns to them. All of the currently available theories and models begin with the assumption that the content of rights and the content of culture are an immutable "given," rather than understanding them to be a dynamic product of the complex set of interactions between them. Joint governance opens up the possibility that our agency as members of a culture and our agency as citizens of a state may be mutually reinforcing, and that cultural accommodation may actually enable this mutual reinforcement to occur. Not only does joint governance point to the possibility for members of minority cultures to redefine their rights as citizens, so that those rights do not marginalize them as culture-bearers; it also heralds a new opportunity for individuals within minority groups to consciously employ (or refrain from employing) their rights as citizens in ways that increase their agency as participants in the internal reproduction – or transformation – of their culture.[3]

The plurality of joint governance

Once we reject the misguided premise that a single entity be granted *exclusive* jurisdiction over the individual in all aspects of life, it becomes apparent that there are many possible ways to re-allocate powers between the state and the group. The authority to make law encompasses a bundle of distinct capacities. Therefore creating joint governance arrangements is an immensely complex process that can assume multiple different forms. This chapter outlines and evaluates some of these creative innovations, classing them into four different schemes for the division of jurisdiction: federal-style accommodation, temporal accommodation, consensual accommodation, and contingent accommodation. (A fifth variant of joint governance, transformative accommodation, will be discussed in the following chapter.) I offer a taxonomy of these legal-institutional models, and appraise the capacity of each scheme to resolve the paradox of multicultural vulnerability.[4]

---

[3] I am grateful to Melissa Williams for her written commentary on my Shachar 2000c paper at the Conference for the Study of Political Thought (Toronto, March 2000). The shape of my current presentation owes much to her careful elucidation of these themes.

[4] Joint governance takes cues from the world around us as we find it, imperfect as it is. It does not purport to be a process of design *de novo* so much as an interpretation of the

Each of these solutions suggests a different understanding of, and commitment to, the values of accommodating cultural diversity and protecting citizenship rights. Each involves a different kind and degree of limited autonomy to the minority community. Each configuration must be analyzed on its own merits, in terms of its own particular advantages and disadvantages. Further, each of these accommodation schemes requires great sensitivity to context-specific factors in their application in different social arenas, such as education, family law, criminal law, and the like, arenas that have recently moved to the forefront of the multicultural debate.

What all of these solutions have in common is the rejection of the simplistic "either/or" understandings of group membership, multicultural identity, and state authority. What is more, each scheme contributes a new angle to our way of thinking about individuals' multiple affiliations and their relationships to different sources of authority.[5] This enables a potentially richer and more fulfilling institutional design for multicultural accommodation which will succeed in reducing power disparities at two levels: *between* identity groups and the wider society, and *within* these cultural communities as well.

Jurisdictional solutions

Joint governance asks us to refocus our gaze from a multiculturalism that views the ultimate level of accommodation as territorially grounded, to one that is grounded in the idea of jurisdiction *per se* as the central factor. What we term "jurisdictional autonomy" is the idea that a *nomoi* group can hold responsibility for certain legal or social matters of special concern to its members without tying those powers to territorial self-government. Three of the four accommodation schemes in this chapter conform to the jurisdictional autonomy approach (the exception being

lessons of actual experience. As such, it is also necessary to acknowledge that certain very specific historical and practical realities (not all of them desirable) may have led to the adoption of the practices that I explore here. Still, we can draw general lessons from them about how to accommodate simultaneous belonging, along with adequate safeguards for the interests of at-risk group members. In the discussion that follows, the example of family law remains the primary and concrete illustration of the multiculturalism paradox in action. Possible applications of these schemes are also suggested in the realm of education.

[5] Such innovative schemes are far less rigid than the normative and legal paradigms that we have seen in the last chapter. Of course, joint governance-inspired approaches cannot boast the same historical staying power as the secular absolutist model, nor can they carry the richness and diversity of the religious particularist model. They can only remain more modest conceptual outlines at this point, although they can potentially yield new ways of thinking about the division of legal authority that may eventually rival the old ways.

federal-style accommodation).[6] Indeed, jurisdictional autonomy is often a more flexible, accountable, and broadly applicable solution for the division of authority because it promises the "possibility of self-legislation, although neither unlimited nor sovereign."[7] This more nuanced understanding of law and cultural membership, identity and jurisdictional authority, thus forms the foundation of a new system of joint governance.

Variants of joint governance

Federal-style accommodation

One point of departure for considering multiple affiliations consists in "federal-style accommodation," where power is allocated between several sub-units and among different branches and levels of government. *Nomoi* groups, like other sub-units, can enjoy potentially considerable autonomy under a federal scheme. But like other sub-units, they are also subject to certain overarching constraints applicable to all governmental levels within the system, such as compliance with basic constitutional principles.

Federal-style accommodation is an attractive option because it permits the division and sharing of power between different communities, making a certain kind of autonomous jurisdiction a viable option for minority communities, yet without threatening to dissolve the united multicultural state. Federal states may – and often do – bring together political units, each with different ethnic bases.[8] Moreover, federalism connotes an agreement between the different constituent units to enter into a multi-tier-style government ("coming together" federalism), or an agreement to devolve authority from a unitary government to different sub-units of a multi-national state ("holding together" federalism).[9] In either case, it is necessary that all parties find the arrangement advantageous in order for the federal system of power division to thrive. As William Riker observes, when all parties are known to benefit from the federal arrangement, then each can reasonably rely on the others to honor their obligations and duties. Ideally, the enforcement mechanism is not coercion so much as the mutual rational self-interest of the different units constituting the federation.[10]

---

[6] Aside from the special case of Aboriginal peoples and of regionally concentrated national minorities, jurisdictional autonomy appears to be a more fitting way to respond to many religious- and culture-based *nomoi* groups' claims for public recognition and institutional accommodation.   [7] See Vitta 1970, p. 193.   [8] See Riker 1995, p. 508.

[9] On the distinction between "coming together" and "holding together" federalism, see Stepan 1999, pp. 21–23.

[10] Usually federalism also requires nourishing shared institutions and values which can hold together a multi-level system of governance at times of crises. For further discussion, see Norman 1994.

Proponents of federalism often emphasize that it reduces the danger of tyrannical centralized law, "recognizes the *pluribus* within the *unum*," permits sub-units to retain their regional autonomy and unique cultural identities, ensures the advantages of an economy of scale, and, finally, provides room for creative public policy and a healthy measure of experimentalism.[11] In many ways, then, federal-style joint governance appears to be the ideal mechanism for accommodating cultural differences.

However, there are some thorny problems which cloud this rosy picture. This model crucially depends on how precisely the boundaries of the sub-units are drawn, as well as on which powers are retained exclusively in the hands of the sub-units, and which are subject to the jurisdiction of the central federal government. A further related difficulty is that federal-style accommodation rests on the presumption of a territorial division of authority. So a precondition of acquiring self-governance under this scheme is that the *nomoi* group must be regionally concentrated.

Then again, the division of authority between territorial sub-units can follow one of two patterns: region based or nation based.[12] In region-based federalism, the boundaries of the territorial sub-units are drawn according to regional or administrative lines (not ethnic or national lines), with a view toward serving the goals of governmental efficiency by means of sensitivity to local interests, structural closeness of the legislator–constituency relationship, and enhanced accountability. The United States is a classic example of this approach.

In nation-based federalism, on the other hand, the boundaries of the sub-units are drawn so as to ensure that a preexisting ethnic or national community is the majority in a given territorial sub-unit. The province of Québec in Canada is a classic example of this idea at work. According to the system of nation-based federalism, control over linguistic and possibly other distinct (cultural, national, etc.) components is assigned to the minority-governed sub-unit.[13] In addition to furnishing all of the services that other regional sub-units provide, the nation-based sub-unit thus serves to accommodate the desire of a regionally concentrated ethnic or national community for some degree of autonomy, within a larger political union.[14]

Yet just as the religious particularist model institutionalizes preexisting

---

[11] For a defense of federalism as a "social laboratory" in which different legal approaches can emerge in different jurisdictions, see Wildavsky 1979, ch. 6. See also Cover 1981.

[12] Kymlicka points out the distinction between "region-based" and "nation-based" federalism: Kymlicka 1998, pp. 136–141.   [13] See Stepan 1999, p. 31.

[14] Some countries accommodate both region-based and nation-based federalism under the same roof. On the complexities of balancing region- and nation-based conceptions of federalism in such mixed systems, see Kymlicka 1998, pp. 141–143.

group differences, the model of nation-based federalism runs a similar risk of inadvertently promoting the rigidification and fundamentalization of a sub-unit's identity. For example, if what justifies the claims of a given sub-unit in a federation is its national or cultural differences, then it is reasonable to expect that policy-makers in that sub-unit will increasingly insist on such differences. In an already competitive environment, where each sub-unit must look out for its own interests when it comes to dividing the common spoils, it simply makes strategic sense for policy-makers to capitalize on national identity by using it to lay claim to additional powers, services, or resources. In other words, there is a strategic aspect to identity claims that might be further exacerbated by a federal-style accommodation scheme. Even if we can overcome this problem by introducing some restraint mechanism designed to curb excessive identity-based accommodation claims, we are still faced with another very significant set of problems.

In order for a *nomoi* group to be recognized as a semi-autonomous sub-unit under federalism, it must be politically powerful, territorially concentrated, and sufficiently confident to bargain effectively with the federal government and with the other competing sub-units. It also helps to have been historically fortunate, since it requires some significant scope of opportunity to become part of a "coming together" or a "holding together" federal compact – opportunities which do not present themselves every day. Moreover, a group must be capable of providing a whole array of services to its residents in order to qualify for federal-style accommodation, ranging from schooling, policing, and taxing to employment, health services, and infrastructure management. Few *nomoi* groups are in the position to meet this challenge.[15]

These practical difficulties further beg a deeper question: is it truly desirable for *all* minority communities to seek federal-style accommodation? What losses or benefits does an identity group accrue in the process of acquiring so many of the symbols of statehood? Federal-style accommodation may be attractive for certain minority communities, especially those that view control over land as constitutive of their self-definition and essential to their self-government.[16] In fact, a federal-style accommodation solution is sometimes thought to be particularly well suited to the

---

[15] Yet this does not imply that federalism is not the right solution for resolving *certain* kinds of conflicts. For a comprehensive defense of pluralistic federal arrangements in the context of resolving specific group-based tensions within multi-national polities, see Bauböck 2000.

[16] Aboriginal peoples claim that their lands hold fundamental resonance for them, as just one such example. From the vast literature that recounts this special relationship, see, for example, Anaya 1996; Havemann 1999.

identity needs of indigenous populations, with their close relationship to the land. It has been suggested that they could constitute, in a country like Canada, for example, a "third order of government." But this concept is not so simple to implement; Kymlicka himself points out that Aboriginal communities may lack the territorial or financial resources, perhaps even the basic numbers, to support such a solution.[17] What then can it offer to other *nomoi* groups, particularly non-territorial religious communities, which traditionally assert their identity by loyalty to sacred texts or shared beliefs?

For this latter type of groups, there may be other more suitable means of accommodation than territorial self-government in the federal style. Jurisdictional autonomy might be one way to sever the Gordian knot represented by the link between territoriality and sub-national sovereignty, which is part and parcel of federal-style accommodation. As such, it allows us to allocate self-governing powers based on jurisdictional rather than territorial considerations. This means that *nomoi* groups can hold power in matters crucial for the preservation of their collective identities such as education, minority-language instruction, or membership demarcation, without governing the entire territory they inhabit. Under this alternative scheme of accommodation, the group does not have to be regionally concentrated, since the application of its laws is personal (i.e. attached to the person) rather than territorial in nature (i.e. based on physical presence in a given territorial unit). Nor does it have to shoulder a complete range of governmental responsibilities – just those appropriate to its situation.[18]

However, even if a given minority population has the critical numerical mass to permit it a majority in a carefully drawn territorial sub-unit, there is still no guarantee that the dismantlement of systematic patterns of intra-group power disparities will be the first concern of negotiators as they pursue talks to create a new inter-governmental political order. Extrapolating from the relevant experience with multilateral negotiations in existing federal systems like the United States and Canada, as well as from the "social engineering" of still embryonic supranational entities like the EU,[19] it is safe to predict that the power implications of definitions of status in the family will be among the very last items on any list of issues drawn up by inter-governmental policy-makers.

Even if such subjects are at the top of the agenda, certain hard

---

[17] Kymlicka 1998, p. 145.
[18] For arguments in favor of adopting a "non-territorial" conception of federalism, see, for example, Elkins 1995; Howse 1996, p. 315; Choudhry forthcoming.
[19] For a comprehensive overview of the harmonization reforms in the European Union context, and the related debates on issues such as "subsidiarity" and the democratic deficit, see, for example, Weiler 1999.

questions remain unresolved under the federal-style accommodation system. Should individuals who live in territorial sub-units (structured around their group) have direct access to "outside" courts when the group is alleged to have violated their citizenship rights? Or does respect for cultural difference require indirect access, meaning that insiders must first turn to a court within their sub-unit, and only then can they turn to the national (or supranational) court system for remedy? This may look like a mere technicality, but in practice it has significant consequences. Different procedural rules affect the relative openness of any legal system, and shape to a large extent the way in which justice is administered. Indirect access to state courts, for example, not only requires considerable resources (since the individual must first exhaust the proceedings within the sub-unit prior to turning toward the state); it also fails to recognize the potentially paralyzing fear that an insider may experience if she must initiate her challenge against dominant forces by starting off in a group-controlled legal forum in her community. A larger provision of direct access to state courts for group members is not a risk-free policy either. After all, the individual who initiates a legal proceeding against her *nomoi* group is potentially exposed to severe pressures to withdraw the legal claim from the state court in order to protect the group.[20]

Given this array of problems, federal-style accommodation seems to offer only a limited promise to vulnerable group members as well as to cultural minorities that are not regionally concentrated or nationally defined, and whose collective identities are not manifested primarily in relation to specific lands. Leaders of these groups that do not fit the federal mold are better off focusing their political energies on other modes of accommodation. Practices based on partial jurisdictional autonomy can more effectively ensure a degree of control over contested legal arenas such as education, family law, immigration policy, resource development, environment protection, cultural heritage, or language instruction.

Temporal accommodation

Another way to slice the jurisdictional pie is along the lines of what I term "temporal accommodation." This alternative view invites us to

---

[20] A third option is to establish a mixed-entry system, in which certain claims must first be heard by a forum internal to the group, while other issues, especially those concerning the safety of the person, can be automatically directed to an outside legal authority. Unfortunately, no technical solution (however sophisticated) can overcome the basic problem: the very real concern that due to intra-group power relations, an injured individual might be too intimidated to seek *any* legal recourse. As I have pointed out elsewhere, granting *amici curiae* standing to administrative bodies or non-governmental organizations to speak for or along with the individual can to some degree mitigate, but not fully resolve, this problem. See Shachar 1998, p. 298.

think of accommodation as time bound and issue specific. According to this temporal accommodation approach, certain life events crucial to the continuation of the group's collective identity (such as the creation of a family or the early education of children) are governed by group tradition as the sole and definitive source of authority. Outside of these crucial moments, individuals must turn to state law.[21] The novelty of this approach lies in its consideration of the likelihood that a group member's sense of affiliation can and will shift across time. Thus, in the case of education, a minority community enjoys the exclusive authority to inculcate its members with its traditions for a certain specified number of years in the child's life, but only under the understanding that these children will eventually be exposed to a broader set of perspectives, meet children from a background different than their own in the more diverse environment of state-sponsored schools, and acquire some degree of citizenship education necessary to political participation in a democracy.

The American landmark case of *Wisconsin* v. *Yoder* (1972) can be read as exemplifying this type of temporal accommodation.[22] In *Yoder*, members of the Old Order Amish community challenged a Wisconsin law that required them to send their children to a state-sanctioned school until they reached the age of sixteen. The Amish parents claimed that "the modern high school is not equipped, in curriculum and social environment, to impart the values promoted by the Amish society." More specifically, they claimed that if Amish children were exposed during their formative years to a schooling experience outside their community, they might decide against continuing in the demanding and heavily regulated Amish way of life.[23] After a long legal dispute, the Amish parents unilaterally removed their fourteen-year-old children from the school upon their completion of the eighth grade (or equivalent) – in violation of the state's compulsory school attendance law. Wisconsin sued, and the Amish parents turned to the US Supreme Court in order to seek exemption from an otherwise universal state law based on their right to the free exercise of religion. In the end, the Court ruled in favor of the Amish parents, holding that "enforcement of the State's requirement of compulsory

---

[21] As with federal-style accommodation, this model also depends on a precise definition of time- and issue-based jurisdictional boundaries between the state and the group.

[22] 406 US 205 (1972). *Yoder* is one of the relatively few cases in the American constitutional tradition in which a court granted a request for religious exemption from a valid law. See Sarat and Berkowitz 1994, p. 298.

[23] The Amish parents were concerned that formal high school education beyond the eighth grade would "place Amish children in an environment hostile to Amish beliefs with increasing emphasis on competition . . . and with pressure to conform to the styles, manners and ways of the peer group," and would "take them away from their community, physically and emotionally, during the crucial formative adolescent period of life."

formal education after the eighth grade would gravely endanger if not destroy" the Amish community.[24]

What often goes unnoticed in the vast body of literature predominantly lambasting the *Yoder* decision is that the Amish parents indicated to the Court that they would *not* seek to remove their children from the public schools *prior* to the eighth grade. As Arenson and Shapiro carefully note, "some of the judges made it clear that they would find differently, were that issue [of removing the children from public school prior to the eighth grade] present."[25] The Court's ruling, then, can be read as establishing in *Yoder* a temporal accommodation approach: Amish children must study in state-sanctioned schools for an extended period of time – eight years – before they are exempted for a two-year period from otherwise compulsory state education law.

This accommodation scheme avoids the "either/or" trap, since it establishes a system whereby the state has authority over the education of Amish children for eight full years, while the community secures the authority to define their education in the two subsequent years which it considers crucial. Neither the state nor the group has full and exclusive jurisdiction over these children. In defense of this accommodation scheme, it can be argued that eight years in the state school system must allow enough time to ensure that Amish-born children have sufficient basic skills, practical knowledge, and familiarity with the world outside their community in order to make a meaningful choice. This includes the choice of whether to be baptized into the faith, which most young people usually undergo toward the end of adolescence. In other words, a well-drafted and carefully implemented temporal accommodation scheme in the educational arena must ensure that individuals develop the capacities required for "exit" to be a real possibility.[26] Equally important, such a temporal accommodation scheme must also allow individuals sufficient "inside" knowledge of their culture, so that they can also stay in the group and make a meaningful decision to follow a traditional way of life. If temporal accommodation is to be effective both state and group authorities must respect the other's authority, and not undermine its influence on the citizen group member.

---

[24] Among the many other complexities of the *Yoder* case there is the question whether parents are indeed the best parties to represent their adolescent children's interests, or whether children should be given an independent voice if their position differs substantially from that of their parents. The German educational system currently allows children to self-select their religious education at the same age of fourteen. For further discussion, see the Appendix, pp. 154–160.   [25] See Arneson and Shapiro 1996, p. 372.

[26] In the case of the Amish community, young people who decide against baptism are not shunned, since they never took the vow and therefore have not failed to live up to it. See Arneson and Shapiro 1996, p. 369.

In the family law arena, temporal accommodation might allow the group formal legal authority over certain aspects of membership demarcation activities. But these powers are balanced by other relevant powers retained by the state. For example, if the group is awarded jurisdiction over individuals at the time of deemed entry, then the complementary authority over individuals at the time of recognized exit is granted to the state. Such accommodation in the family law arena is also likely to demand that the state recognize marriage ceremonies performed by an authorized group official as valid and legally binding, so long as the parties have voluntarily consented to the solemnization – even if no civil ceremony (following the procedures of marriage in state law) is performed. In this way, the group's tradition is adapted from a ceremonial, extra-legal practice which takes place in civil society, to a more widely recognized and legally binding norm.[27]

According to the temporal accommodation scheme, the family law division of powers system does not always follow the pattern suggested by the more clear-cut education example. The "temporal" aspect comes into play with regard to family law like this. The involvement of the state is triggered by significant life events, but ones which can happen at any time, like separation, divorce, or death. It is at that time that the state can become involved, because of the special circumstances accompanying such events. For instance, in the event of a death, state law will govern matters such as inheritance, or the rights of group members *vis-à-vis* third parties (such as employers or insurance companies). This system also anticipates conflicts which might occur.[28] For example, an employer might refuse to pay survivors' benefits on the grounds that a marriage recognized by the group's traditions is not legally valid, since it does not follow standard state procedures. This is precisely what happened in the US in the case of *Parkinson* v. *J. & S. Tool Company* (1974),[29] and the case is instructive for its temporally defined problems specific to family law.

[27] In contradistinction to the secular absolutist model, this approach awards the group the power to publicly define how individuals become officially accepted as family members in the multicultural state. Certain limitations such as minimal marriage age will be applicable to group procedures, just as they are applicable to state procedures.

[28] Conflicts can arise because of the time-bound and cycle-of-life event-driven switches in jurisdictional authority. Such shifts in jurisdictional authority can follow different sequences: the group might first gain authority over regulating individuals' conduct in a given sphere of life, only to later transfer this power to the state (as in the marriage scenario just described); or the state might exercise its authority by defining the rights and obligations of group members at a certain stage of life (e.g. their initial years of schooling) with the understanding that the group will later have an opportunity to consolidate its jurisdiction over these individuals (as illustrated in the balance struck in *Yoder*). Whatever the specific temporal-sequencing technique chosen, the hallmark of this accommodation scheme is that it dovetails with developments in the human life cycle, and uses them as cues for breaking the either/or deadlock. [29] 313 A.2d 609 (1974).

In *Parkinson*, two lifelong Roman Catholics, Ruth and Richard, were legally married before a Roman Catholic priest in 1927. Two children were born from this marriage, which terminated in 1939 when Ruth obtained a divorce decree in a state court. Richard then left the home but returned in 1950 to resume life with Ruth and their children. Prior to cohabitation, and as a step toward remarriage, the couple visited the pastor of their local Roman Catholic church, informed him of the divorce and requested that he marry them. Consent to remarriage was withheld, however, because as the priest explained, they were "already married in the eyes of God." Since they now assumed that they were (still) married, they resumed cohabitation without performing a civil marriage ceremony in accordance with state law.

Years later, when Richard died from a work-related accident, Ruth turned to her husband's employer, J. & S. Tool Company, requesting workers' compensation benefits as Richard's dependent wife. The company denied her entitlement to such compensation benefits, because it claimed that Ruth and Richard were not legally married. And since the precondition for compensation was that the surviving dependent must be the employee's wife at the time of death, Ruth could not qualify for these benefits.[30]

An Appellate Division court affirmed the company's position and denied Ruth the compensation benefits. She then turned to the New Jersey Supreme Court. This Court held that it made perfect sense for Ruth, as a "simple person with [an] inveterate Roman Catholic background," to seek a priest when she wanted to get married, and to turn to a lawyer (i.e. to the jurisdiction of state law) when she sought divorce. Hence, when Ruth and Richard re-united after the divorce, they again turned to the church to formalize their relationship. It was the priest, not Ruth and Richard, who wrongly thought that no new ceremony was required to remarry the couple now divorced under state law. Showing compassion to Ruth, as a devout religious person who acted in good faith, the Court held that "[t]o deny her benefits for the unintentional mistake of another is seriously to penalize her for a wrong she did not willfully commit." The Court reversed the decision of the lower court, and held that Ruth was entitled to receive workers' compensation benefits as Richard's wife.

While the Court in *Parkinson* v. *J. & S. Tool Company* avoided the pitfall of formalism, and granted Ruth the remedy that she sought, this case nevertheless illustrates one of the drawbacks of temporal accommodation. It

[30] Today, given the expansion of the rights guaranteed to opposite- and same-sex cohabiting couples, Ruth would have probably qualified for such benefits based on common-law marriage or non-marital cohabitation.

shows how difficult the translation of standards can be when it must pass from a group-based set of norms to the governing state's understanding of what constitutes "validity." It also points out how the cost of bridging such inevitable gaps tends to fall upon vulnerable group members who must negotiate for their rights on a case-to-case basis, and often against ingrained prejudices and suspicions regarding their *nomoi* groups' traditions besides.

Another illustration of how a temporal accommodation scheme might play out in practice is found in a recent South African Court of Appeal decision in the case of *Amod* v. *Multilateral Motor Vehicle Accidents (MMVA) Fund* (1999).[31] In *Amod*, as in *Parkinson*, the dispute was about a wife's entitlement to compensation after the death of her husband, in this case in a car accident. The insurance fund (MMVA) claimed that it was under no obligation to pay compensation to Ms. Amod since she and her husband married according to the provisions of Islamic law, but failed to register the marriage according to the provisions of state law. The insurance fund further claimed that a marriage solemnized solely by Islamic law was against the *boni mores* of society because an Islamic marriage is potentially polygamous. Even though there was no suggestion that the marriage between Ms. and Mr. Amod was anything other than a monogamous union, the insurance fund still claimed that the *possibility* of polygamy should relieve it from the duty to compensate the wife.[32]

The Court of Appeals, however, offered a different perspective. It suggested that the important question was whether the right contested in this case (the right to compensation from a liable third party, in this case the insurer, for loss of support due to death in a car accident) was a right deserving state protection. Once it answered this question affirmatively, the Court held that the same state protection accorded to a monogamous marriage solemnized in keeping with the Christian faith (in terms of holding the insurer liable) should also be accorded to a monogamous marriage solemnized in keeping with the Islamic faith.

Furthermore, the Court in *Amod* explicitly stated that its ruling should not be "understood as saying that if the deceased had been party to a plurality of continuing unions, his dependants would necessarily fail in a dependant's action [against the liable third party]."[33] As the Chief Justice put it: "I prefer to leave that issue entirely open." In other words, the Court made a distinction between the norms and proceedings which applied at the point of entry into marriage (religious and customary law), and the

---

[31] 444/98 *Amod* v. *Multilateral Motor Vehicle Accidents (MMVA) Fund*, 1999 4 SA 1319 (SCA).
[32] Muslim marriage contracts were recognized in South Africa in 1997 in the case of *Ryland* v. *Edros* 1997 (1) BCLR 77. [33] *Amod*, p. 24.

(secular) legal consequences of marriage as a set of state-sanctioned rights and duties between the marriage partners, and between them and any relevant third parties. Under this accommodation scheme, these rights and duties, as uniformly defined by state law, become applicable in the event of certain life events. As it happened in the *Amod* case, this was at the time of premature death.

The temporal accommodation scheme clearly creates the opportunity for groups with traditions significantly different from those of the dominant majority to maintain certain distinct aspects of their *nomos*.[34] They are able to do so even in the face of the significant encroaching powers of the modern administrative state.[35] In this way, the temporal accommodation approach provides minority groups with the leeway to maintain much valued practices, and the freedom to escape (at least partially and temporarily) from the heavy hand of the regulatory state.

However, this scheme is problematic for several reasons. Besides the burden of proof that it places on individuals seeking recognition of their group's distinct practices, temporal accommodation is also inherently unstable from an institutional point of view. The task of specifying the precise boundaries of issues to be governed by the group versus the state, as well as the necessity of defining the precise temporal periods involved, combine to form a daunting challenge. It can also create interminable legal controversies, and it is not necessarily clear who will ultimately decide these fundamental questions.

Another set of concerns relates to the potentially negative effects of time-bound yet otherwise unregulated accommodation on at-risk group members. For example, if the group is granted exclusive control over the education of children in their early years (with the understanding that these children will later be exposed to state schooling), and subsequently utilizes harsh disciplinary measures, then the fact that the state can *later*

---

[34] Practices such as polygamy, for example, can be accommodated under this scheme so long as they are voluntary, and consent has been given by all relevant parties – including the already married spouses. In this case, state powers are still applicable to these relationships at different points in time, determining, for instance, the eligibility of spouses to state-guaranteed rights at divorce or death (as in *Amod*), or perhaps holding that according to state law each partner is entitled to a share of his or her spouse's property at separation or death (regardless of the plurality of unions). The possibility of such multicultural accommodation does not necessarily mean that *any* group-based marriage practice should be permitted. All determinations of this issue require a context-specific analysis in a given community and within the dominant legal system, which will allow a sound evaluation of the effects of recognition (or non-recognition) of a given legal procedure upon potentially vulnerable insiders.

[35] On the modern state's craving for ever-greater power and control over the citizenry body, see Scott 1995, p. 231. As Scott puts it: "[M]any state activities aim at transforming the population, space and nature under their jurisdiction into the closed system without surprises that can best be observed and controlled." See also Shaskolsky-Sheleff 1993.

affect the education of these children does not suffice to ameliorate any psychological or physical harm already caused. The temporal accommodation scheme therefore fails to provide effective limiting principles or regulatory mechanisms for detecting and preventing harm that could later prove irreversible.

Similarly, if the practice of arranged marriage is permitted by the group's established traditions, and is occasionally practiced by its members, then the fact that the parties to an arranged marriage (performed according to the group's tradition) can eventually turn to the state to terminate the marriage (according to civil law) provides little remedy – because it may be too late to correct the more intangible damage already done. Even if a state court later declares an arranged marriage null and void due to duress or coercion, this subsequent intervention cannot always undo the social effects of "temporal" accommodation. For example, if matters of virginity and sexual purity are significant to the accommodated community, we can reasonably predict that there will be strong pressures to remain in an arranged marriage, regardless of the question of full or original consent in the first place. Recourse to state law under such circumstances can also prove cold comfort, if for example it leads to threats of shunning or excommunication.

Finally, the temporal accommodation scheme fails to create an incentive for the group or the state to establish some form of meaningful and lasting cooperation that can provide systemic answers rather than erratic crisis resolution, or to ease some of the hardships that fall on group members who must navigate between these two normative systems. Instead, it unwisely imposes the full weight of negotiating such transitions upon the individual.

Consensual accommodation

A seemingly more attractive scheme is that of "consensual accommodation." Here the idea is to permit individuals with multiple affiliations to exercise choice and make their own determinations about which legal authority – the state or the group, for example – will have jurisdiction over their personal affairs. In the case of family law, such a scheme will permit each citizen to determine whether to enter marriage in accordance with the procedures of a uniform state law, or to follow the principles encoded in her own group's tradition. This one-time choice of legal framework will govern the individual's relevant affairs from the beginning to the end of her intimate relationship in a given family. Thus, if a marriage is celebrated by a secular authority following the terms and procedures of state law, it can later be dissolved only by an official state authority. However, if a marriage is solemnized by an official of the relevant *nomoi* group according to that group's marriage procedures, it can later be dissolved only in accordance with that *nomoi* group's governing divorce traditions. Unlike state regulation of the group's separate jurisdiction under a multi-layered federal-style accommodation scheme, or the time-bound autonomy granted to the group under the temporal accommodation scheme, the consensual accommodation scheme provides strong and lasting self-governing powers to the group. Once the individual has chosen to submit herself to the group's jurisdiction in lieu of submission to state law, no player in this triad can reverse the original choice of jurisdiction.

This accommodation design has several important advantages. For one, recognized *nomoi* groups' traditions can attain a status equivalent to that of state-created legal norms. Moreover, the consensual accommodation scheme seems to offer a simple and elegant solution to the vexing complexities that other multicultural accommodation schemes encounter when attempting to seriously respect the different facets of a group member's multiple affiliations: it delegates the decision of which facet of identity to emphasize in a given legal arena to the individual herself. Another advantage is that consensual accommodation allows the norms encoded into state law – which in most countries still reflect the interests and social perceptions of the dominant majority – to go unchanged, yet it also provides comprehensive self-governing powers to recognized minority communities in areas crucial for the preservation of their *nomos*.

Another appealing feature of consensual accommodation is that it permits real choice among different normative systems – a choice given to the individual prior to entering an important and binding legal relationship like marriage. This model institutionalizes private choices in the form of publicly enforceable legal obligations. For example, in countries which currently follow a strict secular absolutist model, this accommodation scheme requires the recognition of parallel powers in religious communities which regulate their members in certain legal affairs such as family law or education, followed by a transfer to the individual of all responsibility for any withdrawal from the standard normative system of state law and toward the more diverse terrain of *nomoi* groups' established traditions.[36] In countries that currently exercise a religious particularist

---

[36] Under this scenario, state law serves as the norm (or the default rule), but individuals can reverse this default rule through the expression of voluntary acceptance of the jurisdiction of their respective community. This expression can take different forms, such as the filing of a written affidavit with a civil authority or a local court. In countries that do not permit this freedom to "opt out" (i.e. where religious and customary traditions are not formally recognized as official law), the state itself may offer the choice between different tiers of "regular" or "heightened" marriage commitments. According to this variety of option, individuals must declare which route they wish to follow prior to their entrance

model, consensual accommodation involves transferring to the individual the responsibility to "opt out" of her community's jurisdiction if she prefers to be governed by state law.

The latter variant of the consensual accommodation scheme has recently been advocated by women's groups in Lebanon, for example, since they concluded that it seems unlikely that the religious particularist system prevailing in that country will be abolished anytime in the foreseeable future. Under such circumstances, it is argued that "a viable alternative would be to make [religious marriage] optional by providing a secular system for those who prefer it."[37] Even though such consent-based measures are intended to respect group differences and individuals' autonomous choices, consensual accommodation must still provide an institutional setting that can ensure that vulnerable group members will have the resources to choose *against* the tenets of their faith, family, or community, if they so desire. Otherwise, rather than resolving the multiculturalism paradox, consensual accommodation may just lead to the opposite result: a reformulation of internal power structures in ways that will curtail the applicability of the exit option that this scheme formally seeks to establish.[38]

The South African Law Commission has recommended a related pattern of choice, according to which parties in a customary marriage can convert their marriage into a civil marriage, but not vice versa. The adoption of this selective "opt in" choice, which is skewed toward movement

into marriage. Once they have made a decision, they cannot later revoke it. This type of choice model is currently exercised in Louisiana, which in 1997 was the first American jurisdiction to establish a two-tier system of marriage: a regular marriage, which can be terminated at the will of either of the parties, and a heightened "covenant" marriage which is indissoluble, unless one of the parties breaches the covenant and the other party seeks to terminate the marriage. As the critics of this new model have rightly pointed out, this change in law (which in effect rolls back the "no-fault" divorce revolution) can adversely affect women who may become "trapped" in a dysfunctional marriage relationship.   [37] See Shehadeh 1998, p. 516.

[38] Scattered empirical evidence verifies this concern. While retaining a religious particularist system of family law, Indian law also recognizes civil marriages according to the provisions of the Special Marriage Act. The original Special Marriage Act of 1872 had provided a code of state law by which individuals could choose to marry and divorce, but in order to utilize this option they had to affirm that neither was a Christian, Jew, Hindu, or Muslim. In effect, they had to renounce their religious and property relations with their families: the return of the same "either/or" dilemma. In 1954 a new Special Marriage Act was passed by the Indian Parliament, with an eye toward eliminating the onerous renunciatory costs of entering a civil marriage. The new Act institutes marriage as a civil contract which is based on the principle of equality. The Act is optional: choice is given to the parties to determine whether they wish to marry under this secular law or under the religious-based personal law. While not legally enforcing the "either/or" choice, this law still bears traces of this social meaning. It is not surprising, then, that very few people in India opt for marriage under the Special Marriage Act. See Sagade 1996, p. 17.

from customary to civil marriage, was accompanied by the recommenda-
tion that customary marriage must be fully recognized. The Commission
was careful to note that the selective freedom to "opt in" which it favored
was "based not on the alleged superiority of any one marriage system, but
rather on the practical consideration that movement from a more open-
ended and facilitative arrangement to a stricter and more highly-regu-
lated regime makes better sense than the reverse would do."[39]

The introduction of such "opt in" provisions is not conceptually new;
they were historically favored by colonial rulers. The adoption of such
measures was presumably an outcome of strategic public-policy considerations, namely to avoid directly altering the status quo – "so as to avoid
unrest in the native populations."[40] However, this historic baggage does
not preclude the possibility that these same choice provisions may yet
acquire new meanings in contemporary diverse societies. But to do so,
choice might require a two-way recognition process:

In colonial times the possibility of a choice was intended to increase the application of the civil laws of European origin, by permitting the option only to such
laws from native laws, and not the contrary, while at present [in the post-colonial
period], as a general rule, the interested parties, when granted a right of option,
may opt either from religious or ethnic laws to so called "modern" laws, or vice
versa.[41]

By investing the individual with the power to choose between competing systems of state- and group-based norms, the consensual accommodation scheme respects individual agency. It can be viewed as offering a
sensible solution to one of the deepest problems that any multicultural
policy will inevitably face: the definition of the boundaries for the accommodated community. Instead of following a rigid primary affiliation criterion, and granting too much power either to state officials or to group
authorities (as is the problem with both the secular absolutist and the
religious particularist models), the consensual accommodation scheme
rests on an altogether different and more democratic idea. It assumes that
it is the group members themselves who are in the best position to evaluate their attachments to the group, and to determine whether or not they
wish to be subject to its jurisdiction. Unlike the other two schemes that we
examined so far, the consensual accommodation scheme does not fall
prey to the very real problem of locking individuals into semi-essentialist
identities.

However, the issue of consent becomes more complex when we think
of children who are too young to express their jurisdictional preferences.
Who will have priority in determining their "situatedness" – their parents

---

[39] See South African Law Commission 1998, p. 39, para. 3.3.6.
[40] See Vitta 1970, p. 182.   [41] Ibid., p. 183.

or legal guardians, the group to which these parents belong, or the state? This problem figures prominently in adoption cases, especially where a conflict arises between the will of the parents and the interests of the community. This is precisely what happened in the much-debated US Supreme Court case of *Mississippi Band of Choctaw Indians* v. *Holyfield* (1989).[42] In *Holyfield*, the US Supreme Court had to decide whether the actions of an individual tribe member "who went to some effort to see that [her children] were born outside the confines of the Choctaw Indian Reservation," and who voluntarily consented to the adoption of her twin babies by a non-tribal family, should override the tribe's interest in having jurisdiction over the custody decisions concerning the children. The Court held that the Indian Child Welfare Act of 1978 (ICWA) clearly favored the interests of the tribe over those of individual Indian parents, and created a jurisdictional scheme which granted exclusive or preferred powers to the tribe in custodial decisions.[43]

A consensual accommodation approach, on the other hand, might have lent more weight to the fact of the parents' expressed consent to adoption, and to the fact of the mother's conscious plan to avoid the tribe's jurisdictional mandate by giving birth outside the territory of the reservation. Consensual accommodation does not reserve for the group (or the state) the ultimate power to determine whether a person is "inside" or "outside" the *nomoi* community. Instead, the state and the group must compete for the legal allegiance of individuals who *simultaneously* belong to both – individuals who are granted the power to make independent choices regarding their submission to one or another set of norms at least in theory. This provision can likewise extend to children by taking into consideration the preferences of the parent for the child's future, until such time as he or she can express his or her own preferences. In this way, it might be argued that consensual accommodation overcomes problems that can arise when multiculturalism forces a minority group affiliation on those who, by accident of birth, may be counted as belonging to specific religious, ethnic, or tribal communities. But while it is surely undesirable to "force" an identity on any unwilling individual, it is also misleading to assume that simply providing a one-time (and forever binding) legal opportunity to express consent will overcome the problem of in-group power relations.[44]

---

[42] 490 US 30.
[43] For a comprehensive analysis of the 1978 Indian Child Welfare Act (ICWA) which designates tribal courts as the exclusive or preferred forum for certain child custody proceedings involving Native American children, see Davis 1993; Graham 1998.
[44] Since it overlooks the problem of in-group power relations, and simply assumes that all group members have an equal opportunity to make choices, the consensual accommodation scheme is informed by a specific and highly atomistic perception of the self, which contributes relatively little to addressing the concerns of at-risk group members, especially women.

So ultimately this scheme too fails to adequately resolve the paradox of multicultural vulnerability. It has several crucial problems. First, the scheme is insensible to the possibility of direct or indirect social pressures to conform with the procedures of a given group's *nomos*. These pressures are likely to be felt by all group members, but especially by women – given their crucial contribution to the reproduction of the collective.

Second, one must have sufficient information about the foreseeable consequences of one's decisions in order to arrive at a meaningful choice, and that information must be transparent to all of the parties involved. However, under the consensual accommodation scheme there is no guarantee that the parties will have equal and adequate knowledge about the consequences of their once-in-a-lifetime choices. It might seem like a merely symbolic and natural decision at the time, to preserve the tradition of one's forebears by celebrating marriage in accordance with the group's practices rather than in the secular, and possibly less familiar, environment of the town hall. Perhaps this problem could be ameliorated by means of state-imposed procedural rules, such as the requirement that both spouses sign a document declaring that they fully understand the implications of their choice of legal system. However, such procedures cannot address the heart of the problem: the potential for the power differential between the parties may still be so great that it effectively circumscribes the range of choices for the less powerful participant. This is reminiscent of the access-to-the-legal-system problem encountered with the federal-style accommodation scheme.

Third, from an institutional point of view this model frees the state from any responsibility for in-group violations of group members' citizenship rights. All that the state must do is ensure that the individual is not subjected to duress and not forced into an unwanted religious or customary marriage – two legal categories that require such a high level of proof that they can rarely be established in a courtroom. If problems arise down the road, it can often seem as if individuals have no one to blame but themselves, even when things go very badly wrong. This holds true even if the individual's original choice was made under difficult circumstances. It is easy to imagine how a person might choose to remain under traditional authorities out of submission to familial, cultural, and group-based pressures, or because insufficient knowledge or resources limited his or her ability to imagine a life outside the *nomoi* group.[45]

Finally, to aggravate the matter further, the group and the state are placed in direct competition for the individual's loyalty, in a "winner takes

---

[45] The consensual accommodation design, like other choice-focused approaches, pays too little attention to the constraints imposed upon the individual by the institutional context in which her choices are made.

all" fashion. Although it appears to consider group members' multiple affiliations, this model actually repeats the either/or mistake. Ironically, the consensual accommodation scheme may in fact severely limit at-risk members' ability to meaningfully exercise the right of jurisdictional choice that this model formally guarantees. For example, the fear that young women may be introduced to corrupting "outside" influences, and might decide against their group's traditions as a consequence, may be terrifying for some. In an effort to avoid this outcome, the community might then attempt to manipulate the choices of its members, for example, by lowering the age of consensual marriage. Of course, there should be certain limits as to how far the community can impose such controls. Economic, social, and state-imposed legal factors (such as mandatory criminal prohibition on child marriages) assist in restricting the ways in which the group can act to coerce loyalty to its traditions.[46] Still, in the delicate balance of power between the group, the state, and the individual, the consensual accommodation scheme forces individuals into an untenable all-or-nothing choice by setting out two exclusive yet competing legal routes. It thus fails to do justice to the reality of group members' multiple, manifold, and potentially conflicting affiliations.

Contingent accommodation

A more interesting and promising approach to dividing jurisdiction between the state and *nomoi* groups is found in the "contingent accommodation" scheme. Here the state yields jurisdictional autonomy to *nomoi* groups in certain well-defined legal arenas, but only so long as their exercise of this autonomy meets certain minimal state-defined standards. If a group fails to meet these minimal standards, the state may intervene in the group's affairs and override its jurisdiction by applying the state's residual powers. These powers grant the state the authority to intervene and protect the interests of all its members no matter where, or by whom, their interests are violated.

Thus, for example, a given *nomoi* group is free to set up its own sectarian schools which will advance a specific cultural (or religious, linguistic, or other) attachment. However, if state-defined minimal standards are deemed to have been violated, the state reserves the right to revoke the license of such sectarian schools, interfere with the group-mandated curriculum, or withdraw children from these schools. This scheme is attractive in that it does not require all children to be subject to precisely the same curriculum, thus allowing for several parallel systems of schooling

---

[46] For more on the relationship of traditional loyalties vs. broadened life experience for women, see Lim 1990.

to exist within a single state. Room is allowed for diversity because minority groups can in fact exercise a relatively high level of jurisdictional autonomy. This approach thus respects cultural differences and encourages individual choice by allowing for a healthy measure of competition between different schools, where each can provide children with educational standards that are at least equal to, and in certain cases are higher than, those specified by state law.

Yet this accommodation scheme also requires a complex regulatory regime because information must be gathered (presumably by state authorities) about the actual performance of alternative schooling programs and their compliance with minimal standards. This may create far-reaching review powers for the state, raising serious concerns about possible bias and discrimination in the exercise of such regulatory powers, especially in cases of significant schisms between the dominant majority and certain minority communities.

Important lessons about this model can also be drawn by examining how contingent accommodation has been applied in Anglo-American law concerning issues of child welfare.[47] By and large, Anglo-American law grants parents autonomy in child-rearing practices. But there are certain things that they must do, and others they cannot do, even within the protected realm of the private home. And if their parenting falls below the benchmark set by the state's minimal standards, it enters the category of abuse or neglect and state authorities can intervene, relying on *parens patriae* jurisdiction to act on behalf of the child's interests. *Parens patriae* jurisdiction describes the power of the state to act *in loco parentis* for the purpose of protecting the interests and the person of the child.[48] Almost every country in the world today has a statute which allows a state court to assume jurisdiction over abused or neglected children and, where necessary, to remove them to a safer environment and away from the authority of their parents. However, the legal standards that govern child protection are often broad and vague, and fail to fully define the precise conditions under which the state may intrude into the family and control child-rearing through coercion.[49] In practice, then, the exact distribution of power between the family, the group (where there is devolved authority), and the state is often determined at the discretion of a host of bureaucratic officials including, but not limited to, social workers, police officers, and court personnel. Little thought is given to the accommodation of families whose cultural traditions differ significantly from those of main-

---

[47] I thank Bob Goodin for suggesting that I explore the contingent accommodation scheme in the context of child welfare issues.

[48] See, for example, the American case of *In re Gault*, 378 US 1 (1967).

[49] See Mnookin 1975.

stream society. For example, there is a damning historical precedent in the United States and other countries, whereby "Indian children [were] removed from the custody of their natural parents by nontribal government authorities who [had] no basis for intelligently evaluating the cultural and social premises underlying Indian home life and child rearing."[50] Clearly, in applying a model of contingent accommodation to the *nomoi* group arena, we must be concerned with how "minimal standards" will be defined. We must also ask who will define them, and how.

Sophisticated variants of the contingent accommodation scheme attempt to address these pivotal questions by creating a "mutual policing structure." Authority is thus divided between the state and the group by assigning a different province of legitimate authority to each entity. But with this new power comes a new responsibility – responsibility for monitoring the performance of one's counterpart in the counterpart's jurisdiction. Ian Shapiro offers one such proposal in *Democratic Justice*.[51] In a chapter entitled "Governing Children," Shapiro argues that in order to protect children's interests, the best way to divide and share responsibility between parents and the state is to create a mechanism of overlapping safeguards, one which gives parents primary jurisdiction over their children's "best interests" and secondary authority over their "basic interests," while giving the state primary jurisdiction over children's "basic interests" and secondary authority over their "best interests." Each entity then focuses on its primary jurisdictional duties. However, each authority also has the responsibility to act as a "back-up" or secondary authority. This is essentially a failsafe measure intended to compensate for any failures of the primary authority and to help preserve integrity in the absence of any other regulatory checks.[52]

Leaving aside the inevitable complexities involved in defining the precise boundaries of each entity's primary and secondary jurisdictions, Shapiro's proposal is attractive because it contains a simple and elegant principle: Any initial allocation of primary authority, whether to the state, the group, or the family, may be reversed if one or more of the parties fail to uphold their fiduciary responsibility to protect their

---

[50] Chief Calvin Isaac of the Mississippi Band of Choctaw Indians in his statement to Congress in 1978, Hearing Before the Subcommittee on Indian Affairs and Public Lands of the House Committee on Interior and Insular Affairs, 95th Cong. (1978), 191–192, quoted in *Mississippi Band of Choctaw Indians* v. *Holyfield*, 490 US 30 (1989), 34–35.

[51] See Shapiro 1999, ch. 4. Shapiro develops a fiduciary model for dividing legal authority over children and youth between parents and the state. While full-fledged citizens are not analogous to children, this scheme offers a workable outline for dividing authority. My application of Shapiro's fiduciary model, as a variant of the contingent accommodation design, is therefore limited to a consideration of the methods of jurisdictional allocation.

[52] See Shapiro 1999, pp. 85–99.

members' interests.[53] In other words, this variant of the contingent accommodation scheme creates a "kinetic" separation of powers, whereby each side can theoretically assume the responsibilities of the other authority. This potential removal of responsibilities creates an incentive for each level of governance to properly exercise its own original mandate and to simultaneously monitor the behavior of other power-holding authorities.

Applied to the *nomoi* group context, this model can establish a dynamic division of power. The group and the state both have certain limited spheres of authority over individuals, who are recognized as bearing multiple affiliations. Because the initial allocation of jurisdiction is always subject to reversal, both group and state are placed under an institutional incentive to perform well in their respective spheres of authority. Should they fail to do so, an individual can turn to the complementary authority and seek redress by appealing to its responsibility as a secondary, safeguard protector of her interests. For example, if a group is granted primary authority over matters of family law, but systematically fails to provide shelter, legal remedy, or assistance to battered spouses, then a group insider can legitimately turn to the state and request its intervention on the basis of the group's failure to act within its original jurisdiction. But the devil is in the details here, like everywhere else. For we still have to ask when precisely responsibility must be reversed. Who is to determine this moment? And can this scheme overcome deep differences in perspectives between the norms of the group, and the laws of the state? These differences are significant because they will predictably color the question of what constitutes a violation. No legal scheme can ever be sufficiently detailed to cover all of the possibilities. So in practice, disagreements over the initial allocation of jurisdiction, the definition of minimal standards, and any subsequent re-alignment of responsibility can all too easily lead to deadlocks. Even this promising "kinetic" mechanism for dividing legal authority between the group and the state seems prone to end in paralysis.

The contingent accommodation scheme also suffers from at least three other major deficiencies. First, given the inevitable power asymmetries between the state and the group, it is hard to see how this (analytically attractive) model of mutual "mirror-image policing" can be applied in practice. While it is easy enough to imagine how the state might apply its powers if an individual claims systematic violation of her best interests by a group, it is harder to envision the type of sanction that the group might apply if the circumstances are reversed.

Second, unlike the consensual accommodation scheme which provides

---

[53] I briefly discuss this variant of contingent (or "conditional") accommodation in Shachar 1998, pp. 298–299.

those living in *nomoi* groups with the opportunity to decide which author-ity will have jurisdiction over them in given legal areas, the contingent accommodation scheme relegates individual group members to a more passive position. According to the scheme, they are forced to play the role of whistleblowers (informing the other jurisdictional authority of viola-tions of their rights by the other entity), instead of being allowed to work as authors of the legal-institutional separation of powers intended to protect their multiple interests.[54]

Furthermore, when it comes to the authority over those matters most crucial for at-risk group members – ranging from the protection of their bodily integrity to access to education, vocational training, marriage, or control over independent means of livelihood – nothing in this scheme ensures that these powers will be allocated between the state and the group in a way that maximizes these members' interests. Here again, there is no necessary positive correlation between the enhancement of the self-governing powers of the accommodated group *vis-à-vis* the state, and the improvement of the status of *all* group members. Unless they are granted a formal voice in the original negotiation process, there is little guarantee that the concerns and interests of traditionally vulnerable group members will be heeded or consulted in decisions to split jurisdic-tions between the two membership communities. As with any other multicultural scheme, we must be alert to the potentially injurious effects of well-meaning external protections upon different categories of group members here – effects which may unwittingly exacerbate preexisting internal power hierarchies.[55]

Summary

The four different variants of joint governance which I have outlined in this chapter offer a rich panoply of measures for overcoming some of the

---

[54] See the arguments developed in a different context by McCubbins and Schwartz 1984.

[55] On this last point see, for example, the case of *Native Women's Association of Canada* v. *Canada*, [1994] 3 SCR 627, where the Native Women's Association of Canada (NWAC) launched a court case to gain access to inter-governmental talks between the federal, pro-vincial, and territorial ministers responsible for Aboriginal affairs. NWAC was concerned that the exclusion of Aboriginal women from direct participation in these multilateral talks denied them a voice in decisions significantly affecting their future. Specifically, the dispute between the NWAC and other Aboriginal organizations pivoted around the ques-tion of whether or not the Charter of Rights and Freedoms (the Canadian Bill of Rights) should be made applicable to any form of Aboriginal self-government which might be negotiated. NWAC held a pro-Charter view, and claimed that women's interests would be threatened if the future of enhanced self-government for bands was negotiated solely by male-dominated Aboriginal organizations. The launching of this case at an "outside" forum (the Supreme Court of Canada) eventually won Aboriginal women a seat at the inter-governmental bargaining table.

major problems entrenched in the prevailing normative and legal approaches to dividing jurisdiction in diverse societies. As we have seen, federal-style, temporal, consensual and contingent accommodation all share a commitment to overcoming the oversimplified "either/or" understanding of identity and the division of legal authority that it entails. Instead of rigidly and artificially predetermining the set of rights and duties assigned to an individual in a given legal arena based on her conceived primary affiliation (a mistake committed by the religious particularist and secular absolutist models), these four schemes suggest more sophisticated methods for the mediation of group members' multiple and potentially conflicting affiliations. None of the four assumes that the complex facets of a group member's affiliations can be reduced to a single quasi-essential and idealized identity, nor do they assume that only one source of authority will solely affect group members. Each proposes a different jurisdictional structure to reflect this multiplicity, thus opening the door to newer, more complex, and more attractive possibilities for constructive dialogue between state and group.

Aside from the special case of national minorities, the vast majority of religiously and culturally defined *nomoi* communities are most likely to operate within larger political entities. What they often seek is not what Kymlicka sees as the most expansive (or "fullest") form of accommodation, perceived as territorial self-government. Rather, these groups often seek a narrower measure of public recognition for their practices. Once we reject the premise that *either* the state *or* the group must be granted *exclusive* jurisdiction over the individual in all aspects of a given legal dispute, it becomes apparent that there are many possible ways to reallocate powers between the state and the group to accommodate different facets of individual identity. We can thus work to overcome the ultimatum of "either your culture or your rights."

Our rethinking of the tangled relationship between the state and its non-dominant cultural minorities enables us to resist allocating absolutist notions of jurisdictional authority to *either* of them. As this chapter has shown, a greater promise lies in envisioning new ways of dividing and sharing jurisdictional authority between them. All four approaches to accommodating multiple affiliations attempt to imagine structures of authority which require the state and the group to coordinate their exercise of powers. Each approach responds differently to the challenge of finding new ways to share the pieces of jurisdictional authority in our increasingly diverse societies. The federal-style accommodation scheme advances a multi-layered understanding of authority, which is attractive in that it does not collapse the group into the state. However, it ultimately places too much emphasis on territoriality and so significantly restricts the type and number of *nomoi* groups that can seek accommodation within its parameters. This scheme is not tailored to accommodate the needs of minority cultures that do not or cannot wish to imitate the set of powers associated with a semi-independent sub-unit, but which still seek a level of jurisdictional autonomy that is greater than mere non-discrimination (or public financial support) of certain cultural practices.[56]

Moving away from the emphasis on territoriality means a move toward jurisdictional autonomy, an approach which underlies the other three schemes.[57] The temporal accommodation scheme, for instance, splits jurisdiction along the time line and keys it to significant life events. In this way it addresses the issue of multiplicity by employing the idea that at different points in time the interests of the group, the state, and the individual bear different weight. According to this scheme, a good accommodation policy is one which creates a strong correlation between the issue-specific, time-bound jurisdiction allocated to the group, on the one hand, and the substantive matters that the group understands to be crucially related to the preservation of its identity, on the other. The third scheme we have seen – that of consensual accommodation – adopts yet another perspective. It effectively devolves the decision over jurisdictional allocation to the individual herself. While on first blush this appears an ideal approach to navigating the rough waters of multiculturalism, and while it has the virtue of respecting a person's own jurisdictional preferences, this scheme encounters the same set of problems that plague other contractual models. Foremost among these problems is a blindness to unequal bargaining positions. Ironically, of all the models discussed in this chapter, it is the consensual accommodation model that most echoes the "either/or" fallacy, having simply transferred it to the realm of private preferences.

The fourth and final scheme, of contingent accommodation, operates on the assumption that any initial allocation of jurisdiction is always provisional, and subject to reversal by a complementary jurisdictional authority. The idea of simultaneous belonging is thus fundamental to this design, and provides the underlying rationale for establishing its "reversal" option, which is supposed to ensure that poor performance will by itself justify the transfer of power from one authority to the other. Yet despite its alluring sophistication, the contingent accommodation design is plagued by the "minimal standards" problem: who is allowed to define them, and how is one supposed to enforce them in a way consistent with

---

[56] Therefore, their claims do not fall neatly within the boundaries of Kymlicka's "polyethnic rights" category. See Kymlicka 1995, pp. 30–31.

[57] Some scholars have also suggested that federal-style accommodation should be reconceptualized along non-territorial lines. See, for example, Elkins 1995.

the accommodation of deep cultural differences? It also fails to take into account the asymmetrical power relations that exist between the group and the state, besides assigning too little agency to individuals to affect their jurisdictional environments unless or until they have a grievance.

Evidently each joint governance scheme possesses its own particular strengths and weaknesses; each of these innovations represents a distinct evolution in the development of multicultural theory and practice. Their examples of strategies and solutions, while still provisional, point to the possibility of still another variant of joint governance whose success has yet to be tested. This new and more effective variant to come is called transformative accommodation.

6   Transformative accommodation: utilizing external protections to reduce internal restrictions

This chapter outlines and assesses what I consider to be the most attractive variant of joint governance – *transformative accommodation*. This is a variant that takes the two different locuses of authority – the *nomoi* group and the state – and, instead of viewing their conflict of interests as a problem, considers it as an occasion for encouraging each entity to become more responsive to *all* its constituents. Through an arrangement of *non*-exclusive competition for the loyalties of those citizens who overlap both jurisdictions, transformative accommodation seeks to adapt the power structures of both *nomoi* group and state in order to accommodate their most vulnerable constituents. Each intersection of jurisdictions provides each authority with an opportunity to increase its accountability and sensitivity to otherwise marginalized group members, since each entity must now "bid" for these individuals' continued adherence to its sphere of authority rather than take it for granted.

We can observe such positive dynamics at work in other examples of joint governance. For example, federal-style accommodation of territorially concentrated national minorities marked by historic, cultural, or linguistic difference has led to considerable internal transformations among these national minorities.[1] Granting non-territorial *nomoi* communities certain self-governing powers can similarly result in greater accountability and responsibility among accommodated group leaders. This measure enables the internal re-examination of traditional restrictions (such as those disproportionately burdening women), precisely because the group (or its leaders) acquires certain public powers over its respective members. According to this analysis, the very public recognition of "private" group traditions can exert effective pressure on group leaders to amend these traditions in ways that are loyal to the *nomos*, but are also

---

[1] See Bauböck 2000, pp. 385–387. This internal transformation has been compatible with a stronger assertion of "difference" by the accommodated national minority, as in the case of Québec in Canada, for example.

more compatible with the democratic standards of the larger state in which they dwell.[2]

A truly comprehensive solution to the multiculturalism paradox must therefore identify and defend only those state accommodations which can be coherently combined with the improvement of the position of traditionally subordinated classes of individuals within minority group cultures. Transformative accommodation can rise to this challenge by allowing cultural differences to flourish, while creating a catalyst for internal change. In this sense, it is more radical than the other joint governance schemes that we have examined so far. It aims to establish an ongoing dialogue between different sources of authority as a means of eventually improving the situation of traditionally vulnerable group members without removing them from their *nomoi* groups. In so doing, transformative accommodation incorporates some of the more dynamic attributes of other joint governance schemes in overcoming the "either/or" stalemate, thereby moving toward a meaningful resolution of the paradox of multicultural vulnerability.

Principles of transformative accommodation

Transformative accommodation relies on four key assumptions. First, group members living within a larger political community represent the intersection of multiple identity-creating affiliations. Second, in many real-life circumstances both the group and the state have normatively and legally justifiable interests in shaping the rules that govern behavior. Third, the group and the state are both viable and mutable social entities which are constantly affecting each other through their ongoing interactions. Fourth, it is in the self-professed interest of the group and the state to vie for the support of their constituents. These assumptions form the foundation of a joint governance structure which might finally succeed in granting influence to group members, in order for them to be able to participate effectively in state/group decisions which directly concern them.

Upon the foundational assumptions of transformative accommodation stand three core principles. They are:

1. the "sub-matter" allocation of authority;
2. the "no monopoly" rule; and
3. the establishment of clearly delineated choice options.

These principles define how authority can be usefully divided, how trans-

---

[2] State recognition of group-based authority therefore provides significant powers to *nomoi* community leaders, but it also imposes certain responsibilities upon them. As will be explained below, when this is reinforced by the "no monopoly" rule of a competitive jurisdictional environment and clearly delineated choice options, it increases the pressure on group leaders to maintain a level of accountability to their citizens.

formative accommodation can maintain the separation of powers, and most importantly, how members of groups can exercise some agency once jurisdiction has been shared.

Allocating jurisdiction along "sub-matter" lines

Since it assumes that group members can be attached to more than one membership community and subject to more than one legal authority, transformative accommodation seeks to sustain a circulation of power between authorities, rather than allowing its systemic unequal accumulation. Like other separation-of-power models, transformative accommodation intentionally eschews the idea of exclusive or absolute authority.[3]

Instead, transformative accommodation envisions a new way of allocating jurisdiction. It observes that contested social arenas (such as education, family law, criminal justice, immigration, resource development, and environmental protection) are internally divisible into "sub-matters": multiple, separable, yet complementary legal components. Existing legal and normative models rarely recognize that most contested social arenas in the multicultural state encompass multiple functions, or diverse sub-matters. Rather, they operate on the misguided assumption that each social arena is internally indivisible and thus falls under the full and exclusive jurisdiction of one authority, *either* the state *or* the group. On this account, there is always a winner and loser in the jurisdictional contest.

Transformative accommodation, on the other hand, capitalizes on the divisibility of each social arena by allocating jurisdictional authority along sub-matter lines. The salient feature of sub-matters is this: only when they are addressed together can any legal dispute in a given social arena be resolved. If only one sub-matter comes into play, no complete decision can be made.[4] The fact that power can be divided along sub-matter lines *within* a single social arena makes it possible to have a more creative, nuanced, and context-sensitive allocation of jurisdiction.

The principle of sub-matters can be clearly seen in the arena of family law. The complexities of family life create several legal sub-matters within this single social arena. For example, in the context of marriage, there are at least two sub-matters which come into play. There is a demarcating function which regulates, among other things, the change of one's marital status

---

[3] Thomas Hobbes is perhaps the political theorist most closely associated with deep-seated modern assumptions about the exclusivity of state legal authority. See Hobbes 1955, ch. 18.
[4] It may be useful to think of different sub-matters in a single social arena as pieces of a larger jigsaw puzzle. Each piece of the puzzle (each sub-matter) has limited value when standing on its own, but when these pieces are properly aligned they offer a full and coherent picture, which is greater than the sum of its parts. I develop this metaphor in greater detail in Shachar 2000c.

or one's entitlement to membership in a given community.[5] And then there is a distributing function which covers, among other things, the definition of the rights and obligations that married spouses are bound to honor, together with a determination of the economic and custodial consequences of this change in marital status (in the event of divorce, for example).[6] These "demarcating" and "distributive" functions parallel the two key legal aspects of marriage and divorce rules: status and property relations. While often intertwined in practice, status and property are two legally distinct sub-matters. Meaningful consideration of marriage and divorce rules thus requires an examination of both jurisdictions: the authority which governs each distinct legal sub-matter, as well as the complementary authority which jointly governs (or "co-prevails") in a contested social arena.

The exciting uniqueness of the transformative allocation of authority lies in its capacity to subvert the "either/or" dichotomy/monopoly. It also relieves us from the semi-essentialist categorization of individuals' "primary affiliation" (in contrast to the secular absolutist and religious particularist models), because it encourages us to refocus our attention on the content of the accommodation claim and its situational context. Transformative accommodation does not begin by appraising the type or nature of the group seeking accommodation. Instead, it begins by exploring a specific social arena where accommodation is needed. Then it proceeds to analyze the unique interrelated sub-matters involved in that arena, while taking into account the possibility that different actors may attach different values to specific sub-matters.

The special feature of sub-matters – the fact that each is necessary to making a given social arena work as a whole – provides an important new way to slice the jurisdictional pie, so that each competing entity has a vital share in the governance of a social arena, yet none gets a monopoly over it. This leads to the second principle of transformative accommodation: the "no monopoly" rule.

The "no monopoly" rule

The "no monopoly" rule draws from the rich tradition of modern democratic theory that advocates separation of powers in the political realm. Regardless of their other disagreements, Montesquieu, Madison, and more recently, Dahl, Riker, and Weingast all firmly agree that mecha-

---

[5] See chapter 3 for an enlarged discussion of the demarcating function in family law practice. On a highly controversial construction of this function in the American context, see *Miller* v. *Albright*, 523 US 420 (1998). See also my discussion of the *Martinez* case, in chapter 2.

[6] Other issues are also included under the rubric of family law sub-matters, such as those pertaining to adoption, inheritance, trusts, and estates. But these fall beyond the purview of the present discussion.

nisms for the separation of powers and concomitant limitations on majority rule can prevent tyrannical power.[7] Transformative accommodation institutes the "no monopoly" rule by recognizing the potential rivalries between jurisdictions over legal sub-matters, and by considering the intersections of multiple affiliations among individuals. According to this rule, neither the group nor the state can ever acquire exclusive control over a contested social arena that affects individuals both as group members and as citizens.[8] Since neither can fully override the other's jurisdictional mandate, the "no monopoly" rule re-defines the relationship between the state and its minority groups by structurally positioning them as complementary power-holders.

Thanks to this interdependent balance, decision-makers in contested social arenas can benefit from a broader pool of precedent and autonomy, especially in the arenas of state law and group tradition. They can also benefit from a simultaneously cooperative and competitive situation between authorities, which are now forced to work that much harder to win the support of their constituents.[9] According to this system of joint governance, centers of authority can still exercise significant discretion and public policy decision-making functions, but they operate in an institutional environment where each authority's powers are constrained.

We saw earlier how family law is separated according to the sub-matters of demarcation and distribution. Since neither the state nor the group holds exclusive authority over both sub-matters, the group and the state are permitted to acquire official and binding authority over marriage and divorce rules, that is, once again, never exclusive. The "no monopoly rule" requires certain aspects of a given dispute to be within group jurisdiction, as well as linked to aspects within state jurisdiction. For instance, the group authority may prevail over the demarcating aspects of family law while the state authority may prevail over its distributive aspects. Such a process of division along sub-matter lines allows the group to draw on traditions of lineage rules and distinct personal status laws, while allowing the state to address the societal concerns surrounding distribution (i.e. the effect on women, children, employers, taxation, and social services). Alternatively, the group might hold the authority over distribution

---

[7] Philip Pettit sketches at least three ways in which majority rule may tyrannize minority groups or certain individuals within those groups. See Pettit 1999, pp. 176–178. For an overview of the development of the separation of powers doctrine, see generally Elazar 1987; Vile 1998. For Riker's now classic contribution to this literature, see Riker 1964.

[8] Not all social arenas fit this dual qualification requirement. However, the social arenas most pertinent to the present discussion are those where conflicts have already arisen in practice, such as family law, education, resource development, immigration, and criminal justice. Conflicts tend to arise in precisely these arenas because *both* the state *and* the group have a stake in the legal norms and procedures which govern individuals' behavior.

[9] Cooperative and competitive relationships are also often present in federalist arrangements. See Breton 1998; Watts 1999, pp. 60–61.

(drawing on a group's desire to maintain property within the community), and the state might hold the authority over demarcation (drawing on state traditions to protect the status of certain individuals).[10]

The distribution of authority in this new separation of powers is designed to ensure that no collective entity may ever acquire unlimited powers in a jointly governed social arena. Instead, non-monopolist power-holders are forced to compete for the loyalty of their shared constituents in each different social arena. If carefully designed and implemented, transformative accommodation can thus create incentives for both state and group to serve their citizenry better.[11] Since they can no longer rely on exclusivity as the basis for authority over individuals with manifold affiliations, they must discover other means of appealing to their constituents.[12] This leads to the third principle of transformative accommodation: establishing clearly delineated choice options through which constituents can express approval or disapproval of state or group decisions.

The establishment of clearly delineated choice options

In order for constituents to register their response to the competition between state and group, they must have clear options which allow them to choose between the jurisdiction of the state and the *nomoi* group. Choice here means that they can remain within the sub-matter jurisdiction of the original power-holder (approval) or that they can resist that jurisdictional authority at predefined "reversal" points (disapproval). These options allow constituents to bring influence to bear on both jurisdictions by emphasizing in different social arenas the citizenship or group membership aspect of their manifold identity. As a last resort, they can discipline the relevant power-holder by "opting out" of a jurisdiction if the jurisdiction power-holders fail to effectively respond to constituent needs. It is precisely the fact that members are no longer "locked in" (within their group jurisdiction or under the monopolist power of the state) that ensures the capacity for "change from within". In other words, one important way of encouraging the group and the state better to serve

---

[10] It is worth noting that joint governance does not reflect any natural or predefined symmetry inherent in either the state or the group. Rather, it is in specific contextual and historical settings that problems arise between competing authorities regarding the allocation of power between them. Joint governance is always an innovative and dynamic response to such specific situations.

[11] Once we recognize the competitive streak in legal sub-matters for what it is, we are that much freer to imagine a wider range of jurisdictional authorities. Faced with an array of specific choices and possibilities, the individual group member is much better equipped to potentially influence the division of authority. If a state or a group hopes to hold meaningful authority over a legal sub-matter, it will need the support of its constituents to do so.

[12] This process is strengthened when individuals are granted powers to use their mobility within the system, as discussed below.

their citizens, each in its respective sub-matter of authority, is to provide citizens with viable mechanisms for exercising choice: by delegating to them the ultimate power to determine whether to "switch" their jurisdictional loyalty from the original power-holder to the rival power-holder. Such participation must proceed on an issue-by-issue basis, once the initial jurisdictional boundaries have been set, thus allowing *nomoi* group members to meaningfully choose between jurisdictions.[13]

Such opportunity for individual choice opens up a new window on our perception of group membership. Where most accommodation models only allow membership to be "entirely in" or "entirely out," the possibility to "opt in" or "opt out" of specific group positions produces a decisive shift in group influence from dominant power-holders to individual members. Individuals can now bring more effective pressure to bear on the *nomoi* groups supposed to represent them.[14] And since these group leaders depend on their constituents' support for survival, they will be that much more motivated to attune themselves to the needs of their members. Once the old balance of power shifts from power-holders to individual members, a dynamic new space for meaningful participatory group membership is thus created.[15]

Such "reversal" provisions cannot be taken lightly. The purpose is not to fracture group solidarity so that members can opt out at the slightest opportunity. The initial division of authority between group and state must still remain meaningful and presumptively binding on its individual members. "Opting out" is justified only when the relevant power-holder has failed to provide remedies to the plight of the individual; only then can the individual instigate a fair claim against that authority. Instead of

---

[13] A clearly negative response can in turn provoke the group or state to transform their own internal practices with regard to the particular sub-matter at issue. In most cases, the ability of these constituents to choose between jurisdictions should be enough to encourage such transformation. However, they may actually exercise their right to "opt out" of a jurisdiction in the last resort if there is systemic failure on the part of the responsible jurisdictional power-holder to provide effective remedies.

[14] Such internal attempts at changing the practices, policies, and outcomes of a given collective represent a resort to voice rather than an escape from an objectionable state of affairs. The effectiveness of the resort to voice is strengthened by the possibility of exit. This is particularly true when the threat of turning to the competing jurisdiction is raised by someone for whom exit is costly, such as a "loyalist" member who has much to lose by withdrawing from her minority community, and is therefore more likely to exhaust all internal means of dissent first, as long as any possibility for improving matters "from within" still exists. Fostering such an internal discussion may frustrate the short-term interest of group leaders to entrench themselves (by hiding behind the old ways of doing things), but it clearly serves the long-term interest of the collective by countering the ills of entrenched inequality and in-group repression. Albert Hirschman makes a similar point in his discussion of the power of the "loyalist's threat of exit." See Hirschman 1970, pp. 82–86.

[15] The threat of selective exit by significant numbers of constituents can therefore make group leaders more accountable to the needs and interests of traditionally less powerful group members.

forcing group members to fight for a partial exit (on a case-by-case basis), the "opt out" provision enables them to reverse the jurisdiction of a given authority in relation to a particular sub-matter of authority if that authority has already failed to offer them meaningful remedy. In this way, the provision of an "opt out" clause offers a structural remedy through its potential to bring about social change over and above its resolution of the immediate grievance between the disputing parties.[16]

By "structural remedy" I mean that transformative accommodation is future oriented. It not only refers to finding more just and equitable resolutions to specific disputes. It also seeks to create new conditions where historically vulnerable group members can challenge the established doctrine of their tradition by raising the stakes of a failure to revoke norms that maintain their systemic discrimination. To encourage such conditions for re-evaluation of the *nomos*, a credible threat of exit must be made available to traditionally less powerful group members. This requires establishing clear "reversal" points through negotiation between the state and the group as a precondition for establishing a joint governance regime in the first place. Once an agreed-upon reversal condition has been breached, the individual is automatically entitled to the protection of the competing jurisdictional authority (either group or state). Clearly delineated and selective "entrance," "exit," and "re-entry" options are thus a crucial component in improving the situation of traditionally vulnerable group members, for at least two reasons. In the short term they serve as a stopgap for the individual, when the relevant power-holder fails to provide answers to the needs of certain categories of citizen insiders who are subject to its jurisdiction in a given sub-matter of authority. In the long term, the allowance for "reversal" in jurisdiction following failure in performance can generate significant internal changes, because it raises the collective risks and costs in maintaining discrimination and subordination within the *nomoi* group.[17]

When the system is working effectively to make power-holders more accountable to their constituents, the onus is on group leaders to respond to "alternative" voices within the group, and thus lead to the internal transformation of the group's *nomos*. If they systematically fail to address the concerns of group members who bear a disproportionate burden of the costs of accommodation, and these members are granted at least minimal (educational or material) resources through the state's exercise of

---

[16] Owen Fiss, perhaps more than anyone else in the North American legal literature, has championed the cause of structural remedies as a means of eradicating social patterns of systemic inequality. See, for example, Fiss 1974.

[17] This pressure will occur only when group leaders become convinced that those bearing the disproportionate brunt of accommodation might indeed begin to relocate their jurisdictional loyalty away from the group and toward the state by emphasizing the citizenship facet of their multicultural identity.

authority in its designated sub-matters, then these "peripheral" members can, perhaps for the first time, pose a real threat of selective exit.[18]

The fact that such reversal points are predefined by the state and the group as a condition for the creation of joint governance is significant for another reason. It relieves the vulnerable insider from the need to nego-tiate individually the transition between group and state norms on a case-by-case basis (as we have seen in the examples of *Parkinson* and *Amod*), thus overcoming one of the thorniest problems of other models of accom-modation. Equally important, it creates an impetus for finding an *internal* resolution to the dispute, because the mechanism of reversal (or the pos-sibility of "partial exit") is known to all parties: the individual, the group, and the state. Since the latter two now engage in a competitive relation-ship (where the result of failure to address their constituents' needs can lead to the strengthening of the other power-holder), both authorities are put under that much more pressure to serve and retain their constituents *within* their respective spheres or sub-matters. Ample evidence shows that the best catalyst for settlement in civil litigation (even in the case of severe power disparities) simply lies in setting a firm trial date. It is the matter-of-fact concreteness of this public event which encourages the parties to negotiate in good faith. Unlike a court decision, which takes the form of an all-or-nothing resolution, a mutually arranged settlement allows the parties to at least ensure that the outcome protects their most salient interests. Each party in this scenario prefers a risk-reduction strategy over the peril of losing its case altogether.

By analogy, the introduction of clearly delineated reversal options can create a similarly strong incentive for resolving long-standing in-group problems. Avoiding the reversal of jurisdiction becomes a matter of self-interest to the group, since it allows the group to protect whatever degree of self-regulating power it has already secured over its members, rather than risk losing it piecemeal. The beauty of this model lies in its simplicity. In contrast to the secular absolutist approach, joint governance refrains from forcing externally imposed norms on the group. At the same time, it avoids the pitfalls of granting full immunity to group practices (as per the religious particularist model). Instead of forceful intervention or full immunity, transformative accommodation seeks to create institutional conditions where the group recognizes that its own survival depends on its revoking certain discriminatory practices, in the interests of maintaining autonomy over sub-matters crucial to the group's distinct *nomos*.

---

[18] The advantage of this model is that disproportionately burdened members can realisti-cally reject one certain position of the *nomoi* group, whereas betraying their own tradi-tions and beliefs by leaving the group entirely behind is an unrealistic and arguably undesirable expectation.

The object of harnessing this individual–group–state dynamic is not to strip communities of their distinctive *nomos*. Rather, the goal is to make in-group subordination more costly to the group (especially when at-risk members begin to challenge their traditionally marginalized position) – for only in this way, can the system create incentives for the group to transform the more oppressive elements of its tradition.[19] Instead of tacitly condoning persistent inequalities within a group in deference to cultural differences, transformative accommodation labors toward more justly redistributing the internal costs of preserving the group's *nomos*.[20]

Transformative accommodation vs. other variants of joint governance

Like the federal-style accommodation design, transformative accommo-dation does not grant jurisdiction in an "all or nothing" fashion. However, it diverges from the federal design in two important ways. First, transformative accommodation does not require a territorial basis for the *nomoi* group to acquire a degree of jurisdictional autonomy. Second, since it ensures that no sub-unit accumulates authority over all aspects of its members' behavior, it avoids the risk of exacerbating differences (to which the federal solution of territorial self-government is susceptible). Furthermore, transformative accommodation shares with federal-style accommodation the assumption that although group leaders may want to hold complete power over all group members, they can be convinced of the practical advantages of compromise when faced with the alternative of receiving no public legal authority at all.

As a jurisdictional scheme that aims to reflect in law the real diversity of multicultural identity in practice, transformative accommodation follows a logic similar to that of the temporal accommodation design, which allo-cates jurisdiction over the individual for a set period of time or according to specific life events. Both systems specify that certain matters arising in a controversial social arena will be governed by the group, while others will be governed by the state. Yet unlike the temporal accommodation design, transformative accommodation does not allocate complete powers to the group even for a given period of time. Instead, it allows standards arising from a range of sources to govern the matters arising in

---

[19] Transformative accommodation entrusts each community with the capacity to articulate its own solutions for overcoming such entrenched power inequalities.

[20] This can be seen as indirect intervention into the group's "private" affairs, a multicultural state acting *ultra vires*. However, this arrangement must build on the realities of a pre-existing state of affairs. We have already seen in previous chapters that group and state are constantly interacting, and that multicultural accommodations inevitably exert an impact on both the political expressions of a culture and the power relations it propagates.

a social arena simultaneously. It does this by permitting input from both state law and group tradition according to their relevance to the single event in question, be it a matter of education, immigration, criminal proceeding, family law, or other contested social arenas in the multicultural state. While conflict-of-law principles already recognize that it is not always necessary for one legal system to govern all aspects of a single social arena, the question still arises as to how to determine which aspect of a given dispute will be governed by which standard.

Like all other variants of the joint governance model, transformative accommodation takes a context-sensitive approach. Instead of providing a strict and comprehensive master plan, like the grand civil codes of old that sought to anticipate all legal problems in one governing document, transformative accommodation seeks to negotiate and set in motion a dynamic system of complementary multicultural jurisdictions, which leaves room for social experiment and historical development. Yet this built-in potential for organic change does not mean that we automatically forgo a governing principle. Rather, it means that the principles adopted – the sub-matter allocation of authority, the "no monopoly" rule, and the establishment of clearly delineated choice options – must be reflexive and flexible, thus leaving room for spontaneous, situation-specific innovations.

Drawing on the principle of choice encoded in the consensual accommodation scheme, transformative accommodation allows individuals to make significant choices about the jurisdictions under which they wish to be governed. However, individuals are no longer trapped in a fixed allocation of power between the group and the state, and instead have more leverage in shaping the precise legal regime that will affect them in each social arena. The impact of individual preferences and experiences therefore contributes to the dynamism of the system.

Finally, like contingent accommodation, which introduces the idea of a kinetic or dynamic separation of powers tied to the adequate performance of the authority in question, transformative accommodation establishes an initial allocation of authority in different social arenas, yet allows adjustments to be made to those jurisdictions as needed. However, by dividing and sharing authority along sub-matter lines, the transformative accommodation model, rather than relying on a mechanism of mutual policing that only comes into play when one of the parties falls below some "minimal standards," instead establishes a regime of ongoing mutual adjustments by both the group and the state. In this way, transformative accommodation avoids the very real problems surrounding the definition, interpretation, and application of "minimal standards," thereby overcoming one of the major difficulties that plagues the contingent accommodation scheme.

Moreover, since the transformative accommodation model deals with an array of social arenas and with a multitude of groups, it is in fact far more dynamic than the contingent accommodation scheme. If we think of the former as operating on a two-dimensional plane, with two players, then joint governance is a model which operates in three-dimensional space, with three players – the group, the state, and the individual – which can each simultaneously interact on different planes and in different social arenas. In this latter model, the potential for dynamism is far greater, and so it provides for a far richer multicultural system. While transformative accommodation operates according to a constant and stable inner logic as dictated by its three guiding principles, it also has the capacity to actively adapt as the different players interact.

Decision-making across jurisdictional boundaries: tensions and possibilities

Assuming that neither state nor group can fully control all aspects of a given social arena, decision-making must begin by recognizing the multiple, complexly situational, and often conflicting affiliations for individuals in contested social arenas. From this premise, the three principles of transformative accommodation must guide any law-maker's or policy-maker's attempt to redesign the allocation of powers in a multicultural state.

Decision-makers must consistently recognize the presence of legal sub-matters in every contested social arena, as well as the importance of providing group members with opportunities to influence state and group policy. The hope is to create jurisdictional boundaries between state and group to best accommodate the different affiliations and facets of individual group members. In cases where both state and group have a legitimate claim to authority, the specific allocation of power between them depends on the justifications that each can provide for its preferred position in governing a specific sub-matter.

Because of the careful balance that needs to be struck in each arena, it will be necessary to negotiate the precise jurisdictional boundaries between competing authorities such as the group and the state. And more often than not, both parties will naturally work to reach an agreement that maximizes their respective interests. To reach an agreement, however, they must also bend toward meeting each other. Thus, even if the group truly prefers to control all aspects of its members' legal affairs, group leaders will nevertheless have to settle for less than full control.[21] Faced with this necessity, responsible group leaders will predictably seek deci-

---

[21] This is an outcome of the "no monopoly" restraint, imposing a structural limitation on co-prevailing parties: under no circumstances should either gain authority over *all* sub-matters in a jointly governed social arena.

sion-making power over the sub-matters that they consider most significant for group survival. For example, if the group views control over the
demarcation aspects of family law as crucial to its *nomos*, it will probably
seek to acquire jurisdictional influence over this sub-matter.[22] Similarly,
while for the sake of simplicity, efficiency, and uniformity the state might
prefer to exercise full control over all legal aspects of family law (or education, immigration, and criminal law, as discussed in the appendix), it too
will have to compromise. The state must determine which sub-matters
are most relevant to the interests of group members as participants in the
larger body politic. The state must then aim at acquiring preferred jurisdiction over those particular sub-matters.

At the negotiation stage, power asymmetries between the group and the
state must be taken into account before establishing the initial allocation of
authority. Since the state is the more powerful entity, the presumption in
the negotiations must be in favor of the group. This presumption requires
goodwill on both sides, but it must also be translated into more concrete
guarantees. For instance, the group might be given the advantage of setting
the agenda for negotiations, or it might receive a commitment from the
state that it will receive first priority in identifying and securing the sub-
matter most crucially concerned with the preservation of its *nomos*, in at
least one social arena.[23] Careful attention must especially be paid to the
precise definition of "reversal" options. These clearly delineated choice
options will be defined according to not only the input of group representatives and state officials, but also to the input of those constituents who are
most likely to need option protection in each specific sub-matter (such as
students and parents in the education arena, women and other historically
disempowered group members in the family law context, and so forth).

Once an initial agreement is reached, day-to-day operations then

---

[22] Each *nomoi* group will be able to follow its own decision-making procedures in pursuing
such jurisdictional choices. However, if these internal decision-making procedures deny
voice and representation to a specific category of member (such as women), these citizens
will be given the option to participate directly at the inter-governmental bargaining table.
See, for example, the *NWAC* case (discussed in ch. 5, note 55). Similarly, if representatives of the state fail to take the interests of vulnerable citizens into account, these group
members will then be able to demand that their specific interests be represented by their
groups as well as by human rights or non-governmental organizations (NGOs). Such
advocacy groups regularly participate in the legislative process: they too may deserve a
place at the negotiating table when dramatic constitutional changes such as joint governance are introduced. In addition, procedures and remedies for resolving potential conflicts between an individual member and her accommodated community must be
defined *ex ante*, before any changes in the jurisdictional boundaries take effect.

[23] Joint governance must therefore secure some advantage to the group in negotiating jurisdictional boundaries, yet also avoid the trap of accepting *whatever* demands are presented. It must further ensure representation of different contingents of group members
in the negotiations, so as to provide an unmediated voice to those who will be most
affected by the change of policy.

require the parties to engage in a process of jurisdictional dialogue, since the "no monopoly" rule dictates that neither has sufficient legal power to resolve a dispute single-handedly. In turn, reaching a resolution means appealing to, and integrating, the operations of two value systems – that of the state and the *nomoi* group – both of which have a claim to consideration in the jointly governed legal arena.

It is foreseeable that disagreements may arise over the initial allocation of authority between group and state in a specific legal arena. In this event, generosity at the negotiation stage is required from the state as the stronger party. At the same time, responsible negotiators for *nomoi* groups will be aware that if the dominant majority so chose, it could turn its back on accommodation and impose a secular absolutist-type model, perhaps even criminalizing certain of the group's practices. This gives the state considerable clout in all negotiations of whatever style. However, the state's undeniable power to impose cultural conformity on its minorities does not come without its own risks in practice. Such measures can arouse objections among members of the majority who view them as morally unjust; acts of cultural fiat can equally incite social upheaval and violence by members of minority groups subjected to a "cultural crackdown." There are incentives firmly in place for both parties to engage in constructive dialogue once they have embarked on the path of joint governance.

Arguably, however, the leveling tendencies inherent in joint governance lack the efficiency and utility that is gained when power is consolidated in the hands of a sole jurisdictional-holder.[24] We need not shy away from admission that addressing complex and multi-layered problems such as the paradox of multicultural vulnerability is never an easy enterprise. It requires both imagination and a strong political will to advance a multicultural institutional design that respects differences and protects rights, while empowering individual agency. Although joint governance in the guise of transformative accommodation is admittedly limited in terms of immediate and practical judicial economy, it nevertheless offers major advantages of a more lasting import. It promises to decentralize power, in the process establishing conditions that help break the vicious circle of reactive culturalism and thus encourages *nomoi* groups to re-examine

---

[24] One could argue that the sheer loss of bureaucratic efficiency that presumably attends the joint governance approach constitutes a limitation unto itself. Yet similar concerns could equally be raised about *any* multi-level governance scheme, ranging from federalism to supra-nationalism, since they also lead to complex and concurrent dispute resolution mechanisms. See Pennock 1959. Moreover, the practical examples of joint governance that are already operative in the world (as discussed in the appendix) do not support suspicions of increased inefficiency. If anything, these examples provide heartening proofs of the powers to be gained from well balanced incentive structures: when the most salient interests of all involved parties are so met, increased cooperation between them is the result – due to their mutual rational self interest in sustaining a transformative accommodation system of shared jurisdictions.

internally the more hierarchical elements of their traditions. It generates dialogue between non-monopolist power-centers, and ultimately empowers disproportionately burdened group members caught in the crossfire between competing jurisdictions. In this way, joint governance seeks not only to provide a solution to the paradox of multicultural vulnerability, but also to contribute to a broader contemporary endeavor to re-define the role of state law in relation to competing sources of authority from "above" and "below" the national level.

The transformative potential of joint governance thus allows us to place it within a larger context by thinking about it as a special case in a broader set of institutional challenges which are prevalent in contemporary public-policy debates worldwide, and which ask us to reflect on the level of authority best suited to govern each set of activities. Emerging patterns of shared jurisdictions escape the idea that binding legal norms must originate in a single source of authority.[25] They demonstrate an open field of possibilities, since different normative systems now tend to overlap and interact without necessarily requiring that one be subordinate or hierarchically inferior to the other.[26] Transformative accommodation, as a fresh approach to multicultural accommodation, illustrates the promises and challenges encapsulated in any ambitious institutional design that aims to enhance the jurisdictional autonomy of religious/cultural minorities, while seeking to address the severe problem of sanctioned intra-group rights violations at the same time.

As will be illustrated in the family law example discussed in the following section (and in other social arenas as well, such as immigration, education, and criminal justice, all of which are discussed in a separate appendix), there are some existing arrangements that are suggestive and instructive of ways in which partial accommodation by the state of a minority group tradition seems to have initiated an ongoing legal dialogue. And, in the long run, such a system of dialogue can not only alter the often "hierarchical" relations between the state and the group; it can contribute to improving the status of once-vulnerable insiders within the group as well.

Family law revisited: fostering change "from within"

In the family law arena, transformative accommodation can translate into a division of jurisdictional powers whereby the group exercises

---

[25] In the modern era, this single source of authority was consolidated primarily by the state through its sovereign powers. See Weber 1978. Any joint governance system involves a revision of existing political traditions that are based on exclusive sovereign powers. But to a great extent, this change has *already* occurred in our current socio-global reality. No state authority can still credibly claim to have absolute and unilateral control over all norms and regulations that affect its territory and citizenry.

[26] See MacCormick 1993, p. 8. For a detailed discussion, see Helfer 2000.

authority over the sub-matter of demarcation (including questions of status regulating marriage or offspring affiliation to the group), and the state exercises authority over the sub-matter of distribution (including questions of how material resources are allocated in certain relationships, and which public benefits flow from one's family and group membership status).[27] As a result of this initial division of authority, the state and the group each possesses partial and contingent authority in the field of family law. In addition, individuals have the opportunity to change their jurisdictions themselves. In order to exert any impact on significant life events in the families of their shared citizens, both of these authorities must then overcome whatever mutual suspicions they might have, and exercise their complementary powers in tandem.

But transformative accommodation is not only designed to create an ongoing dialogue between group and state authorities. It is also designed as a way to empower at-risk group members. This empowerment can occur in immediately tangible form, such as the provision of better protection to female group members' property and custodial rights at divorce. And empowerment can also assume the less tangible but no less important form of fortifying their agency.

Dividing demarcation from distribution

It is readily demonstrated that transformative accommodation, when put into action in the family law arena, better protects female group members' entitlements to property rights, since it has already been tried out in practice. A sub-matter style of division of authority has been used within the family law arena to improve the circumstances of traditionally disadvantaged women. One such example of a joint-governance style sub-matter allocation of authority is already employed in Malaysia, where the Muslim population is subject to the jurisdiction of *shari'a* courts for matters of family law.[28] In the 1980s, the federal government in Malaysia introduced legislation in an attempt to ameliorate the status of women after divorce, but the object was to do so without violating the power of religious courts

---

[27] The state has a strong and lasting jurisdictional connection to both the parties and the cause of action which supports its interest in governing the sub-matter of distribution in the family law arena. Change of marital status for group members is an event with effects beyond the boundaries of the group, touching on such issues as tax benefits and access to certain public services (including child care, health services, and welfare benefits). The state therefore has at least as strong an interest as the group in adjudicating some aspects of a given family law dispute, such as those concerning distributive aspects of a divorce settlement (i.e. property rights, division of joint ownership, maintenance, and child support).

[28] A related development toward a sub-matter allocation of authority also occurred in Israel, in the aftermath of the 1992 Israeli Supreme Court landmark decision in *Bavli v. the Rabbinical High Court*. I discuss this case and its significance for the protection of women's rights in Shachar 1998.

to define marriage and divorce. The Malaysian Islamic Family Law (Federal Territories) Act of 1984 contains provisions regarding the division of property acquired during marriage in the event of separation or divorce. This state law holds that in making such distributive decisions, courts "shall incline towards equality of division"[29] – and this state-guaranteed provision is to be implemented by the religious courts. Interestingly, the religious courts have not only followed the state's provision, but have in fact extended the mandate of protecting the property interests of women by reviving a traditional (pre-Islamic Malay) custom called *harta sepencarian*. This custom holds that property acquired or improved during the marriage by means of joint labor of husband and wife belongs to both, even if it is registered only under the husband's name.[30] By creatively using this custom as an interpretive tool, recent Malaysian court decisions have broadly defined the term joint labor to include housework by the wife because it leaves a husband free to acquire property, as well her companionship or connections because they assist the husband's business. In this way, the separated or divorced wife is entitled to a significant share of the property acquired during marriage, typically a one-half share.[31]

The Malaysian legislative reform thus created a "no monopoly" rule where both the state and the group jointly govern the arena of family law in ways that improve women's distributive interests and create the basic conditions necessary for women to remain fiscally afloat after divorce. Yet it does so within a framework that defers to their group's jurisdictional autonomy in demarcating membership boundaries through control over marriage and divorce. This arrangement, which is effectively joint governance in action, brings to bear co-prevailing norms from both the state law and the group tradition to resolve the status and property aspects of divorce proceedings.

To further illustrate this point, consider how under transformative accommodation the power imbalance between spouses in an *agunah* situation can be significantly modified by ensuring that the religiously observant woman has recourse to certain economic and custodial rights which are administered under the jurisdiction of the state in its distributive range of authority. As Robert Mnookin and Lewis Kornhauser have shown, divorcing couples often "bargain in the shadow of the law,"[32] and

---

[29] See section 58(1) of the Islamic Family Law Act of 1984 (Malaysia).
[30] Custom has become an important source of law in some Muslim countries. In Malaysia, for example, as Ahmad Ibrahim explains, "the *adat* [custom] has played an important part in the development of the Islamic law and there would appear to be no reason why it should not continue to do so, especially in those spheres where it helps . . . the status and position of women in society." See Ibrahim 1968, p. 204.
[31] For a concise overview of these developments, see Horowitz 1994a, pp. 557–562.
[32] See Mnookin and Kornhauser 1979, pp. 975–976. Mnookin and Kornhauser use much the same divorce example as that discussed above.

are consequently affected by the rules and norms set by the legal system, or systems, that govern them. These rules shape the parties' assessments of their options, and enable them to work out the possible outcomes of demarcation and distribution questions concerning marital property, maintenance, child support, etc., even before they involve either the group or the state court in their dispute.

Assume that a Jewish Othodox divorcing couple has entered marriage through a religious solemnization.[33] A few years later, their relationship has soured. This couple have no children and the only issue they have to resolve is how to divide the $10,000 they have accumulated during the marriage. Suppose it was clear that the state distributive rules would award one-half of the sum to each spouse. This property allocation rule would apply as soon as proof was established that the couple has been separated for a minimum period of perhaps one year, even if the parties were still considered married by the group's demarcation rules. One might expect that the parties would normally settle for $5,000 each and save themselves the time and cost of litigation. The husband cannot get more than $5,000 regardless. But without the separation of authority along sub-matter lines, this divorce could degenerate into an unnecessary legal battle where group-specific gender-biased demarcating-status rules are used to achieve material gain. In the process, the ex-wife is made to pay emotionally and financially for the accommodation of her group's traditions, as the ex-husband is not.

By allowing the *agunah* woman to pursue basic capacities and freedoms in the wake of a separation, some of her husband's exclusive power will be dissolved. The underlying connection between the state- and group-controlled sub-matters that jointly affect individuals subject to both sources of authority can thus help women acquire greater leverage in their relationships and their communities. The divorce example just discussed is significant because it can provide real solutions under the majority of circumstances, but it still leaves unresolved those cases where the more powerful party simply abuses a discriminatory demarcating group tradition in order to cause pain and disadvantage to the other party. Some partners who deny their spouses the religious divorce decree (the *get* or the *khula*, for example) are not motivated by a cost–benefit analysis in abusing their power, so much as a basic spite or vengeance. In such circumstances, even if there is no material or custodial motivation to refuse the divorce, a recalcitrant husband may still refuse to consent to the dissolution of his marriage.

[33] State law will recognize this union as binding, so long as the parties have freely chosen this path and followed the recognized procedures of solemnization as defined by their group tradition (i.e., the marriage was celebrated by a recognized representative of that group).

Transformative accommodation can offer a practical response to this impasse by carefully drafting specific "opt out" provisions, thus allowing individuals an alternative to the group's sub-matter authority – even if they have voluntarily subjected themselves to that jurisdiction in the first place. This last resort safeguard option cannot be used lightly. As established earlier, it is justified only if the group has failed to provide internal remedies to the plight of the individual (in this case, the woman trapped in a marriage relationship because of discriminatory demarcating practices sanctioned by her own community). In such a case, she has a fair claim against that community. But forcing each woman to fight her case in court amounts to an expensive, time-consuming, and cumbersome legal procedure, which can lead to social ostracism of that individual. The consequences of legal action can be so burdensome that a woman may ultimately revoke her claim, and such recourse will most likely fail to lead to internal revision of the discriminatory practice itself. The better solution is to ensure that group insiders have a choice in acquiring a pre-defined remedy through the complementary power-holder (in this case the state), after the original jurisdiction (the community) has failed to offer a meaningful remedy.

If the group fails to provide an answer in the marital context – if it cannot devise some effective internal mechanisms to apply pressure to the recalcitrant husband – then the "trapped" insider is given the option of appealing to the state's jurisdiction instead, after a specified separation period. At this point, the state will acquire (group backed) authority to enforce the removal of all barriers to remarriage (even if the marriage was originally created by religious solemnization). This type of reversal of authority offers a structural remedy, by carving out (upon consultation with the group's representatives) the exact terms for such last resort "opt out" options in each social arena.[34] In short, the idea is to "transfer" the costs of accommodation to the level of the collective, instead of disproportionately imposing them on certain individuals within the group, whether in family law, education, or any other related social arena where the group and the state vie for control in the multicultural age.

Breaking the property–status extortion cycle

We have just seen how the underlying connection between state- and group-controlled sub-matters can help women acquire greater leverage in their relationships and their communities, even under restrictive cultural

---

[34] Clearly, the group stands to lose if the individual finds no resort but to turn to the "reversal" option, because it loses jurisdiction over a sub-matter crucial for its self-determination and survival.

regimes that have a history of subordinating women. In the case of family law, status and property are still closely connected, and any change on one side of the equation can affect the state of affairs on the other. Historically, this connection was used to preserve women's subordination. But there is nothing inherent in the relationship that necessitates this outcome. In fact, evidence from the field of family economics shows how the improvement of women's status within the family is often closely tied to, and in certain cases is a direct result of, her capitalization on property-enhancing activities outside the home.[35]

Of interest to our discussion are studies that explore the web of mutual interactions between women's positions in intra-household bargaining and their positions in extra-household setting. The term "bargaining" is employed here to describe the degree of freedom (or some might simply say the power)[36] that an individual has in affecting the distribution of goods, resources, and obligations in a situation that requires cooperation with others, but may also contain certain elements of conflict between them.[37] This approach to the idea of bargaining has been developed in the family economics literature,[38] most notably in the work of Bina Agarwal.[39]

Accepting Amartya Sen's treatment of the family as a realm of both cooperation and conflict, where many different cooperative outcomes are possible in relation to who does what, who receives what goods and services, and how each member is treated, Agarwal shows how the ability of women to challenge norms that disadvantage them within the family (i.e. to "bargain" for a better allocation of intra-household duties and benefits) is affected, at least in part, by their "fall-back position," i.e. by the outside options available to them.[40]

Generally, we can expect an improvement on one's fall-back position to correspond to an improvement in one's intra-household positioning. The basic logic operating here is that the enhancement of women's legal, educational, and other participation and choice options in both group and state contexts can make a difference (for the better) in their positioning within the family, even if the household (and the community) still remain traditional. It is not the fact that women spend more or fewer

---

[35] For a concise overview of the development of bargaining models in the study of family economics, see Lundberg and Pollak 1996.

[36] On the different dimensions, or faces, of power, see Bachrach and Baratz 1962; Lukes 1974; Isaac 1987; Hayward 2000.   [37] See Sen 1990.

[38] This literature adapts John Nash's formulation of cooperative "bargaining problems" within game theory to the family arena. See Nash 1950; Nash 1953.

[39] See, for example, Agarwal 1994; Agarwal 1997. For further exposition to this field of research, see McElroy 1990.   [40] See Agarwal 1997, p. 4.

hours working in the home, but the fact that they are not fully dependent on others in order to maintain themselves that transforms the power balance in the home in their favor.[41] Specifically, three outside factors are identified as having profound significance in defining the "fall-back position" of women within the family: (1) their economic situation; (2) the link between command over property and control over institutions and decision-making processes that shape cultural and religious norms; and (3) the ability to engage in collective action with other women when contesting norms that disadvantage them.[42] While these three factors are instructive, family economists have tended to pay relatively little attention to legal-institutional parameters, that is, to the direct exploration of how changes in the allocation of authority between state and group over specific arenas of life (such as family law) may significantly affect the access that women have to economic and symbolic resources (such as property entitlements, educational opportunities, and marital status definitions).[43]

The transformative accommodation approach, on the other hand, speaks precisely to this challenge: it reconceptualizes the move toward differentiated or multicultural citizenship as an important opportunity to affect the complex matrix of conditions that affects the degree of freedom, or the "bargaining" position of historically vulnerable group members.[44] Accepting this new approach may not necessarily mean that the life circumstances of vulnerable group members will be dramatically or instantaneously altered, but it does certainly provide for such a *potential* outcome.[45] According to this model, the sub-matter allocation of authority, the "no monopoly" rule, and the establishment of clearly

---

[41] See Sen 1990, p. 139.   [42] See Agarwal 1997, p. 21.

[43] However, most of the family economics literature (especially Agarwal's work) is well suited to such institutional explorations, since it accepts as a basic premise the fact that parameters *outside* the home dramatically affect women's bargaining power *within* it. See Agarwal 1997, pp. 28–36.

[44] The significance of capacity-enhancing conditions is an important facet in Martha Nussbaum's recent writings on women's rights. See, for example, Nussbaum 2000. Other scholars also suggest that greater attention should be given in the multicultural debate to examining the actual practice of freedom by individuals. See, for example, Peled and Brunner 2000.

[45] Unlike the "re-universalized citizenship" response, which attempts to speak for women (because they are viewed either as victims or as coopted agents) by forcing their "redemption" from their cultural traditions and communities, transformative accommodation leaves room for the agency of at-risk group members themselves. It is capable of doing so thanks to the "no-monopoly" rule and the sub-matter allocation of authority, which provide these group members with the power to select between competing jurisdictional authorities in different social arenas, as well as the access to realistic resources allowing them to challenge their traditionally subordinated status.

defined "reversal" options ensure that women (and other categories of historically vulnerable group members) acquire the tools, knowledge, and resources needed to exercise greater leverage within the group. It can only strengthen women's position within the *nomoi* group if they already know that they have acquired the basic capacities needed to live effectively outside it.[46] Even if a woman is not keen to activate the "reversal" option, and will only consider this option as a last-ditch resort, the fact that she has greater leverage available to her will likely prompt her group's leaders and fellow group members to ensure that her experience within the group is congenial, in order to maximize the chances that she will choose to stay under its sub-matters of jurisdiction.

Empowering the once vulnerable

This alignment of interest between the group and the once-vulnerable individual must be complemented by attention to the basic problem of unequal access to resources. Dividing jurisdictional authority along sub-matter lines can assist in this process too by equipping disproportionately burdened group members with new in-group leverage.[47] If group members have certain protections guaranteed to them as citizens (through the state's jurisdiction in sub-matters within social arenas such as family law, education, and the like), then these protections will further strengthen their potential bargaining power as group members. All other things being equal, transformative accommodation endows vulnerable individuals with the power to question their situations, and to seek ways of challenging and changing them for the better.

"Empowerment" here means that women (as well as any other group systematically put at risk by their *nomos*) can gain access to the resources and capacities needed to exercise and initiate change from within their communities. This cannot be achieved by simply allowing these insiders access to an "outside" state court. (Unfortunately, this solution to the multiculturalism paradox can backfire, particularly in a *nomoi* group that has adopted a reactive culturalist interpretation: such an external form of

---

[46] Related approaches that emphasize agency and empowerment as the best venues to create significant and lasting change in the situation of traditionally vulnerable segments of the population are found in the "gender and development" literature. For a concise overview, see Moose 1993, pp. 152–176.

[47] Such leverage is created, in part, by the underlying connection between the state- and group-controlled sub-matters. This underlying connection means that change in one side of the equation (for example, property relations) can affect the other (status relations), just as enhancement of a woman's extra-household options can lead to an improvement of her positioning within the family as well.

recourse may merely entail a deeper silencing of internal dissent, by sin-
gling out those who dare to challenge the conventional interpretations of
the tradition as cultural traitors.) Instead, transformative accommodation
can allow historically subordinated categories of individuals to participate
in the improvement of their situation by ensuring that they have an
improved "fall-back" position. Not only are they guaranteed access to
minimal material protections, as well as to other capacity-enhancing
resources (educational, legal, institutional, and so on), it is these same
group members who also hold the ultimate decision-making power concerning the "reversal" of jurisdiction. This power is vested in them by
nature of their manifold affiliations through a joint governance division of
authority across different social arenas.

In this respect, the empowerment potential of joint governance lies in
its ability to make visible the enduring structures of in-group power relations. The mechanism of divided jurisdictional powers is crucial to this
process because it allows individuals to see their situation from an
enlarged ("insider/outsider") vantage point. Once historically vulnerable
group members have been given the means to withstand the oppressive
tendencies of their traditions and the opportunity to self-select their jurisdictions, group leaders may finally start recognizing the need to avoid
internecine conflict. This in turn can stimulate *nomoi* communities to
earn their allegiances, rather than merely inheriting them, because the
stakes of group survival have become so much higher.

If, on the other hand, the group systematically fails to address the concerns of members who hold manifold affiliations to different sources of
authority, it runs the risk of making its tradition obsolete; it will (inadvertently) encourage those most vulnerable to the multiculturalism paradox
to use the "partial exit" alternative in growing numbers. However, by
availing themselves of the new institutions of joint governance that gauge
which traditional practices are deemed oppressive by factions within
the group, certain authorities within the group may prefer to lead a progressive transformation of the tradition.[48] In other words, in a choice
between losing group members incrementally to the state's jurisdiction,
or attending more swiftly to some of their requests, it is reasonable to
predict that at least some group leaders will prefer the latter option over

---

[48] Such internal transformation can be justified substantively as protecting the *nomos* due to
the fact that group members who seek to promote a more egalitarian theology (for
example, by reviving traditions of internal re-interpretations) clearly wish to highlight the
group membership facet of their manifold identity, not to ignore it. Providing a home for
them in the community can therefore be defended as enhancing the group's strength and
relevance to its members.

the former.[49] Transformative accommodation thus suggests that the best way to effect a lasting transformation in the position of once-vulnerable group members is to create incentives for the *nomoi* group, in order to ensure that these (now empowered) individuals who may see themselves as belonging to more than one membership community will indeed find value in upholding and following the group's distinct cultural traditions.

Harnessing group survival instincts

Nomoi communities are living entities. They are not suicidal in nature. Most have ample resources for re-interpretations which permit them to preserve their *nomos* while adaptively responding to change.[50] Transformative accommodation critically challenges discriminatory internal norms and practices by delegating to the group's authorities themselves the power to decide whether to risk such alienation and exit by following group traditions to the letter. It creates conditions whereby the improvement of the status of those most vulnerable to the multiculturalism paradox becomes positively aligned with their group's self-interest in survival, under conditions where the group must operate within the boundaries of a larger multicultural state.

By including the group in the state process of defining key issues for its self-definition, transformative accommodation creates a strong incentive for authorized group leaders to seek solutions for overcoming entrenched power inequalities encoded in the group's traditions. But it entrusts each community with the capacity to articulate such solutions. It is precisely that allocation of non-monopolist jurisdictional authority to the group that encourages group leaders to consider the interests of those long mal-

---

[49] The recent changes in Egypt's family law codes support this claim. After a long political battle, a group of feminist advocates succeeded in securing the endorsement of the country's religious establishment in order to enact one of the Muslim world's most far-reaching reforms of family law. The new Egyptian law makes divorce an equal-opportunity alternative to an unhappy marriage. Under the new law, a woman will be able to divorce her husband with or without his assent. This re-interpretation of the *shari'a* was possible with the support of an alliance of moderate Muslim clerics, women advocates, civil court judges, and divorce lawyers, who avoided resistance for change from hard-liners by working within the boundaries of the tradition. For, unlike the hard-liners, the coalition offered an alternative reading of the tradition, rendering the new law as a modern reading of the equal rights that Islam bestows on women. Similar efforts for change are under way in other countries, where the Women Living Under Muslim Law (WLUML) network is trying to achieve greater equality for women within the boundaries of Muslim law, by exposing the tremendous variety of rulings and customs concerning women, and endorsing a rereading of Muslim law in ways that are more favourable to women. On Egypt, see Zuhur 2001. On the WLUML network, see Shaheed 1994.

[50] On the possibility for such internal change in religious tradition which holds fidelity to the group's *nomos*, see, for example, An-Na'im 1990; Anwar 1999; Heschel 1995; Richards 1999; Satha-Anand 1999.

treated by the established tradition – even when such re-interpretation requires reviewing and revitalizing the *nomos*. This is the case because failure to find meaningful answers to the needs of vulnerable group members can lead to a "reversal" of jurisdiction. Hence if group leaders fail to act appropriately, not only do they lose some of their power (because of the smaller base of supporters they now have); the collective also stands to lose because of the risk that it no longer controls key identity-defining sub-matters, such as the power to demarcate who is inside and who is outside the group's membership boundaries.

Minority cultures operating within a wider society are rightly concerned with the problem of assimilation, and in certain cases this fear has pushed groups to assert their identities "reactively" via rigid interpretations of crucial traditions. Yet responsible group leaders will be equally concerned with regeneration – that is, with ensuring that the group has enough members in the foreseeable future to preserve its norms and practices. The existence of culture is important, but it needs the existence of group members to perpetuate it as a living tradition. It is this rational and legitimate concern which, under a transformative accommodation system of joint governance, will motivate groups to re-examine their treatment of women and other at-risk group members, and to reform and revitalize their traditions where necessary. While some groups may continue to enforce compliance with tradition by further increasing the subjection of female group members, no cultural community intent on self-preservation in the multicultural age can afford to maintain authority over half its members solely on the basis of fear and internal punishment.

Given that women are responsible for constituting the *nomos* of many groups (through matrilineage, domestic cultural tradition, or specific female transmission of lore), female group members have tremendous potential power. Without them, the group simply cannot survive. Their continued participation is essential for cultural and biological reproduction; they are central to the group's social and economic fabric; and politically, their sheer numbers in a given minority community guarantee them a considerable presence. The maltreatment of women by the group therefore becomes a self-defeating strategy as soon as it explicitly and obviously starts to threaten their continued membership in the group, or their children's qualification for, or interest in, full group membership. From that point onward it is clear to the minority group that it is in its best interests as a collective to reinterpret the group's tradition in a way that recognizes claims for improving the situation of women within their own cultural community.

Unlike the other accommodation models we have seen in previous chapters, the pressure here is on the group to transform its laws from within, since it has already secured the sub-matter authority over the formal definition of key issues such as status or property – and it stands to lose it if it fails to address the needs of its members who now have the power to turn to the state's jurisdiction instead. This dynamic works precisely because of the manifold nature of multicultural identity. That is, the bearers of rights are also the bearers of the *nomos*. Differently put, the intersection of different sources of authority occurs in the lives of persons who belong to both the group and the state, and who are thus subject to their competing jurisdictions.[51]

Once set in place, transformative accommodation may also have another welcome effect. It can help free minority cultures from their ongoing struggle with the ever-encroaching bureaucratization of the modern state, because certain crucial aspects of their *nomos* will be granted publicly enforceable authority. Yet in providing this guarantee to the group, transformative accommodation also imposes its limiting principles: the "no monopoly" rule, the division of jurisdiction along sub-matter lines, and clearly delineated choice options. The purpose of such an arrangement is not for the state to externally impose state norms on the group. If that were the goal, there would be no reason to invest so much in a system that institutionally guarantees that identity-preserving aspects of different social arenas will be governed by the group. Instead, the point of this strategy is to break the vicious cycle of "reactive culturalism" whereby the group adopts an inflexible interpretation of its traditions precisely because of the perceived threat from the modern state. Transformative accommodation thus creates conditions of sufficient security so that the group may revive its own *nomos* and make it once again a vital, dynamic tradition that can engender viable answers to the present-day challenges that its members encounter in their manifold identity.[52] Such transforma-

---

[51] According to this account, Mrs. Martinez (discussed in chapter 2) could have turned to the state and not the group in order to ensure that her children received the same health benefits to which other residents of the Pueblo reserve were entitled. Similarly, Mrs. Shah Bano (discussed in chapter 4) would have been entitled to her maintenance payment according to state law, if the group failed to ensure that she receive equivalent support. In both cases, the three principles of transformative accommodation could have ensured that these women were not left without remedy after all: the sub-matter allocation of authority (in this context, between demarcation and distribution), the "no monopoly" rule (which forbids the possibility that the group controls *both* status *and* property issues), and the establishment of clearly delineated choice options (here allowing vulnerable insiders to turn to the "outside" if their group fails to address their basic needs).

[52] Susannah Heschel makes a similar point in a powerful way. Speaking of the failure of Orthodox Judaism today to resolve the problem of the *agunah* – a woman whose husband has deserted her without granting a divorce – she says: "A living legal system never has the luxury to ignore a serious conflict; it must respond in one way or another. Only when a legal system dies can problems be ignored or passed over." See Heschel 1985, p. xlii.

tion is anything but easy, but at least it seems possible, if not downright urgent, under the condition of cooperative yet competitive jurisdictional relationships between the group, the state, and the individual.

The innovation in such an approach lies in the fact that it does not expect change to necessarily occur because of the "goodwill" of a given minority group's leaders. Rather, joint governance draws upon a *realpolitik* consideration: it may be better to accommodate women (or any other category of group member who is structurally put at risk by the group's sanctioned traditions) so as to ensure that they follow the group's self-defined traditions, rather than run the risk that significant numbers of insiders will emphasize the citizenship identity aspect alone and break their loyalty to the group altogether. Group leaders, perhaps more than anyone else, have much to lose if their members (or "constituents") turn in growing numbers to state law in lieu of the group tradition. This type of pressure for change can be created only when group members' continued loyalty can no longer be taken for granted. It must instead be earned by deed. Joint governance allows individuals the opportunity to self-select their jurisdictions. It does not promote the exit of vulnerable insiders from their home community as a preferred policy solution. Instead, it recognizes the need to increase their in-group leverage (including the power to make credible threats of exit) as effective means to bring about much-needed internal change. In this way, joint governance attempts to take the very real concerns that responsible group leaders have in practice – those relating to issues of regeneration and the continued existence of their group's unique worldview in the foreseeable future – and turn them into a viable incentive for protecting the vulnerable within.

Summary

Through the avoidance of jurisdictional monopoly, the division of authority along sub-matter lines, and the establishment of competing but complementary jurisdictions, transformative accommodation yields several important advantages over the other proposed alternatives. This multicultural separation of powers forces the state and the group to each recognize the legitimacy of the other jurisdiction-holder. Even when both jurisdictions can furnish strong arguments for laying exclusive claim to the norms and procedures governing each individual, a single cohesive system of checks and balances guarantees that neither the state nor the group is enabled to govern alone. Both the state and the group are consequently forced to abandon their perfectionist and maximalist jurisdictional aspirations, which are so often the source of conflict.

By stipulating that in certain social arenas the group will have authority

over sub-matters it views as crucial for cultural survival, and by permitting the accommodated group an advantage in the negotiation process,
transformative accommodation significantly restricts the power of the
state. At the same time, however, it also imposes limits on the *nomoi*
group: it denies it a monopoly over its members in each of these social
arenas. Not all minority cultures will be happy with this basic principle. It
denies groups absolute regulation and control over all aspects of their
members' lives, and it does not allow a *nomoi* group to insulate its
members fully from the effects of state law. Some might argue that in
order to truly respect cultural differences, multicultural accommodation
must defer to the group's practices, even when they may injure some. We
have encountered this "non-interventionist" argument before, but it
remains clear that the last word on the "reversal" of jurisdiction belongs
to those group members who are at most risk from oppressive group practices. Furthermore, although the state may try to disassociate itself from
responsibility for internal restrictions imposed by the group, the disproportionate injury that some members suffer at the hands of their *nomos* is
inextricably related to the external measures of accommodation adopted
by the state. In other words, the state always affects *nomoi* groups, even if
it is only the result of turning a blind eye to in-group violations of
members' rights as citizens.

Given this analysis, the fundamental problem ceases to be *whether* the
state must interfere in the "private affairs" of *nomoi* groups – because it
inevitably will. Rather, the central question becomes *how* the state must
intervene to protect the interests of individuals put at risk by their *nomos*,
while still allowing their group maximum jurisdictional autonomy. The
transformative accommodation approach respects both the citizenship
and the group membership aspects of individuals' manifold identity, and
it employs these intersecting power hierarchies to empower historically
vulnerable group members that are affected by them. Thus, rather than
tacitly condoning in-group subordination in the name of respecting cultural differences, transformative accommodation explicitly accepts the
challenge of redistributing the internal costs of preserving the group's collective identity.

I do not want to suggest that any mere legal formulas or institutional
designs can single-handedly resolve the paradox of multicultural vulnerability. Clearly, no single jurisdictional writ can fully encompass the
complex sets of tensions that are embedded in the legal terrain of asymmetrical power relationships within the state, between different constituent communities, and among different groups of individuals who share a
given culture.[53] Instead of ignoring these complicated problems, transfor-

---

[53] See Parekh 1999.

mative accommodation recognizes these intersecting power hierarchies as an inevitable starting point. To overcome these problems, transformative accommodation creates specific institutional conditions (including the sub-matter allocation of authority, the "no monopoly" rule, a healthy measure of rivalry between jurisdictional power-holders, and clearly delineated choice options), which then perform as incentives for group leaders themselves to reduce internal restrictions.

7   Conclusion

"Power," as Lord Acton famously put it, "tends to corrupt, and absolute power corrupts absolutely." Our rethinking of the tangled relationship between the state and its non-dominant cultural minorities should lead us to resist allocating absolutist notions of jurisdictional authority to *either* of them. Greater promise lies in envisioning new ways of dividing and sharing jurisdictional authority between them. By creating an ongoing dialogue between state- and group-based norms according to the principles of joint governance, it is hoped that a new "horizontal" separation of powers may become established: each entity will now be required to contribute its distinct legal input devoid of monopoly, with each individual self-selecting his or her own jurisdictions. But this will not be an easy transformation. It will demand vigilance and patience to break away from deep-seated modern assumptions about the exclusivity of jurisdictional authority.

We must reject the "hands-off" message broadcast by the "unavoidable costs" approach to multiculturalism, because this often simply cements the group's license to perpetuate preexisting power hierarchies at the expense of more vulnerable group members. At the same time, we must reject the hierarchical enforcement of state law, as it is replayed in the "re-universalized citizenship" response. In rejecting these "either/or" types of solutions to the paradox of multicultural vulnerability, we are opening the door to newer, more complex, and more attractive state- and group-based possibilities for dialogue. As we have seen, any serious attempt to resolve the multiculturalism paradox must attempt to address not only the recognition of cultural differences, but also the sober acknowledgment of their potentially injurious intra-group effects.

The debate over multiculturalism can thus serve as an opportunity to re-examine not only age-old questions about the relations between *nomoi* groups and state, but also the interests and conflicts of at-risk group members. Proponents of both the religious particularist and the secular absolutist models tend to avoid this challenge, given their respective emphases on the exclusive regulation of the citizen-insider. But neither of

146

these models can provide a viable option for vulnerable group members, since they fail to preserve collective cultural identity alongside individual citizenship rights.

However, the transformative accommodation variant of joint governance offers a more complex incentive system because both the state and the group are engaged in constant interaction. And since individuals have leeway in deciding the substantive legal systems to which they are subject in different social arenas, the traditions and conduct of both are held to higher standards: now the group and the state can no longer afford to take the old style of jurisdictional loyalties for granted.

This book offers an exploration of the patterns behind routine in-group violations of individual citizenship rights within a broad range of *nomoi* communities. These exploitative patterns can be traced to the paradox of multicultural vulnerability, whereby well-meaning public policies aimed at accommodating minority cultures actually legitimize the sanctioned and systemic maltreatment of certain group members. The state's current and primary focus on the external aspects of accommodation tends to overlook their injurious internal effects. Thus an official public policy of respect for cultural differences often ends up camouflaging persistent in-group persecutions. And within these hidden scenes of strife, it is the women who generally shoulder the bulk of the *nomos*-specific burden.

These patterns of disadvantage and vulnerability demand a sober appreciation of the fact that we fail to effectively practice the purposes of multiculturalism. While there are no "one-size-fits-all" solutions, this book has charted the development of several joint governance schemes which may one day successfully resolve the tension between accommodating differences and protecting rights. These joint governance models all share the recognition that the group, the state, and the individual are inevitably intertwined in a complex web. Once we recognize this interdependence, we can pursue the goal of reducing injustice between groups as well as enhancing justice within them. This then becomes the basis for the new institutional design of transformative accommodation.

Transformative accommodation creates a legal system of mutual checks and balances which varies according to the prevailing legal model already in place. For example, in countries where the secular absolutist model prevails, this variant of joint governance requires the state to relinquish some of its legal powers and delegate them to *nomoi* groups operating within its borders. Political pressure must be brought to bear in order to persuade the state to part with regulatory powers. Conversely, in countries where the religious particularist model prevails, *nomoi* groups must be convinced to voluntarily surrender their power over family law or other issues. The deeper the cleavages run between the communities comprising a body politic, the more difficult it becomes to alter the current balance of power between the state and the group. In both cases, a serious political commitment must precede any hopeful implementation of joint governance in its several guises, regardless of the relationships between state and *nomoi* groups in a given polity. But despite the obvious obstacles, the alternatives are surely unacceptable: either abandon all hope of multicultural accommodation, or abandon all hope of protecting at-risk group members from the paradox of multicultural vulnerability.

This lack of ready-made answers should not surprise us, because the practical and theoretical problematics of multiculturalism have served as this book's guide. The multiculturalism paradox challenges us to critically evaluate existing models of accommodation, and creatively envision new and more promising legal-institutional approaches. Transformative accommodation respects and preserves cultural differences and individual rights through the application of the "no monopoly" rule, the sub-matter division of authority, and the creation of well-defined choice options, since these institutional conditions can be reasonably expected to reduce power disparities *between* the group and the wider society as well as *within* the accommodated community. Joint governance thus offers new answers to the paradox of multicultural vulnerability by shifting the debate about differentiated citizenship. It re-defines solutions that emphasize "non-interference" between groups, as strategies that reduce domination within groups. It exchanges the "right of exit" and its enforced abandonment of one's culture for a dynamic incentive structure, which encourages groups to re-examine their discriminatory traditions while enhancing their jurisdictional authority. It discards the legitimizing of intra-group subordination in favor of empowering once-vulnerable insiders. And instead of an "either/or" ultimatum, it embraces the recognition that group members are both culture-bearers and rights-bearers, who must exercise their connections to and choices between more than one source of authority in order to re-negotiate their position from within the group.[1]

We saw earlier how federal-style, temporal, consensual and contingent accommodation-innovations have attempted to overcome the multiculturalism paradox. The transformative accommodation variant of joint governance builds on the strength of these innovations, but because it establishes a more comprehensive and dynamic institutional framework,

---

[1] In this way, joint governance rejects the view that in order to resolve the multiculturalism paradox, vulnerable group members must leave their *nomoi* community and assimilate into the wider society. Nor does it accept the proposition recommended by proponents of a hands-off, "non interventionist" multiculturalism, that each vulnerable group member is to be left on her own to assure a balance between her culture and her rights within the state.

it entails four distinct advantages. First, it creates a direct linkage between the enhancement of minority communities' jurisdictional autonomy and the strengthening of at-risk group members within their own *nomoi* communities. Second, it guarantees access to the state and its institutions via the state's sub-matter authority in each contested social arena. In this way, transformative accommodation is designed to provide at-risk group members with realistic tools to exercise in-group leverage and to challenge established traditions that disproportionately burden them, yet without jeopardizing their community's opportunities for jurisdictional authority.[2] Third, transformative accommodation is not an *ad hoc* solution. It is designed as a permanent and comprehensive mechanism for joint governance that is intended to transform the jurisdictional, and therefore also the basic political, relationship between the state and its minority *nomoi* communities. However, it can only exert a meaningful impact if it is effectively applied to various contested social arenas such as family law and education. Fourth and finally, group members' manifold, overlapping, and potentially contradictory affiliations are treated as part of the solution, not as part of the problem. Neither the state nor the group has a monopoly over these situated individuals: each must earn the individual's continued attachment.

Although we dwell in a world where interlocking power relations exist between and within groups, and where such relationships are likely to persist for the foreseeable future, we are not relieved from the obligation to envision a better way of practicing multiculturalism. The new joint governance approach tries to "operationalize" the justice claims put forward in support of respecting cultural differences, as defended by leading proponents of accommodation. For example, it follows Taylor's advocacy of public recognition for non-dominant cultural traditions because of their significance to individual self-respect. It also adopts Kymlicka's commitment to autonomy-enhancing multicultural accommodation. And it embraces Young's view of justice as fundamentally enabling. But it further expands the goal of eradicating inequalities by examining the relations between groups, as well as the relations within them.

Joint governance thus provides a way to conceptually expand the boundaries of what is included under the mandate of multiculturalism, while also honoring the basic justifications behind the adoption of such policies

---

[2] Clearly, some of these tools and resources can also make exit a more viable option for group members. However, I do not view exit as an adequate solution to the multiculturalism paradox (though it might be the preferred solution by some insiders). Rather, I view the *potential* for exit (especially as it translates into the potential to exercise leverage) as an important bargaining chip that can be utilized by traditionally subordinated categories of group members who wish to remain loyal to their *nomos* yet still fight for the improvement of their in-group status.

in the first place. The move toward differentiated citizenship therefore has a radical element in it: if we follow the joint governance path, we find a structural framework that works to reduce internal restrictions by the very same system of external protections that it creates for accommodating cultural difference. Based on the recognition that the positioning of historically vulnerable group members within their accommodated communities may be affected by changing the institutional context in which they operate, joint governance opens up the possibility to empower women (and other disproportionately burdened classes of group members) by ensuring that neither the group nor the state authority is shut out of the decision-making process when the individual has a legitimate interest in being governed, and served, by both. Even if they do not change anything in their traditional lifestyle, they still gain an improved "fall-back position" through the introduction of the principles of transformative accommodation: the sub-matter division of authority, the "no monopoly" rule, and the establishment of clearly delineated choice options.

Of course, joint governance does not provide a perfect solution to the multiculturalism paradox. What it does do, however, is take into consideration the interests of all three participants in the multicultural triad, and establishes a dynamic and multi-level division of authority. If carefully implemented, joint governance can provide historically vulnerable group members with realistic options and enhanced bargaining powers which they can then use to improve their in-group situation. While there are no magic formulas that can neatly abolish the paradox, joint governance remains the most potentially effective strategy to coax both the group and the state to work for the individual, rather than forcing her to choose one or the other. By making internal empowerment a real option, joint governance overcomes the "your culture or your rights" ultimatum. It suggests a more compelling way out of the multiculturalism paradox, one where historically subordinated group members can remain full participants in their *nomos*, but transform the conditions of their membership at the same time. This, I believe, is the path we must follow to escape the paradox of multicultural vulnerability. Instead of resorting to so many already established, tired, and misguided approaches toward a just and workable multiculturalism, we must follow the road less traveled. For only that may make all the difference.

Appendix: How transformative accommodation works in different social arenas

We have already seen what the necessary assumptions are for transformative accommodation to work and what the principles are by which it works. In this section we will discuss examples in three different social arenas where the principles introduced above will lead to (or have led to) a progressive transformation of the state and/or the *nomoi* group involved. The discussion will illustrate how this variant of joint governance can be applied in different social arenas which have become highly contested in the multicultural state, such as immigration, education, and criminal justice.

IMMIGRATION LAW

In immigration law, a basic division is made between the activities of "admission" and "selection." Admission refers to the rules shaping the overall immigration policy of a given state in determining how many people can be admitted to a given country in a given year, and based on what considerations (family re-unification, humanitarian grounds, professional qualifications, etc.). Admission criteria also set the procedures to be followed, in order for someone outside the polity to apply for immigration status in it. Selection, meanwhile, is a complementary authority. It involves the administrative activity of selecting *who* will actually enter a given country as an immigrant within a given annual quota from a pool of applicants who must also fulfil the admission threshold. Each legal immigrant entering a country must have both qualified for admission, *and* been selected to enter the host country by an official of that country's immigration authorities.

In certain countries, most notably the United States, both admission and selection processes are the preserve of the national government.[1] But in other countries, authority over immigration is divided along sub-matter lines. This distinction between admission and selection allows for accommodation of regional or national sub-units, where they have special

[1] See Manheim 1995.

demands. In Canada, for example, in recognition of Québec's concern with maintaining a distinct French-speaking society, that province has a direct input in selecting a proportional share of the annual immigration intake into Canada from among the federally defined pool of admissible applicants.

In a set of agreements negotiated and modified between the 1970s and the early 1990s, Canada and Québec arrived at a division of authority in the field of immigration that follows the lines of the two major sub-matters of selection and admission, by instituting a "no monopoly" rule, and establishing clearly delineated choice options. Under the current 1991 Canada–Québec Accord, the federal government retains authority to determine national standards and general objectives relating to immigration, as well as to define who is inadmissible on grounds of criminality, health, national security, and so on. In this way, it retains responsibility for the *admission* of all immigrants. The Québec provincial government, then, has the responsibility of *selecting* from among the federally defined pool of potential immigrants to Canada, and decides who will be allowed immigrant status in that province.[2] Canada and Québec must cooperate if Québec is to receive any immigrants at all, since Québec must comply with Ottawa's numerical caps and admission criteria for any immigrant it selects. Also, both share the goal of accepting immigrants who score highest on their mutual agendas (for example, giving priority to candidates with higher education and professional credentials over those who lack them).

Yet in recognition of Québec's concern with maintaining a distinct French-speaking society, the Accord also allows the province greater leeway in defining the selection criteria for immigrants. Québec is entitled, for example, to give extra weight to knowledge of French in its selection criteria, or to prefer applicants who declare in their applications that they are committed to partaking in its distinct society, so long as it complies with Ottawa's admission criteria.[3] This type of power-dividing and -sharing is designed to allow a sub-state authority (in this case, a territorial sub-unit with a distinct cultural and linguistic heritage) the opportunity to co-govern a social arena that greatly affects its ability to preserve its distinct cultural identity.[4] Yet it does so according to the "no monopoly"

[2] Or, alternatively, Québec's immigration officials can recruit candidates for immigration based on the province's selection criteria, and then refer them to the federal immigration officials who have to determine whether these candidates qualify by Canada's admission criteria.   [3] See Hanna 1995.

[4] This joint governance policy was originally introduced in the 1970s, in response to a declining birthrate within Québec, and a growing out-migration (by members of the anglophone community), which led that province to seek increased influence on the number and types of immigrants entering into its jurisdiction.

rule which requires close cooperation with the larger political community to which Québec citizens also belong.

This variant of joint governance is certainly not a perfect one. It creates a cumbersome bureaucracy and involves costly duplication, since Canadian immigration officers must deal with the same cases that are also separately re-evaluated by Québec's officials. But it is part of a complicated political relationship between Canada and Québec, and, no less importantly, it may also benefit the immigration applicants themselves. To be more specific, the Canadian immigration process allows both "opt in" and "opt out" protections for the individual, the third party in the multicultural triad, who is effectively given the final powers to make determinations about which part of the country she wants to join.

For example, when applying to immigrate to Canada, individuals are given the opportunity to specify which province they wish to reside in, and can therefore select themselves for special consideration by Québec.[5] Furthermore, once these immigrants become residents of Québec, as citizens of Canada they cannot be obliged to remain in that province; as individuals they enjoy constitutionally protected freedom of movement, i.e. they have a protected "opt out" option, which permits them to establish their new life in whichever part of Canada they may wish to reside.

What is most significant for our discussion is that this freedom of movement has pushed the Québec government to invest heavily in services for immigrant newcomers (services which are better funded and considered superior to those provided by the other provinces), so that they have compelling reasons to remain members of its distinct society, rather than exercise their protected "exit" option. In other words, this competitive jurisdictional environment creates incentives for the accommodated national minority to listen to the voices and address the needs of newcomers in its midst (persons who are not yet citizens, and who belong to a class that is often vulnerable to discrimination in any new host society).

This version of joint governance applied to the realm of immigration regulation is not immune from occasional political controversies, nor is it free from bureaucratic inefficiencies. However, as we have seen, it uses the principles of transformative accommodation to preempt the ways in which the shifting power relations between the group and the state may

---

[5] Applying to Québec provides an advantage in the selection process to individuals who are French-speaking, assuming that they otherwise comply with Canada's admission criteria. If they wish to immigrate to any other part of the country, their application will be subject solely to the federal government's discretion in both sub-matters of admission and selection.

adversely affect sub-communities within the accommodated community. It thus helps protect their interests by empowering individuals to use their agency to partly define which substantive legal rules will affect them. In the process, transformative accommodation may also create a coalescence of values that is not imposed from above, but rather is the outcome of promoting the intersection of the minority community's self-interest with that of the larger political entity to which it belongs (in this case, the self-interest of advancing the demographic and economic growth of Québec *and* Canada, and selecting and admitting the best qualified immigration applicants).[6]

By dividing jurisdiction along sub-matter lines, this immigration system divides authority between non-monopolist power centers, while at the same time establishing mechanisms for dialogue and shared decision-making between them. It induces cooperation because the accommodated sub-unit will not be able to promote its demographic and economic growth through immigration if it does not cooperate with Ottawa. Canada, too, has an incentive to find solutions to any problems that may occur in the management of this delicate joint governance system. The country as a whole stands to fall into serious decline if it fails to work out differences with Québec, since roughly 30 percent of the annual intake of immigrants is designated to that province (based on the proportion of Québec's population in relation to the general population of Canada). Finally, this joint governance formula has helped to improve the type and level of services provided to individual newcomers, because their membership can no longer be taken for granted. According to this model, the multiple affiliations they bear to different sources of authority is not part of the problem. Rather, it becomes part of the solution: the clearly delineated "opt in" option which they have as applicants is followed by the "opt out" option which they have as citizens, and both of these options progressively transform their internal status within the minority community.

EDUCATION

To illustrate further how clearly delineated choice options can lead to processes of internal change, consider, for instance, an example of power-dividing and -sharing arrangements in education. While the United States maintains a "high and impregnable wall of separation" between

---

[6] As Joe Carens observes, perhaps what is most striking about this division of authority along sub-matter lines is how similar Québec's immigration goals and policies are to those of Canada. See Carens 1995, pp. 27–28.

church and state in the education arena, other countries have taken an altogether different route to meet the challenges of diversity.[7]

Instead of interpreting (dis)establishment as ordering that the state may not favor, encourage, or promote *any* religion (the strict separationist position adopted by the US Supreme Court), many European countries have interpreted the separation of church and state as equivalent to the dictum that the state may not discriminate on the basis of religion and faith.[8] According to this "strict neutrality" approach, the state may not favor, encourage, or promote a particular religion, but it may well recognize diversity in the school system by accommodating *all* established religious communities on an equal basis.[9]

This understanding of church-state relations has translated in the Netherlands and in Denmark into a model that provides financial support on an equal basis to different-faith-based schools which promote specific religious traditions (Roman Catholic, Protestant Christian, Islamic, Hindu, and Jewish schools, for example) or educational philosophies (such as Montessori, Dalton, Jenaplan, and Freinet schools), while also subjecting them to extensive state regulation.[10] But the major concern with this system is that it encourages each community to reach out solely to its constituents (while enjoying state funding), thus creating, as one commentator has put it, a "separate but equal school system."[11]

A more attractive model, which complies more squarely with the joint governance ideal of encouraging input from different sources of authority in co-governing a given social arena, encourages the education of children in a setting that overcomes the "either/or" choice between excluding religion altogether from the curriculum (the strict separationist approach) or fully upholding and sponsoring faith-based schooling (the strict neutrality approach). Joint governance imagines public schools as spaces where children from different backgrounds can learn about their own communities and distinct histories (in a secure and supportive environment), while establishing a minimal level of commonality between them as members of a larger, shared political entity.

---

[7] This strict separation doctrine leads to endless court battles about what is and what is not within the definition of "establishment" of religion in public schools, and about the type of services that the state can provide to children attending private parochial schools. See the landmark case of *Lemon* v. *Kurtzman*, 403 US 602 (1971), where the Supreme Court defined a three-part test for determining whether a state statute or government program violates the establishment clause.

[8] For a comparative study of these different educational policies, see Monsma and Soper 1997.

[9] For a discussion of the socio-historical background that leads to the adoption of these policies in the Netherlands and other European polities, see Walford 1995.

[10] For a detailed account of these policies, see Walford 1995; Monsma and Soper 1997, pp. 67–74.   [11] Walford 1995, p. 250.

Dividing authority in the education arena may mean that religion will be treated as a legitimate educational sub-matter alongside the civic component of the curriculum.[12] We can examine how this model might play out in practice by looking at the example of joint governance education in Germany. There, education is the domain of the *Länder* governments, not the federal government. However, *Länder* governments do not constitute the sole authority over the education experience of young citizens. Rather, they share the sphere of education with established religious communities. In a situation that might seem counter-intuitive to an American eye, the German Constitution permits, and indeed institutionalizes, state-funded religious instruction in public schools. Article 7(3) of the German Basic Law establishes that "Religious instruction shall be part of the curriculum in state schools." The operative word here is "shall," not "may" – making education an arena of joint governance between the state and religious communities and entrenching this relationship as a constitutional principle.[13] "Without prejudice to the state's right of supervision," continues Article 7(3), "religious instruction shall be given in accordance with the doctrine of the religious community concerned."

In other words, as part of these children's general education in the public schools, recognized *nomoi* groups have sub-matter authority over the instruction of school children in religious matters, according to the tenets of their belief. The state neither assigns children to the religious instruction classes, nor controls the content of these classes. Religious instruction classes are generally two to three hours a week, for which students break up into different classes according to their religious affiliation.[14] There need only be six to eight students of a given *nomoi* group to justify a class being held for them.[15] It is the responsibility of the different

---

[12] For some concrete ideas on how this sub-matter of authority might be drawn, see Halstead 1995, pp. 269–271. Halstead distinguishes between education for democratic citizenship (or what I label "civic education") and education for specific cultural education (which corresponds with my usage of the term "religious instruction"). For further discussion on how state and group authorities might cooperate in the education arena, see Spinner-Halev 2000.   [13] Monsma and Soper 1997, p. 179.

[14] Religious instruction classes must be taught by a member of the relevant faith community, who is a regular member of the public school faculty, and who teaches in accordance with the tenets of that faith.

[15] What this arrangement cannot guarantee, however, is that all religiously defined *nomoi* groups have equal access to state funding for the purposes of instruction. A community needs to be large enough in a given area to warrant its own classes, and must reach agreement on the course of study to implement. Thus, difficulties have arisen in accommodating smaller or less organized religious communities in Germany, especially in the case of members of different sects of the Islamic faith, the Jewish community, and small Christian groups. Furthermore, there is great variation between the different *Länder*: for example, some have introduced Islamic instructions, while others have not. In Brandenburg, for example, religious instruction has been replaced with a general course in ethics. Here too, the same principal of choice applies. Hence students can opt out of

religious communities to develop the actual course of study in these classes, and then to implement them in the public school setting. Religious instruction by the group is therefore an integral part of a student's educational experience in the public school system.

However, no one can be forced to attend religious instruction classes. Up to the age of fourteen, children attend religious instruction classes if their parents so desire. If parents object to their participation in such classes, the children need not attend.[16] From the age of fourteen on, the students decide for themselves whether to pursue religious instruction. Outside the specified sub-matter of religious instruction, students are all subject to the same general curriculum which is developed, implemented, and supervised by the state in its sub-matter authority.

Conflicts may still arise under this system. For example, if sex education classes (included in the civic education component of the curriculum) expose students to information about birth control measures, discuss sex graphically, or teach students how to protect themselves against sexually transmitted diseases, this might offend certain members of minority groups who identify with religious or customary traditions that condemn premarital sex. This problem is not specific to public schools that aspire to create joint governance schemes of education, of course. But these schools are in a better position to address these kinds of tensions because they already have in place mechanisms for respecting diversity by allowing "opt in" and "opt out" choices in reference to certain subjects of instruction. If sex education classes are included in the curriculum of the higher grades of secondary school, there is no compelling reason why adolescents (who probably already know more about sex than their parents and teachers ever want to believe) should not be given a clear option to opt in or opt out of these classes at the beginning of the term, once they have been given some preliminary information about the content and educational value of these classes.[17]

Moreover, with the introduction of such clearly delineated choice

the ethics course and enroll instead in a religious instruction class. We find more consistency along provincial lines in Austria, where religious instruction in public schools is guaranteed to twelve "recognized religious congregations," which include *inter alia* Jews, Muslims, Hindus, and Buddhists. My thanks to Rainer Bauböck for calling my attention to the Austrian variant of joint governance in education.

[16] These children who do not attend the religious classes are required to remain at school, and are offered alternative classes in which to participate during the hours that their counterparts are in religious instruction classes.

[17] Accommodation has its limits, however. A student (or her parents) cannot seek to have a choice option concerning each and every subject of instruction because the public school then ceases to function. For this reason, joint governance in education must mark the specific junctures where such choice is available, and justify it in relation to the multicultural goal of respecting cultural differences in common public institutions.

options, this accommodation scheme can eventually transform the ways in which both state and group carry out their educational mandates. For example, a sex education class may be pursued in a way that conveys important information about the prevention of pregnancy or the risks of AIDS, but which does not include explicit and potentially offensive graphic representations. Or, in certain communities, these classes may be best carried out in a non-co-educational setting which will attract students, especially girls, who might otherwise be exposed to pressure by their parents not to participate in these classes out of fear that these classes might somehow "encourage" adolescent sex. The presence of a diverse student body may therefore require certain adjustments in the way that the school's teachers present and discuss certain subjects that fall within the state's civic education mandate.

Conversely, the content, tone, and themes explored in the hours designated for religious instruction are also shaped, at least in part, by the fact that this activity takes place at a *public* school, where members of a given religious group are regularly interacting with students from other communities, and where parents and later the students themselves can make independent jurisdictional choices about their enrollment in the religious instruction class. This institutional setting means that the students are not a "captive audience." Religious communities are thus forced to re-assess the responsibility, decision-making power, and onus of internal renewal that will continue to make their teaching relevant and accessible to the sons and daughters of the twenty-first century, or else run the risk of losing these future members' allegiance and interest in preserving the *nomos*.

In sum, this transformative accommodation scheme treats cultural and religious difference as an issue which need not be shunned or artificially omitted from scrutiny and debate in the public schools, simply because it is a controversial and complicated issue. Instead, this system allows cultural and religious difference to be part of the everyday life of children in state schools. It encourages inclusion in common spaces, thus overcoming the troubling centrifugal and fragmenting effect of both "strict separation" and "strict neutrality." It permits, and indeed fosters, accommodation – but in a non-exclusivist setting.

In short, transformative accommodation creates a common public space where students from different backgrounds can intermingle, exchange ideas, and struggle with the inevitable issues of identity, sexuality, and membership. It shows that even in an arena as complex as education, where both the state and the group have strong and at times contradictory messages, authority can be divided between them along sub-matter lines and in ways so that neither entity gains ultimate control over their shared constituents. This institutional design creates an incentive structure which is best suited for fostering cooperation between state and group, pushing each entity to more carefully design and pursue its educational responsibility in its respective sub-matter of authority, and in ways that respect individuals' manifold affiliations and their jurisdictional choices.

Now assume that at the age of fourteen a girl can choose whether or not to attend a religious instruction class in her public school. No one can force her to take advantage of this resource, which is jointly set up by the state and the group. Also assume that the group to which she belongs has traditionally excluded women from access to, and study of, its sacred texts.

Come the first day of classes, only a few students are enrolled in the religious instruction class. Others are happy to spend an extra two or three hours a week on other activities, be it surfing the net or taking an extra math class. The teacher in the religious instruction class (who must be a member of the relevant community) tells her that she is of course welcome to join that class, but only to listen to the discussion, rather than to participate in it. These restrictive attendance conditions, she is told, are gender based and sanctioned by the group's tradition. It is hard to see why, under such conditions, the female prospective student may still voluntarily wish to attend such a class, where she is treated as a second class citizen. And it is easy to comprehend not only why she might feel alienated, but why the community at large has much to lose if this is the end result of the allocation of jurisdictional authority to its representatives.

However, the teacher may simply insist on these gender-biased attendance conditions (subject to potential constitutional challenge, though). This will most plausibly lead the girl who wanted to learn about her tradition to eventually drop the class. But there is an alternative. The teacher may also, while remaining faithful to the *nomos*, seek guidance from informed religious leaders to find out whether there is a possibility to fully include the student in the class, and whether there were any historical precedents where women participated actively in the learning of the tenets of the faith.

I do not mean to suggest that any problem can be resolved in this way, nor do I wish to be interpreted as championing the watering down of different *nomoi* traditions. Recent examples from the practices of Judaism and Islam show that such re-interpretations are possible, and in fact can greatly enhance the number of group members (including women) who are actively participating in the faith.[18]

---

[18] See, for example, Goodman-Thau 1993, pp. 45–53. Historically, the Second Great Awakening in American history also saw church membership swell with significant female involvement in the revitalization of Protestant Christianity.

On the other hand, a dogmatic teacher might eventually make the experience of religious instruction so sour that the girl might eventually choose to leave the class. With this kind of outcome, all parties lose. A system of transformative accommodation connects the *survivalist* interest of *nomoi* groups to that part of their members' identities which concerns multicultural citizenship. The hope is that by dividing jurisdiction along sub-matter lines in compliance with the "no monopoly" rule, we can create conditions that make it worthwhile for those who care about the *nomos* (such as recognized spiritual leaders) to turn around the process of alienation from the group, by permitting internal change instead.

We can see how this latter type of resolution is significantly more attractive than a system which forces an individual group member to turn to an "outside" court in order to impose gender equality norms in the classroom externally. While this route can provide formal (legal) remedy to the multiculturalism paradox, it does not help (in fact, it can impair) a kind of internal qualitative, transformative change in the community and its self-perception. This is particularly true when we think about *nomoi* communities which raise some of the most difficult dilemmas for multicultural accommodation: those communities that have taken the path of reactive culturalism.

As a matter of institutional design, then, one of the most significant advantages of transformative accommodation is that its allocation of authority along sub-matter lines can inspire more established leaderships of "reactive" *nomoi* communities to rework their discriminatory practices by transforming and revitalizing traditions from within the group.

CRIMINAL JUSTICE

In criminal justice, a basic distinction is drawn between two sub-matters – that of "conviction" and "sentencing." Conviction refers to the legal determination of whether an accused person is guilty or not, while sentencing decides the appropriate means of punishment, protection of the public, deterrence, or rehabilitation of the offender. A criminal case is not completed until these two sub-matters are addressed. If the accused is found innocent, no sentence is imposed. If the accused is found guilty, a sentence must be pronounced.[19]

In practice, a jury is often responsible for the sub-matter of "conviction" whereas a presiding judge controls the domain of "sentencing." In

---

[19] Careful attention is paid to the sentencing aspect of criminal law, since it involves state action that substantively limits an individual's liberty.

recent years, this division of authority has been adopted as the basis for a new joint governance initiative instituted between state authorities and representatives of different Aboriginal communities.[20] This time around, power over the sub-matter of conviction rests in the hands of a presiding judge, while authority over sentencing is vested in the hands of an Aboriginal community, which assumes responsibility for the punishment and rehabilitation of the convicted.

Joint governance makes it possible to grant the people most directly affected by the offender's conduct (such as their victims, family members, and the community at large in cases of domestic violence and sexual abuse) a public voice in the process at the time of sentencing. Without compromising the basic principle of parity at conviction (which demands that criminal law be equally applied irrespective of race or culture), the use of "sentencing circles" has been introduced (as one example) to allow for community input and communal responsibility in dealing with convicted Aboriginal offenders – offenders who are found guilty in a state court and in accordance with state law.

Historically, Aboriginal communities in North America relied upon a complex array of social mechanisms to maintain order in their societies. These mechanisms varied from community to community but often included the warning and censure of particular offenders by leaders or by councils representing the community as a whole. They might also involve the use of ridicule and ostracism by the community to shame offenders and to denounce a particular wrong-doing.[21]

Today, sentencing and healing circles allow a forum for direct community participation in deciding and implementing a sentence. Sentencing and healing circles can call for many different resolutions, but in most cases the sentences involve extensive community-based treatment measures, which may include counseling, public disclosure of the crime, or participation in circles where the offender, representatives of the community, and the victim(s) of the crime are all participants.[22] Sentencing and healing circles often focus on in-group rehabilitation, and are tied to a healing process which involves not only the offender's acceptance of responsibility, but also provides assistance and guidance for the victim,

---

[20] Members of indigenous communities, it should be noted, are over-represented in charges laid, court appearances, and rates of incarceration, so their interest in the workings of the justice system is well grounded. See, for example (in the Canadian context) the Royal Commission on Aboriginal Peoples 1996. Similar statistics are also reported from Australia and New Zealand.   [21] For a detailed exploration, see Coyle 1986.

[22] Sentencing and healing circles "'tap into' local systems of social control, thereby accessing additional resources in their attempt to change offender behavior." Their more holistic approach is explicitly oriented toward resolving the root problems of the criminal behavior rather than merely punishing the offender. See Green 1997, p. 98.

the victim's family, and those others in the community who are affected by the offender's behavior.[23]

Sentencing circles are clearly not your standard state approach to sentencing. The state usually puts a much heavier emphasis on individual punishment and public deterrence, whereas Aboriginal communities have stressed the values of reconciliation, accountability, and healing in a communal setting.

To come under the jurisdiction of a sentencing circle (rather than the state), the offender must consent to participation in the process. The convicted must also have deep roots in the community where the circle is held, and elders and other respected non-political community leaders must be willing to participate. Members of the Aboriginal community in question must themselves assume the responsibility for fulfilling the terms of the sentence that they have imposed on the convicted individual. Finally, if the sentencing circle includes a confrontational stage which requires the participation of the victim, the consent of the victim must be given, and given freely.[24] No person can be brought under the sub-matter authority of the group, then, unless they have specifically agreed to do so.

These alternative dispute-resolution measures transform the state system from within. As one judge put it, "[t]he circle breaks down the dominance that traditional courtrooms accord lawyers and judges . . . [It] denies the comfort of evading difficult issues through the use of obtuse, complex technical language."[25] Punishment by a judge whose authority rests in formal state law is qualitatively different from sentencing by one's community, where offenders must face their sentencers daily, and are subject to disapproval of the criminal behavior by fellow group members.[26] By recognizing Aboriginal justice procedures as binding, i.e. as valid legal alternatives to state-based measures of punishment, trans-

---

[23] Some sentencing circles culminate in a confrontation between the offender and the victim, a confrontation which is intended to make the offender feel responsibility for the hurt he or she has caused to other individuals and to the community.

[24] Determining the free will of an actor, especially when he or she is in a vulnerable situation, is an extremely difficult task which the law has a hard time fulfilling when no physical or extreme psychological evidence is available. In the context of consent to sentencing circles, the state court might be called upon to establish whether consent was given freely or not by the individual. This effectively means that the court is supposed to operate as a safeguard against coercion, an extremely complex task in any social setting.

[25] Justice Stuart Terr, *R. v. Moses* (1992), 71 CCC (3d) 347 (Y.T. Terr. Ct.).

[26] This distinction resembles Max Weber's distinction between formal (bureaucratic) authority and the traditional (*Q'adi*'s) authority. But unlike Weber's argument, the observation here is not complicated by a normative argument about the superiority of state law over community law.

formative accommodation enables the revitalization of a complex array of social and legal mechanisms historically employed by indigenous communities to maintain order in their societies.[27] States and municipalities must now consult with them in developing new crime prevention and crime reduction initiatives. In this respect, joint governance in criminal justice has a significance which extends beyond its immediate reformulation of sentencing functions. It is part of a much broader accommodation process, where relations are re-defined between colonial settler societies and their indigenous populations, in part, by re-instituting Aboriginal customary laws, traditional adjudicatory processes, and indigenous dispute-resolution practices, within a state context.

A re-allocation of authority along sub-matter lines (which complies with the "no monopoly" rule and establishes clearly delineated choice options) can therefore help transform both state and group practices, and the relationship between them, while remaining sensitive to individual preference. However, this joint governance system is not invulnerable to criticism. Some have been concerned that Aboriginal justice initiatives may deprive the offender of due-process rights, such as legal representation, which are part and parcel of the traditional adversarial system. Sentencing and healing circles are by definition non-adversarial. No one can come under their jurisdiction unless they voluntarily choose to do so, either after they have been convicted, or after they have pleaded guilty to charges laid by the state. Yet even after this initial choice of jurisdiction, individuals may "reverse" the jurisdiction of the circle by turning to the state, the failsafe authority, if they believe that their sentence and healing process is not conducted fairly by the community. This "opt out" option means that the state can theoretically take over the responsibilities of the community, if it is too harsh (or too lenient) in its sentencing. Transformative accommodation also grants the community a right to use the "reversal" option as a means of disciplining the offender, if and when it becomes clear that that person is failing to cooperate in the healing process. In such cases, the offender must face the state's punishment apparatus instead. This "kinetic" division of powers thus endows each non-monopolist power center, together with the individual, the capacity to monitor the other power-holder's exercise of authority.

But perhaps most importantly, this non-monopolist division of powers promises to help Aboriginal women, who have consistently suffered from

---

[27] As mentioned above, these mechanisms may vary from community to community. However, they often consist of a warning and censure of particular offenders by leaders or by councils representing the community at large.

extremely high incidence of sexual abuse within their communities.[28] Hardly anyone disputes the fact that the state has failed to provide them with meaningful protection. But no one can predict whether a devolution of authority along sub-matter lines will definitively improve their in-group situation. Serious concerns have been raised about the potentially negative effects of such a move. For example, some have argued that the adoption of sentencing and healing circles might trivialize the offense, because these measures are not focused on punishment and deterrence in the traditional "crime control" way.[29] Others are concerned that group members who suffer domestic violence and sexual abuse (most of them women) may be intimidated and possibly dominated by these informal proceedings.[30]

Evidence gathered on sentencing and healing circles in Canada as well as on Navajo peace courts in the United States presents quite a different picture. The most illuminating findings are those referring to the *active* involvement and agency manifested by women who entered the circle.[31] They were more likely than the offenders to complete the full healing process, which in certain cases lasted between two to three years, during which separate rounds of the circle were convened. In the process, they were considered to have played an important role. Because reconciliation and restorative justice depends on the re-integration and healing of the victim, the offender, and other people who might have been affected by the offense in the community, "[t]he offender needed the victim for forgiveness and understanding, and the victim needed the offender for the recognition of the harm done." In the circle setting, both the victim and the offender were regularly at the center of discussion. The non-adversarial circle process also spared the victim the trauma of testifying in a state court, under a set of procedural rules of examination and cross-examination that are notoriously insensitive to cultural differences. These rules often make it harder for women and minorities to convince the court of the validity of their version of the events at trial. Moreover, state law pro-

---

[28] The statistics concerning physical violence and sexual abuse of women are staggering. In Canada, the Ontario Native Women's Association, for example, concluded that eight out of ten Aboriginal women personally experienced violence, and the majority of those physically injured were also sexually abused. Several public inquiries have reaffirmed these findings, pointing to the police and the justice system's failure to protect Aboriginal women from violence and abuse. See the Royal Commission on Aboriginal Peoples 1996, pp. 269–275.   [29] See, for example, Laroque 1997.

[30] Royal Commission on Aboriginal Peoples 1996, pp. 269–275.

[31] Ibid., p. 166. For a comprehensive empirical study of domestic violence cases decided by the Navajo peace-making courts in the United States, and their effect on women, see Coker 1999. Coker shows how such decision-making processes can be autonomy-enhancing for women, especially when they effectuate change in the underlying material and social conditions that foster battering. See Coker 1999, pp. 38–50.

vides a relatively limited role in the criminal process to the victimized individual, once the testimony (and in certain case, victim-impact statements) have been submitted. There is no duty to inform the victim of the results of the trial, or to provide him or her with psychological or any other forms of assistance. The circle process, on the other hand, does much more for victims and their families by including them as key participants in the sentencing and healing proceedings.[32]

The re-establishment of sentencing authority through healing circles translates into an increase of Aboriginal influence within the larger justice system. Yet absolute authority is still withheld from the accommodated group in the domain of criminal law, although some commentators have urged just such a solution that respects the cultural values of Aboriginal people.[33] Sentencing and healing circles nevertheless provide a preferable solution in that they comply with the "no monopoly" rule and the sub-matter allocation of authority, as well as delegate the ultimate decision-making authority to the individual in choosing between these jurisdictions in a matter of crucial importance to both.

[32] See Roach 1999, p. 275.
[33] For a critical evaluation of such separatist proposals, see Schwartz 1990.

References

BOOKS AND JOURNALS

Abu-Odeh, Lama 1992, "Post-Colonial Feminism and the Veil: Considering the Differences," *New England Law Review* 26, 1527–1537.

Ackerman, Bruce A. 1980, *Social Justice in the Liberal State*, New Haven, CT: Yale University Press.

Addis, Adeno 1997, "On Human Diversity and the Limits of Toleration," *Ethnicity and Group Rights*, Ian Shapiro and Will Kymlicka (eds.), New York: New York University Press, pp. 112–153.

Afshar, Haleh (ed.) 1987, *Women, State, and Ideology: Studies from Africa and Asia*, Albany, NY: SUNY Press.

Agarwal, Bina 1994, *A Field of One's Own: Gender and Land Rights in South Asia*, Cambridge: Cambridge University Press.

1997, "'Bargaining' and Gender Relations: Within and Beyond the Household," *Feminist Economics* 3, 1–51.

Akzin Benjamin 1970, "Who is a Jew? a Hard Case," *Israel Law Review* 5, 259–263.

Al-Hibri, Aziza Y. 1992, "Marriage Laws in Muslim Countries: a Comparative Study of Certain Egyptian, Syrian, Moroccan, and Tunisian Marriage Laws," *International Review of Comparative Public Policy* 4, 227–244.

Anaya, S. James 1996, *Indigenous Peoples in International Law*, New York: Oxford University Press.

Anderson, Benedict 1991, *Imagined Communities: Reflections on the Origin and Spread of Nationalism*, rev. edn., London: Verso.

An-Na'im, Abdullahi Ahmed 1990, *Toward an Islamic Reformation: Civil Liberties, Human Rights, and International Law*, Syracuse, NY: Syracuse University Press.

Anthias, Floya and Yuval-Davis, Nira 1989, "Introduction," in Yuval-Davis and Anthias, pp. 1–15.

Arneson, Richard J. and Shapiro, Ian 1996, "Democratic Autonomy and Religious Freedom: a Critique of *Wisconsin v. Yoder*," *Political Order*, Ian Shapiro and Russell Hardin (eds.), New York: New York University Press, pp. 365–411.

Atkin, Bill and Austin, Graeme 1996, "Cross-Cultural Challenges to Family Law in Aotearoa/New Zealand," *Families Across Frontiers*, Nigel Lowe and Gillian Douglas (eds.), The Hague: Martinus Nijhoff Publishers, pp. 327–345.

Auerbach, Jerold S. 1990, *Rabbis and Lawyers: the Journey from Torah to Constitution*, Bloomington, IN: Indiana University Press.

Australia Law Reform Commission 1986, *Report 31: the Recognition of Aboriginal Customary Law*, Canberra: Australian Government Publishing Service.

Avnon, Dan and de-Shalit, Avner (eds.) 1999, *Liberalism and its Practice*, New York: Routledge.

Bachrach, Peter and Baratz, Morton S. 1962, "Two Faces of Power," *American Political Science Review* 56, 947–952.

Badawi, Zaki 1995, "Muslim Justice in a Secular State," *God's Law versus State Law: the Construction of an Islamic Identity in Western Europe*, Michael King (ed.), London: Grey Seat, pp. 73–80.

Bader, Veit M. 1999, "Religious Pluralism: Secularism or Priority for Democracy?" *Political Theory* 27, 597–633.

forthcoming, "Religious Pluralism: Secularism or Priority for Democracy?"

Bainham, Andrew 1996, "Family Law in a Pluralistic Society: a View From England and Wales," *Families Across Frontiers*, Nigel Lowe and Gillian Douglas (eds.), The Hague: Martinus Nijhoff Publishers, pp. 295–307.

Balkin, J. M. 1995, "Ideology as Cultural Software," *Cardozo Law Review* 16, 1221–1233.

Bano, Samia 1999, "Muslim and South Asian Women: Customary Law and Citizenship in Britain," *Women, Citizenship and Difference*, Nira Yuval-Davis and Pnina Werbner (eds.), London: Zed Books, pp. 162–177.

Barry, Brian 1999, "Statism and Nationalism: a Cosmopolitan Critique," *Global Justice*, Ian Shapiro and Lea Brilmayer (eds.), New York: New York University Press, pp. 12–66.

2001, *Culture and Equality*, Cambridge, MA: Harvard University Press.

Bauböck, Rainer 1999, "Liberal Justifications for Ethnic Group Rights," *Multicultural Questions*, Christian Joppke and Steven Lukes (eds.), Oxford: Oxford University Press, pp. 133–157.

2000, "Why Stay Together? a Pluralist Approach to Secession and Federation," in Kymlicka and Norman, pp. 366–394.

Behrendt, Larissa 1995, *Aboriginal Dispute Resolution: a Step towards Self-Determination and Community Autonomy*, Annandale, NSW: Federation Press.

Beiner, Ronald 1992, *What's the Matter with Liberalism?* Berkeley, CA: University of California Press.

Beiner, Ronald (ed.) 1995, *Theorizing Citizenship*, Albany, NY: SUNY Press.

Bellamy, Richard 2000, "Dealing with Difference: Four Models of Pluralist Politics," *Parliamentary Affairs* 53, 198–217.

Bendroth, Margaret Lamberts 1993, *Fundamentalism and Gender, 1875 to the Present*, New Haven, CT: Yale University Press.

Ben-Israel, Hedva 1992, "Nationalism in Historical Perspective," *Journal of International Affairs* 45, 367–397.

Bennett, T. W. 1981, "Conflict of Laws: the Application of Customary Law and the Common Law in Zimbabwe," *International and Comparative Law Quarterly* 30, 59–103.

Berman, Saul J. 1973, "The Status of Women in Halakhic Judaism," *Tradition* 14, 5–28.

Biale, David 1994, "Classical Teachings and Historical Experience," *The Jewish Family and Jewish Continuity*, Steven Bayne and Gladys Rosen (eds.), Hoboken, NJ: Ktav Publishing House, pp. 133–171.

Biale, Rachel 1984, *Women and Jewish Law: an Exploration of Women's Issues in Halakhic Sources*, New York: Schocken Books.

Bielefeldt, Heiner 1995, "Muslim Voices in the Human Rights Debate," *Human Rights Quarterly* 17, 587–617.

Birnbaum, Pierre 1996, "From Multiculturalism to Nationalism," *Political Theory* 24, 33–45.

Blackstone, William 1765, *Commentaries on the Laws of England*, I, Oxford: Clarendon Press.

Bleich, J. David 1984, "Jewish Divorce: Judicial Misconceptions and Possible Means of Civil Enforcement," *Connecticut Law Review* 16, 201–289.

Borrows, John 2000, "'Landed' Citizenship: Narratives of Aboriginal Participation," in Kymlicka and Norman, pp. 326–342.

Boyle, Kevin and Sheen, Juliet (eds.) 1997, *Freedom of Religion and Belief: a World Report*, London: Routledge.

Bradney, Anthony 1993, *Religions, Rights and Laws*, Leicester: Leicester University Press.

Bredbenner, Candice Lewis 1998, *A Nationality of Her Own: Women, Marriage, and the Law of Citizenship*, Berkeley, CA: University of California Press.

Breitowitz, Irving 1992, "The Plight of the *Agunah*: a Study in *Halacha*, Contract, and the First Amendment," *Maryland Law Review* 51, 312–421.

Breton, Albert 1998, *Competitive Governments: an Economic Theory of Politics and Public Finance*, Cambridge: Cambridge University Press.

Brown, Wendy 1995, "Rights and Identity in Late Modernity: Revisiting the 'Jewish Question,'" *Identities, Politics, and Rights*, Austin Sarat and Thomas R. Keans (eds.), Ann Arbor, MI: Michigan University Press, pp. 85–130.

Brubaker, Rogers 1992, *Citizenship and Nationhood in France and Germany*, Cambridge, MA: Harvard University Press.

Buergenthal, Thomas 1997, "The Normative and Institutional Evolution of International Human Rights," *Human Rights Quarterly* 19, 703–723.

Callan, Eamonn 2000, "Discrimination and Religious Schooling," in Kymlicka and Norman, pp. 45–67.

Cammack, Mark, Young, Lawrence A. and Heaton, Tim 1996, "Legislating Social Change in an Islamic Society: Indonesia's Marriage Law," *American Journal of Comparative Law* 44, 45–73.

Carens, Joseph H. 1995, "Immigration, Political Community, and the Transformation of Identity: Québec's Immigration Policies in Critical Perspective," *Is Québec Nationalism Just? Perspectives from Anglophone Canada*, Joseph H. Carens (ed.), Montreal and Kingston: McGill-Queen's University Press, pp. 20–81.

  2000, *Culture, Citizenship, and Community: a Contextual Exploration of Justice as Evenhandedness*, Oxford: Oxford University Press.

Chandra, Sudhir 1998, *Enslaved Daughters: Colonialism, Law and Women's Rights*, Delhi: Oxford University Press.

Chapman, Bruce 1998, "More Easily Done than Said: Rules, Reasons and Rational Social Choice," *Oxford Journal of Legal Studies* 18, 293–329.

Choudhry, Sujit forthcoming, "National Minorities and Ethnic Immigrants: Liberalism's Political Sociology," *Journal of Political Philosophy*.

Christofferson, Clara 1991, "Tribal Courts' Failure to Protect Native American

Women: a Reevaluation of the Indian Civil Rights Act," *Yale Law Journal* 101, 169–185.

Cleveland, Richard F. 1925, "Status in Common Law," *Harvard Law Review* 38, 1074–1095.

Clifford, James 1988, *The Predicament of Culture: Twentieth Century Ethnography, Literature and Art*, Cambridge, MA: Harvard University Press.

Cohen, Joshua, Howard, Matthew and Nussbaum, Martha C. (eds.) 1999, *Is Multiculturalism Bad for Women? Susan Moller Okin and Respondents*, Princeton, NJ: Princeton University Press.

Coker, Donna 1999, "Enhancing Autonomy for Battered Women: Lessons from Navajo Peacemaking," *UCLA Law Review* 47, 1–111.

Collins, Patricia Hill 1991, *Black Feminist Thought: Knowledge, Consciousness, and the Politics of Empowerment*, New York: Routledge.

Cook, Rebecca J. (ed.) 1994, *Human Rights of Women: National and International Perspectives*, Philadelphia, PA: University of Pennsylvania Press.

Cornelius, Wayne A., Martin, Philip L. and Hollifield, James F. (eds.) 1992, *Controlling Immigration: a Global Perspective*, Stanford, CA: Stanford University Press.

Cott, Nancy F. 1995, "Giving Character to Our Whole Civil Polity: Marriage and the Public Order in the Late Nineteenth Century," *US History as Women's History*, Linda Kerber, Alice Kessler-Harris, and Kathryn Kish Sklar (eds.), Chapel Hill, NC: University of North Carolina Press, pp. 107–121.

1996, "Justice for All? Marriage and Deprivation of Citizenship in the United States," *Justice and Injustice in Law and Legal Theory*, Austin Sarat and Thomas R. Kearns (eds.), Ann Arbor, MI: University of Michigan Press, pp. 77–97.

1998, "Marriage and Women's Citizenship in the United States: 1830–1934," *American Historical Review* 103, 1440–1474.

Cover, Robert M. 1981, "The Uses of Jurisdictional Redundancy: Interest, Ideology, and Innovation," *William and Mary Law Review* 22, 639–682.

1983, "The Supreme Court 1982 Term, Forward: *Nomos* and Narrative," *Harvard Law Review* 97, 4–68.

Coyle, Michael 1986, "Traditional Indian Justice in Ontario: a Role for the Present?" *Osgoode Hall Law Journal* 24, 605–633.

Crenshaw, Kimberlé 1989, "Demarginalizing the Intersection of Race and Sex: a Black Feminist Critique of Antidiscrimination Doctrine, Feminist Theory, and Antiracist Politics," *University of Chicago Legal Forum*, 139–167.

1991, "Mapping the Margins: Identity Politics, Intersectionality, and Violence against Women of Color," *Stanford Law Review* 44, 1241–1299.

Crenshaw, Kimberlé, Gotanda, Neil, Peller, Gary and Kendall Thomas (eds.) 1995, *Critical Race Theory: the Key Writings that Formed the Movement*, New York: New Press.

Dasgupta, Partha 1993, *An Inquiry into Well-Being and Destitution*, Oxford: Clarendon Press.

Davis, Toni Hahn 1993, "The Existing Indian Family Law Exception to the Indian Child Welfare Act," *American Journal of Family Law* 7, 189–206.

Delgado, Richard (ed.) 1995, *Critical Race Theory: the Cutting Edge*, Philadelphia, PA: Temple University Press.

"Developments in the Law: Religion and the State," *Harvard Law Review* 100 (1987), 1606–1781.

Dinstein, Yoram 1976, "Collective Human Rights of Peoples and Minorities," *International and Comparative Law Quarterly* 25, 102–120.

Diwan, Paras 1987, *Muslim Law in Modern India*, 4th edn, Allahabad, India: Allahabad Law Agency.

Edelman, Martin 1994, *Courts, Politics, and Culture in Israel*, Charlottesville, VA: University Press of Virginia.

Eekelaar, John and Maclean, Mavis 1986, *Maintenance after Divorce*, Oxford: Clarendon Press.

Eisgruber, Christopher L. 1997, "Birthright Citizenship and the Constitution," *New York University Law Review* 72, 54–96.

Elazar, Daniel J. 1987, *Exploring Federalism*, Tuscaloosa, AL: University of Alabama Press.

Elkins, David J. 1995, *Beyond Sovereignty: Territory and Political Economy in the Twenty-First Century*, Toronto: University of Toronto Press.

Elon, Menachem 1985, "The Legal System of Jewish Law," *New York University Journal of International Law and Politics* 17, 221–243.

Endelman, Todd M. (ed.) 1987, *Jewish Apostasy in the Modern World*, New York: Holmes and Meier.

Everett, William Johnson 1997, *Religion, Federalism, and the Struggle for Public Life: Cases from Germany, India, and America*, Oxford: Oxford University Press.

Favell, Adrian 1998, *Philosophies of Integration: Immigration and the Idea of Citizenship in France and Britain*, London: Macmillan.

Feldblum, Miriam and Klusmeyer, Douglas 1999, "Foreign-Born Residents in the United States," *Research Perspectives on Migration* 2, 10.

Fiss, Owen 1976, "Groups and the Equal Protection Clause," *Philosophy and Public Affairs* 5, 107–177.

1984, "Against Settlement," *Yale Law Journal* 93, 1073–1090.

Fraser, Nancy 1995, "From Redistribution to Recognition? Dilemmas of Justice in a 'Post-Socialist' Age," *New Left Review* 212, 68–93.

Fredman, Sandra 1997, *Women and the Law*, Oxford: Clarendon Press.

Freeman, Marsha A. 1990, "Measuring Equality: a Comparative Perspective on Women's Legal Capacity and Constitutional Rights in Five Commonwealth Countries," *Berkeley Women's Law Journal* 5, 110–138.

Friedman, Marilyn 1989, "Feminism and Modern Friendship: Dislocating the Community," *Ethics* 99, 275–290.

Friedman, Milton 1955, "The Role of Government in Education," *Economics and the Public Interest*, Robert A. Solo (ed.), New Brunswick, NJ: Rutgers University Press, pp. 123–144.

Galeotti, Anna Elisabetta 1993, "Citizenship and Equality: the Place for Toleration," *Political Theory* 21, 585–605.

Galloway, J. Donald 1999, "The Dilemmas of Canadian Citizenship Law," *Georgetown Immigration Law Journal* 13, 201–231.

Galston, William A. 1989, "Civic Education in the Liberal State," *Liberalism and the Moral Life*, Nancy L. Rosenblum (ed.), Cambridge, MA: Harvard University Press, pp. 89–101.

1995, "Two Concepts of Liberalism," *Ethics* 105, 516–534.

Ginossar, Shalev 1970, "Who is a Jew: a Better Law?" *Israel Law Review* 5, 264–267.

Glazer, Nathan 1997, *We Are All Multiculturalists Now*, Cambridge, MA: Harvard University Press.

Glendon, Mary Ann 1980, "The New Marriage and the New Property," *Marriage and Cohabitation in Contemporary Societies: an International and Interdisciplinary Study*, John M. Eekelaar and Sanford N. Katz (eds.), Toronto: Butterworth, pp. 59–70.

Glenn, Evelyn Nakano 1994, "Social Constructions of Mothering: a Thematic Overview" *Mothering, Ideology, Experience, and Agency*, Evelyn Nakano Glenn, Grace Chang, and Linda Renney Forcey (eds.), New York: Routledge, pp. 1–29.

Glenn, H. Patrick 1997, "The Capture, Reconstruction and Marginalization of 'Custom,'" *American Journal of Comparative Law* 45, 613–620.

Goldscheider, Calvin and Zuckerman, Alan S. 1984, *The Transformation of the Jews*, Chicago, IL: University of Chicago Press.

Goodin, Robert E. 1996a, "Institutions and Their Design," *The Theory of Institutional Design*, Robert E. Goodin (ed.), Cambridge: Cambridge University Press, pp. 1–35.

1996b "Designing Constitutions: the Political Constitution of a Mixed Commonwealth," *Constitutionalism in Transformation: European and Theoretical Perspectives*, Richard Bellamy and Dario Castiglione (eds.), Oxford: Blackwell, pp. 223–234.

Goodman-Thau, Eveline 1993, "Challenging the Roots of Religious Patriarchy and Shaping Identity and Community," *Calling the Equality Bluff: Women in Israel*, Barbara Swirski and Marilyn P. Safir (eds.), New York: Teachers College Press, pp. 45–53.

Gotanda, Neil 1991, "A Critique of 'Our Constitution is Color Blind,'" *Stanford Law Review* 44, 1–68.

Graham, Lorie M. 1998, " 'The Past Never Vanishes': a Contextual Critique of the Existing Indian Family Law Doctrine," *American Indian Law Review* 23, 1–54.

Green, Ross Gordon 1997, "Aboriginal Community Sentencing and Mediation: Within and Without the Circle," *Manitoba Law Journal* 25, 77–125.

Greene, Abner S. 1996, "*Kiryas Joel* and Two Mistakes about Equality," *Columbia Law Review* 96, 1–86.

Grewal, Inderpal and Kaplan, Caren (eds.) 1994, *Scattered Hegemonies: Postmodernity and Transnational Feminist Practices*, Minneapolis, MN: University of Minnesota Press.

Griffiths, Anne 1998, "Reconfiguring Law: an Ethnographic Perspective from Botswana," *Law and Social Inquiry* 23, 587–620.

Gutmann, Amy 1987, *Democratic Education*, Princeton, NJ: Princeton University Press.

1993, "The Challenge of Multiculturalism in Political Ethics," *Philosophy and Public Affairs* 22, 171–206.

1995, "Civic Education and Social Diversity," *Ethics* 105, 557–579.

Habermas, Jürgen 1995, "Multiculturalism and the Liberal State," *Stanford Law Review* 47, 849–853.

Haddad, Yvonne Yazbeck 1998, "Islam and Gender: Dilemmas in the Changing Arab World," *Islam, Gender, and Social Change*, Yvonne Yazbeck Haddad and John L. Eposito (eds.), Oxford: Oxford University Press, pp. 3–29.

Hall, Peter A. and Taylor, Rosemary C. R. 1996, "Political Science and the Three New Institutionalisms," *Political Studies* 44, 936–957.

Halstead, Mark 1995, "Voluntary Apartheid? Problems of Schooling for Religious and other Minorities in Democratic Societies," *Journal of Philosophy of Education* 29, 257–272.

Hamilton, Carolyn 1995, *Family, Law and Religion*, London: Sweet & Maxwell.

Hanna, Scott A. 1995, "Shared Powers: the Effects of the Shared Canadian Federal and Québec Provincial Immigration Powers on Immigrants," *Georgetown Immigration Law Journal* 9, 75–103.

Harris, Angela P. 1990, "Race and Essentialism in Feminist Legal Theory," *Stanford Law Review* 42, 581–616.

1995, "Forward: the Unbearable Lightness of Identity," *African American Law and Policy Report* 2, 207–221.

Hatem, Mervat 1986, "The Enduring Alliance of Nationalism and Patriarchy in Muslim Personal Status Laws: the Case of Modern Egypt," *Feminist Issues* 6, 19–43.

Havemann, Paul (ed.) 1999, *Indigenous Peoples' Rights in Australia, Canada, and New Zealand*, Auckland: Oxford University Press.

Hayward, Clarissa Rile 2000, *De-Facing Power*, Cambridge: Cambridge University Press.

Helfer, Laurence R. 2000, "Forum Shopping for Human Rights," *University of Pennsylvania Law Review* 148, 285–400.

Helfer, Laurence R. and Slaughter, Anne-Marie 1997, "Toward a Theory of Effective Supranational Adjudication," *Yale Law Journal* 107, 273–391.

Hélie-Lucas, Marie Aimée 1994, "The Preferential Symbol for Islamic Identity: Women in Muslim Personal Laws," in Moghadam 1994a, pp. 391–407.

Heschel, Susannah (ed.) 1995, *On Being a Jewish Feminist: a Reader*, New York: Schocken Books.

Hijab, Nadia 1998, "Islam, Social Change, and the Reality of Arab Women's Lives," *Islam, Gender and Social Change*, Yvonne Yazbeck Haddad and John L. Esposito (eds.), Oxford: Oxford University Press, pp. 45–55.

Hirschman, Albert O. 1970, *Exit, Voice, and Loyalty: Responses to Recline in Firms, Organizations, and States*, Cambridge, MA: Harvard University Press.

Hirst, Paul 2000, "Democracy and Governance," *Debating Governance: Authority, Steering, and Democracy*, Jon Pierre (ed.), Oxford: Oxford University Press, pp. 13–35.

Hobbes, Thomas 1955, *Leviathan: or The Matter, Form, and Power of a Commonwealth, Ecclesiastical and Civil*, ed. with an introduction by Michael Oakeshott, Oxford: Basil Blackwell.

Hobsbawm, Eric and Ranger, Terrence (eds.) 1983, *The Invention of Tradition*, Cambridge: Cambridge University Press.

Hooker, M. B. 1975, *Legal Pluralism: an Introduction to Colonial and Neo-Colonial Laws*, Oxford: Clarendon Press.

Horowitz, Donald L. 1985, *Ethnic Groups in Conflict*, Berkeley, CA: University of California Press.

1994a, "The Qur'an and the Common Law: Islamic Law Reform and the Theory of Legal Change, Part II," *American Journal of Comparative Law* 42, 543–580.

1994b, "Democracy in Divided Societies," *Nationalism, Ethnic Conflict, and Democracy*, Larry Diamond and Marc F. Plattner (eds.), Baltimore, MD: Johns Hopkins University Press, pp. 35–55.

Hossain, Sara 1994, "Equality in the Home: Women's Rights and Personal Laws in South Asia," in Cook, pp. 465–494.

Howland, Courtney W. 1997, "The Challenge of Religious Fundamentalism to the Liberty and Equality Rights of Women: an Analysis under the United Nations Charter," *Columbia Journal of Transnational Law* 35, 271–377.

Howland, Courtney W. (ed.) 1999, *Religious Fundamentalisms and the Human Rights of Women*, New York: St. Martin's Press.

Howse, Robert 1996, "Liberal Accommodation," *University of Toronto Law Journal* 46, 311–334.

Huntington, Samuel P. 1968, *Political Order in Changing Societies*, New Haven, CT: Yale University Press.

Hyman, Paula E. 1995, *Gender and Assimilation in Modern Jewish History: the Roles and Representation of Women*, Seattle, WA: University of Washington Press.

Ibrahim, Ahmad Inche 1968, "The Muslims in Malaysia and Singapore: the Law of Matrimonial Property," *Family Law in Asia and Africa*, J. N. D. Anderson (ed.), New York: Praeger, pp. 182–204.

Isaac, Jeffrey C. 1987, "Beyond the Three Faces of Power: a Realist Critique," *Polity* 20, 4–31.

Jayal, Niraja G. 1998, *State and Democracy: Welfare, Development, Secularism*, Delhi: Oxford University Press.

Jeffery, Patricia 1998, "Agency, Activism, and Agendas," *Appropriating Gender: Women's Activism and Politicized Religion in South Asia*, Patricia Jeffery and Amrita Basu (eds.), New York: Routledge, pp. 221–243.

Jessop, Bob 1997, "The Governance of Complexity and the Complexity of Governance: Preliminary Remarks on Some Problems and Limits of Economic Guidance," *Beyond Market and Hierarchy: Interactive Governance and Social Complexity*, Ash Amin and Jerzy Hausner (eds.), Lyme, NH: Edward Elgar, pp. 95–128.

Johnston, Darlene 1989, "Native Rights as Collective Rights: a Question of Group Self-Preservation," *Canadian Journal of Law and Jurisprudence* 2, 19–34.

Joseph, Suad 1999, "Women Between Nation and State in Lebanon," *Between Women and Nation: Nationalism, Transnational Feminisms, and the State*, Caren Kaplan, Norma Alarcón, and Minoo Moallem (eds.), Durham, NC: Duke University Press, pp. 162–181.

Kabeberi-Macharia, Janet 1992, "Family Law and Gender in Kenya," *International Review of Comparative Public Policy* 4, 193–207.

Kamili, Mohammad Hashim 1997–1998, "Islamic Law in Malaysia: Issues and Developments," *Yearbook of Islamic and Middle Eastern Law*, IV, Eugene Cotran and Chibli Mallat (eds.), London: Kluwer Law International, pp. 153–179.

Kandiyoti, Deniz (ed.) 1991, *Women, Islam and the State*, London: Macmillan.

Kates, Gary 1989, "Jews into Frenchmen: Nationality and Representation in Revolutionary France," *Social Research* 56, 213–232.

Katz, June S. and Katz, Ronald S. 1978, "Legislating Social Change in a Developing Country: the New Indonesian Marriage Law Revisited," *American Journal of Comparative Law* 26, 309–320.

Kaufman, Debra Renee 1985, "Women Who Return to Orthodox Judaism: a Feminist Analysis," *Journal of Marriage and Family* 47, 543–551.

Kaviraj, Sudipta 1997, "Religion and Identity in India," *Ethnic and Racial Studies* 20, 325–344.

Kiss, Elizabeth 1997, "Alchemy or Fool's Gold? Assessing Feminist Doubts About Rights," *Reconstructing Political Theory: Feminist Perspectives*, Mary Lyndon Shanley and Uma Narayan (eds.), University Park, PA: Pennsylvania State University Press, pp. 1–24.

Klug, Francesca 1989, " 'Oh to be in England': the British Case Study," in Yuval-Davis and Anthias, pp. 16–35.

Knop, Karen 2000, "Here and There: International Law in Domestic Courts," *New York University Journal of International Law and Politics* 32, 501–536.

Kohli, Atul 1997, "Can Democracies Accommodate Ethnic Nationalism? the Rise and Decline of Self-Determination Movements," *Journal of Asian Studies* 56, 325–344.

Kommers, Donald P. 1997, *The Constitutional Jurisprudence of the Federal Republic of Germany*, 2nd edn, Durham, NC: Duke University Press.

Korsgaard, Christine M. 1993, "G. A. Cohen: Equality of What? On Welfare, Goods and Capabilities, Amartya Sen: Capability and Well-Being," in Nussbaum and Sen, pp. 54–61.

Kukathas, Chandran 1992, "Are There Any Cultural Rights?" *Political Theory* 20, 105–139.

1997, "Cultural Toleration," in Shapiro and Kymlicka, pp. 69–104.

1998, "Liberalism and Multiculturalism: the Politics of Indifference," *Political Theory* 26, 686–699.

Kymlicka, Will 1989, *Liberalism, Community and Culture*, Oxford: Clarendon Press.

1992, "The Rights of Minority Cultures: Reply to Kukathas," *Political Theory* 20, 140–146.

1995, *Multicultural Citizenship: a Liberal Theory of Minority Rights*, Oxford: Clarendon Press.

1996, "Three Forms of Group-Differentiated Citizenship in Canada," *Democracy and Difference: Contesting the Boundaries of the Political*, Seyla Benhabib (ed.), Princeton, NJ: Princeton University Press, pp. 153–170.

1998, *Finding Our Way: Rethinking Ethnocultural Relations in Canada*, Toronto: Oxford University Press.

1999, "Comments on Shachar and Spinner-Halev: an Update from the Multiculturalism Wars," *Multicultural Questions*, Christian Joppke and Steven Lukes (eds.), Oxford: Oxford University Press, pp. 112–129.

Kymlicka, Will and Norman, Wayne, 1994, "Return of the Citizen: a Survey of Recent Work on Citizenship Theory," *Ethics* 104, 352–381.

2000, "Citizenship in Culturally Diverse Societies: Issues, Contexts, Concepts," in Kymlicka and Norman, pp. 1–41.

Kymlicka, Will and Norman, Wayne (eds.) 2000, *Citizenship in Diverse Societies*, Oxford: Oxford University Press.

Lagerspetz, Eerik 1998, "On Language Rights," *Ethical Theory and Moral Practice* 1, 181–199.

Laroque, Emma 1997, "Aboriginal and Treaty Rights in Canada," *Aboriginal Treaty Rights in Canada*, Michael Asch (ed.), Vancouver: University of British Columbia Press, pp. 75–96.

Let's Build Québec Together: Vision, a Policy Statement on Immigration and Integration, Québec: Ministère des Communautés culturelles et de l'immigration du Québec, 1990.

Levey, Geoffrey Brahm 1997a, "Equality, Autonomy, and Cultural Rights," *Political Theory* 25, 215–248.

1997b, "Liberalism and Cultural Toleration: the Ineluctability of Autonomy," paper presented at the Annual Meeting of the American Political Science Association, Washington DC, 28–31 August 1997.

Levy, Jacob T. 1997, "Classifying Cultural Rights," in Shapiro and Kymlicka, pp. 22–66.

2000, *The Multiculturalism of Fear*, Oxford: Oxford University Press.

Lijphart, Arend 1977, *Democracy in Plural Societies: a Comparative Exploration*, New Haven, CT: Yale University Press.

Lim, Linda Y. C. 1990, "Women's Work in Export Factories: the Politics of a Cause," in Tinker, pp. 101–119.

Liu, Tessie P. 1991, "Race and Gender in the Politics of Group Formation: a Comment on Notions of Multiculturalism," *Frontiers* 12, 155–165.

Loomba, Ania 1998, *Colonialism/Postcolonialism*, London: Routledge.

Lopez, Ian F. Haney 1994, "The Social Construction of Race: some Observations on Illusion, Fabrication, and Choice," *Harvard Civil Rights-Civil Liberties Law Review* 29, 1–62.

Lukes, Steven 1974, *Power: a Radical View*, London: Macmillan.

Lundberg, Shelly and Pollak, Robert A. 1996, "Bargaining and Distribution in Marriage," *Journal of Economic Perspectives* 10, 139–158.

MacCormick, Neil 1993, "Beyond the Sovereign State," *Modern Law Review* 56, 1–18.

Macedo, Stephen 1990, *Liberal Virtues: Citizenship, Virtue, and Community in Liberal Constitutionalism*, Oxford: Clarendon Press.

1995, "Liberal Civic Education and Religious Fundamentalism: the Case of God v. Rawls?" *Ethics* 105, 468–496.

1998, "Transformative Constitutionalism and the Case of Religion: Defending the Moderate Hegemony of Liberalism," *Political Theory* 26, 56–80.

Macklem, Patrick 1993, "Distributing Sovereignty: Indian Nations and Equality of Peoples," *Stanford Law Review* 45, 1311–1367.

Mahoney, Martha R. 1992, "Exit: Power and the Idea of Leaving in Love, Work, and the Confirmation Hearings," *Southern California Law Review* 65, 1283–1319.

Mamdani, Mahmood 1996, *Citizen and Subject: Contemporary Africa and the Legacy of Late Colonialism*, Princeton, NJ: Princeton University Press.

Manheim, Karl 1995, "State Immigration Laws and Federal Supremacy," *Hastings Constitutional Law Quarterly* 22, 939–1018.

March, James G. and Olsen, Johan P. 1989, *Rediscovering Institutions: the Organizational Basis of Politics*, New York: Free Press.

Margalit, Avishai and Halbertal, Moshe 1994, "Liberalism and the Right to Culture," *Social Research* 61, 491–510.

Marrus, Michael 1971, *The Politics of Assimilation: a Study of the French Jewish Community at the Time of the Dreyfus Affair*, Oxford: Clarendon Press.

Marx, Karl 1994, "On the Jewish Question," *Marx: Early Political Writings*, Joseph O'Malley and Richard A. Davis (ed. and trans.), Cambridge: Cambridge University Press, pp. 28–56.

Mayer, Ann Elizabeth 1999, *Islam and Human Rights: Tradition and Politics*, 3rd edn., Boulder, CO: Westview Press.

McClain, Linda C. 1992, "'Atomistic Man' Revisited: Liberalism, Connection, and Feminist Jurisprudence," *Southern California Law Review* 65, 1171–1264.

McClintock, Anne 1993, "Family Feuds: Gender, Nationalism and the Family," *Feminist Review* 44, 61–80.

1995, *Imperial Leather: Race, Gender and Sexuality in the Colonial Context*, New York: Routledge.

McClure, Kirstie M. 1990, "Difference, Diversity, and the Limits of Toleration," *Political Theory* 18, 361–391.

McCubbins, Mathew D. and Schwartz, Thomas 1984, "Congressional Oversight Overlooked: Police Patrols versus Fire Alarms," *American Journal of Political Science* 28, 165–179.

McDonald, Michael 1991, "Should Communities Have Rights? Reflections on Liberal Individualism," *Canadian Journal of Law and Jurisprudence* 4, 217–237.

McElroy, Marjorie B. 1990, "The Empirical Content of Nash-Bargained Household Behavior," *Journal of Human Resources* 25, 559–583.

Meiselman, Moshe 1978, *Jewish Woman in Jewish Law*, New York: Ktav Publishing House.

Mernissi, Fatima 1996, *Women's Rebellion and Islamic Memory*, London: Zed Books.

Mertus, Julie 1994, "'Woman' in the Service of National Identity," *Hastings Women's Law Journal* 5, 5–23.

Miller, David 1995, "Citizenship and Pluralism," *Political Studies* 43, 432–450.

Miller, David and Walzer, Michael (eds.) 1995, *Pluralism, Justice, and Equality*, Oxford: Oxford University Press.

Minow, Martha 1985, "Forming Underneath Everything that Grows: toward a History of Family Law," *Wisconsin Law Review* 1985, 819–898.

1990, *Making All the Difference: Inclusion, Exclusion, and American Law*, Ithaca, NY: Cornell University Press.

1995, "The Constitution and the Subgroup Question," *Indiana Law Journal* 71, 1–25.

1997, *Not Only for Myself: Identity, Politics, and the Law*, New York: The New Press.

Minow, Martha, Ryan, Michael and Sarat, Austin (eds.) 1995, *Narrative, Violence, and the Law: the Essays of Robert Cover*, Ann Arbor, MI: University of Michigan Press.

Mnookin, Robert H. 1975, "Child-Custody Adjudication: Judicial Functions in the Face of Indeterminacy," *Law and Contemporary Problems* 39, 226–293.

Mnookin, Robert H. and Kornhauser, Lewis 1979, "Bargaining in the Shadow of the Law: the Case of Divorce," *Yale Law Journal* 88, 950–997.

Moghadam, Valentine M. (ed.) 1994a, *Identity Politics and Women: Cultural Reassertions and Feminisms in International Perspective*, Boulder, CO: Westview Press.

1994b, *Gender and National Identity: Women and Politics in Muslim Societies*, London: Zed Books.

Monsma, Stephen V. and Soper, J. Christopher 1997, *The Challenge of Pluralism: Church and State in Five Democracies*, Lanham, MD: Rowman & Littlefield.

Monsma, Stephen V. and Soper, J. Christopher (eds.) 1998, *Equal Treatment of Religion in a Pluralistic Society*, Grand Rapids, MI: William B. Eerdmans Publishing.

Monture-Okanee, Patricia and Turpel, Mary Ellen 1992, "Aboriginal Peoples and Canadian Criminal Law: Rethinking Justice," *University of British Columbia Law Review* 26, 239–277.

Moodod, Tariq 1998, "Anti-Essentialism, Multiculturalism, and the 'Recognition' of Religious Groups," *Journal of Political Philosophy* 6, 378–399.

Moodod, Tariq (ed.) 1996, *Church, State, and Religious Minorities*, London: Policy Studies Institute.

Moose, Julie Cleves 1993, *Half the World, Half a Chance: an Introduction to Gender and Development*, Oxford: Oxfam.

Morgan, Ed 1995, "Cyclops Meets Privy Council: the Conflict in the Conflict of Laws," *The Canadian Yearbook of International Law* 33, 3–39.

Muli, Koki 1995, "'Help Me Balance the Load': Gender Discrimination in Kenya," *Women's Rights Human Rights: International Feminist Perspectives*, Julie Peters and Andrea Wolper (eds.), New York: Routledge, pp. 78–81.

Narayan, Uma 1997, *Dislocating Cultures: Identities, Traditions, and Third World Feminism*, New York: Routledge.

Nash, John F. 1950, "The Bargaining Problem," *Econometrica* 18, 155–162.

1953, "Two-Person Cooperative Games," *Econometrica* 21, 128–140.

Nasir, Jamal J. 1990, *The Islamic Law of Personal Status*, 2nd edn, London: Graham & Trotman.

Natapoff, Alexandra 1995, "Trouble in Paradise: Equal Protection and the Dilemma of Interminority Group Conflict," *Stanford Law Review* 47, 1059–1096.

Nedelsky, Jennifer 1989, "Reconceiving Autonomy," *Yale Journal of Law and Feminism* 1, 7–36.

1993, "Reconceiving Rights as Relationship," *Review of Constitutional Studies* 1, 1–26.

Norman, Wayne J. 1994, "Towards a Philosophy of Federalism," *Group Rights*, Judith Baker (ed.), Toronto: University of Toronto Press, pp. 79–100.

Nussbaum, Martha C. 1999, *Sex and Social Justice*, Oxford: Oxford University Press.

2000, *Women and Human Development: the Capabilities Approach*, Cambridge: Cambridge University Press.

Nussbaum, Martha C. and Glover, Jonathan (eds.) 1995, *Women, Culture, and Development: a Study of Human Capabilities*, Oxford: Clarendon Press.

Nussbaum, Martha C. and Sen, Amartya (eds.) 1993, *The Quality of Life*, Oxford: Oxford University Press.

Nyamu, Celestine I. 2000, "How Should Human Rights and Development Respond to Cultural Legitimization of Gender Hierarchy in Developing Countries?" *Harvard International Law Journal* 41, 381–418.

O'Brien, Mary 1981, *The Politics of Reproduction*, Boston, MA: Routledge & Kegan Paul.

Oestreich, Joel E. 1999, "Liberal Theory and Minority Group Rights," *Human Rights Quarterly* 21, 108–132.

Okin, Susan Moller 1997, "Is Multiculturalism Bad for Women?" *Boston Review* 22, 25–28.

1998, "Feminism and Multiculturalism: some Tensions," *Ethics* 108, 661–684.

Olsen, Frances E. 1983, "The Family and the Market: a Study of Ideology and Legal Reform," *Harvard Law Review* 96, 1497–1578.

Ostrom, Elinor 1990, *Governing the Commons: the Evolution of Institutions for Collective Action*, Cambridge: Cambridge University Press.

Parekh, Bhikhu 1995, "Cultural Pluralism and the Limits of Diversity," *Alternatives* 20, 431–457.

1999, "Balancing Unity and Diversity in Multicultural Societies," in Avnon and de-Shalit, pp. 106–124.

2000, *Rethinking Multiculturalism: Cultural Diversity and Political Theory*, Cambridge, MA: Harvard University Press.

Parker, Andrew, Russo, Mary, Sommer, Doris and Yaeger, Patricia (eds.) 1992, *Nationalisms and Sexualities*, New York: Routledge.

Parkinson, Patrick 1994, "Taking Multiculturalism Seriously: Marriage Law and the Rights of Minorities," *Sydney Law Review* 16, 473–505.

Patai, Raphael and Wing, Jennifer Patai 1975, *The Myth of the Jewish Race*, New York: Scribner.

Pateman, Carole 1988, *The Sexual Contract*, Stanford, CA: Stanford University Press.

Pearl, David 1995, "The Application of Islamic Law in the English Courts," *Yearbook of Islamic and Middle Eastern Law*, II, Eugene Cotran and Chibli Mallat (eds.), London: Kluwer Law International, pp. 3–11.

Pearl, David and Menski, Werner 1998, *Muslim Family Law*, 3rd edn, London: Sweet & Maxwell.

Peled, Yoav and Brunner, José 2000, "Culture is not Enough: or Democratic Critique of Liberal Multiculturalism," *Ethnic Challenges to the Modern Nation State*, Shlomo Ben-Ami, Yoav Peled, and Alberto Spektorowski (eds.), New York: St. Martin's Press.

Pelikan, Jaroslav Jan 1984, *The Vindication of Tradition*, New Haven, CT: Yale University Press.

Pennock, J. Roland 1959, "Federal and Unitary Government: Disharmony and Frustration," *Behavioral Science* 4, 147–157.

Peterson, Richard P. 1996, "A Re-Evaluation of the Economic Consequences of Divorce," *American Sociological Review* 61, 528–536.

Pettit, Philip 1997, *Republicanism: a Theory of Freedom and Government*, Oxford: Oxford University Press.

1999, "Republican Freedom and Contestatory Democratization," in Shapiro and Hacker-Cordón, pp. 163–190.

Pocock, J. G. A. 1995, "The Ideal of Citizenship Since Classical Times," in Beiner 1995, pp. 29–52.

Poovey, Mary 1988, *Uneven Developments: the Ideological Work of Gender in Mid-Victorian England*, Chicago, IL: University of Chicago Press.

Post, Robert forthcoming, "Democratic Constitutionalism and Cultural Heterogeneity," *Australian Journal of Legal Philosophy*.

Poulter, Sebastian M. 1998, *Ethnicity, Law and Human Rights: the English Experience*, Oxford: Clarendon Press.

Putnam, Robert D. 1988, "Diplomacy and Domestic Politics: the Logic of Two-Level Games," *International Organization* 42, 427–460.

Rawls, John 1971, *A Theory of Justice*, Cambridge, MA: Harvard University Press.

1988, "The Priority of Right and Ideas of the Good," *Philosophy and Public Affairs* 17, 251–276.

1993, *Political Liberalism*, New York: Columbia University Press.

Raz, Joesph 1994, *Ethics in the Public Domain: Essays in the Morality of Law and Politics*, Oxford: Clarendon Press.

Razack, Sherene H. 1998, *Looking White People in the Eye: Gender, Race, and Culture in Courtrooms and Classrooms*, Toronto: University of Toronto Press.

Réaume, Denise G. 1995, "Justice Between Cultures: Autonomy and the Protection of Cultural Affiliation," *University of British Columbia Law Review* 29, 117–141.

Resnik, Judith 1989, "Dependent Sovereigns: Indian Tribes, States, and the Federal Courts," *University of Chicago Law Review* 56, 671–759.

Revesz, Richard L. 1992, "Rehabilitating Interstate Competition: Rethinking the 'Race-to-the-Bottom' Rationale for Federal Environmental Regulation," *New York University Law Review* 67, 1210–1254.

Rheinstein, Max 1953, "Trends in Marriage and Divorce Law of Western Countries," *Law and Contemporary Problems* 18, 3–19.

Riker, William H. 1964, *Federalism: Origin, Operation and Significance*, Boston: Little Brown.

1995, "Federalism," *A Companion to Contemporary Political Philosophy*, Robert E. Goodin and Philip Pettit (eds.), Oxford: Blackwell, pp. 508–514.

Roach, Kent 1999, *Due Process and Victims' Rights: the New Law and Politics of Criminal Justice*, Toronto: University of Toronto Press.

Rodrik, Dani 1997, *Has Globalization Gone Too Far?* Washington, DC: Institute for International Economics.

Rose, Carol M. 1992, "Women and Property: Gaining and Losing Ground," *Virginia Law Review* 78, 421–459.

Rosenblum, Nancy L. 1989, "Pluralism and Self-Defense," *Liberalism and the Moral Life*, Nancy L. Rosenblum (ed.), Cambridge, MA: Harvard University Press, pp. 207–226.

Rosenblum, Nancy L. (ed.) 2000, *Obligations of Citizenship and Demands of Faith: Religious Accommodation in Pluralist Democracies*, Princeton, NJ: Princeton University Press.

Royal Commission on Aboriginal Peoples 1996, *Bridging the Cultural Divide: a Report on Aboriginal People and Criminal Justice in Canada*, Ottawa: Supply and Services.

Ruggie, John Gerard 1993, "Territoriality and Beyond: Problematizing Modernity in International Relations," *International Organization* 47, 139–174.

1998, *Constructing the World Polity: Essays on International Institutionalization*, London: Routledge.

Sagade, Jaya 1996, *Law of Maintenance: an Empirical Study*, Pune: Indian Law Society.

Sandel, Michael J. 1982, *Liberalism and the Limits of Justice*, Cambridge: Cambridge University Press.

Sapiro, Virginia 1984, "Women, Citizenship, and Nationality: Immigration and Naturalization Policies in the United States," *Politics and Society* 13, 1–26.

Sarat, Austin and Berkowitz, Roger 1994, "Disorderly Differences: Recognition, Accommodation, and American Law," *Yale Journal of Law and the Humanities* 6, 285–316.

Sassin, Saskia 1996, *Losing Control: Sovereignty in an Age of Globalization*, New York: Columbia University Press.

Schuck, Peter H. and Smith, Rogers M. 1985, *Citizenship Without Consent: Illegal Aliens in the American Polity*, New Haven, CT: Yale University Press.

Schwartz, Bryan 1990, "A Separate Aboriginal Justice System?" *Manitoba Law Journal* 19, 77–91.

Scott, James C. 1995, "State Simplifications, Nature, Space and People," *Journal of Political Philosophy* 3, 191–233.

Scott, Joan W. 1988, "Deconstructing Equality-versus-Difference: or, the Uses of Poststructuralist Theory for Feminism," *Feminist Studies* 14, 33–50.

Sen, Amartya K. 1990, "Gender and Cooperative Conflicts," in Tinker, pp. 123–149.

1993, "Capability and Well-Being," in Nussbaum and Sen, pp. 30–53.

Shachar, Ayelet 1998, "Group Identity and Women's Rights in Family Law: the Perils of Multicultural Accommodation," *Journal of Political Philosophy* 6, 285–305.

2000a, "On Citizenship and Multicultural Vulnerability," *Political Theory* 28, 64–89.

2000b, "Should Church and State be Joined at the Altar? Women's Rights and the Multicultural Dilemma," in Kymlicka and Norman, 199–223.

2000c, "The Puzzle of Interlocking Power Hierarchies: Sharing the Pieces of Jurisdictional Authority," *Harvard Civil Rights–Civil Liberties Law Review* 35, 385–426.

forthcoming, "The Thin Line between Imposition and Consent: a Critique of Birthright Membership Entitlements and their Implications," *Breaking the Cycles of Hatred: Memory, Law, and Repair*, Nancy L. Rosenblum (ed.), Princeton, NJ: Princeton University Press.

Shaheed, Farida 1994, "Controlled or Autonomous? Identity and the Experience of the Network, Women Living under Muslim Laws," *Signs* 19, 997–1019.

1995, "Networking for Change: the Role of Women's Groups in Initiating Dialogue of Women's Issues," *Faith and Freedom: Women's Human Rights in the Muslim World*, Mahnaz Afkhami (ed.), London: I. B. Tauris.

Shapiro, Ian 1989, "Gross Concepts in Political Argument," *Political Theory* 17, 51–76.

1999, *Democratic Justice*, New Haven, CT: Yale University Press.

Shapiro, Ian and Hacker-Cordón, Casiano (eds.) 1999, *Democracy's Value*, Cambridge: Cambridge University Press.

Shapiro, Ian and Kymlicka, Will (eds.) 1997, *Ethnicity and Group Rights*, New York: New York University Press.

Shaskolsky-Sheleff, Leon 1993, "'Thou Shalt Not Be Too Different': Civil Rights, Social Control and Deviant Religious Practices in the United States," *Israel Yearbook on Human Rights* 23, Martinus Nijhoff: Dordrecht.

Shehadeh, Lamia Rustum 1998, "The Legal Status of Married Women in Lebanon," *International Journal of Middle East Studies* 30, 501–519.

Siegel, Reva B. 1996, "'The Rule of Love': Wife Beating as Prerogative and Privacy," *Yale Law Journal* 105, 2117–2207.

Singh, Kirti 1994, "Obstacles to Women's Rights in India," in Cook, pp. 375–396.

Slaughter, Anne-Marie 1994, "A Typology of Transjudicial Communication," *University of Richmond Law Review* 29, 99–137.

1997, "The Real New World Order," *Foreign Affairs* 76, 183–197.

Smith, Steven B. 1997, *Spinoza, Liberalism, and the Question of Jewish Identity*, New Haven, CT: Yale University Press.

Smith Rogers, M. 1997, *Civic Ideals: Conflicting Visions of Citizenship in US History*, New Haven, CT: Yale University Press.

South African Law Commission 1998, *Project 90, The Harmonization of the Common Law and the Indigenous Law, Report on Customary Marriages*, Pretoria.

Soysal, Yasemin Nuhoglu 1994, *Limits of Citizenship: Migrants and Postnational Membership in Europe*, Chicago, IL: University of Chicago Press.

Spinner, Jeff 1994, *The Boundaries of Citizenship: Race, Ethnicity, and Nationality in the Liberal State*, Baltimore, MD: Johns Hopkins University Press.

Spinner-Halev, Jeff 2000, "Extending Diversity: Religion in Public and Private Education," in Kymlicka and Norman, pp. 68–95.

Stepan, Alfred 1999, "Federalism and Democracy: beyond the US Model," *Journal of Democracy* 10, 19–34.

Stolzenberg, Nomi Maya 1993, "'He Drew a Circle that Shut Me Out': Assimilation, Indoctrination, and the Paradox of a Liberal Education," *Harvard Law Review* 106, 581–667.

Stolzenberg, Nomi Maya and Myers, David N. 1992, "Community, Constitution, and Culture: the Case of the Jewish *Kehilah*," *University of Michigan Journal of Law Reform* 25, 633–670.

Stratton, Lisa C. 1992, "'The Right to Have Rights': Gender Discrimination in Nationality Laws," *Minnesota Law Review* 77, 195–239.

Syrtash, John T. 1987, "Removing Barriers to Religious Remarriage in Ontario: Rights and Remedies," *Canadian Family Law Quarterly* 1, 309–344.

1992, *Religion and Culture in Canadian Family Law*, Toronto: Butterworth.

Tamir, Yael 1993, *Liberal Nationalism*, Princeton, NJ: Princeton University Press.

1995, "Two Concepts of Multiculturalism," *Journal of Philosophy of Education* 29, 161–172.

Taylor, Charles 1991, "Shared and Divergent Values," *Options for a New Canada*, Ronald L. Watts and Douglas M. Brown (eds.), Toronto: University of Toronto Press, pp. 53–76.

　　1994, "The Politics of Recognition," *Multiculturalism: Examining the Politics of Recognition*, Amy Gutmann (ed.), Princeton, NJ: Princeton University Press, pp. 25–73.

Tempelman, Sasja 1999, "Constructions of Cultural Identity: Multiculturalism and Exclusion," *Political Studies* 47, 17–31.

Tinker, Irene (ed.) 1990, *Persistent Inequalities: Women and World Development*, Oxford: Oxford University Press.

Tohidi, Nayereh 1994, "Modernity, Islamization, and Women in Iran," in Moghadam 1994b, pp. 110–147.

Tomasi, John 1995, "Kymlicka, Liberalism, and Respect for Cultural Minorities," *Ethics* 105, 580–603.

Tsebelis, George 1995, "Decision Making in Political Systems: Veto Players in Presidentialism, Parliamentarism, Multicameralism and Mulitpartyism," *British Journal of Political Science* 25, 289–325.

Tully, James 1995a, "Cultural Demands for Constitutional Recognition," *Journal of Political Philosophy* 3, 111–132.

　　1995b, *Strange Multiplicity: Constitutionalism in an Age of Diversity*, Cambridge: Cambridge University Press.

Turpel, Mary Ellen 1991, "Home/Land," *Canadian Journal of Family Law* 10, 17–40.

Van Dyke, Vernon 1975, "Justice as Fairness: for Groups?" *American Political Science Review* 69, 607–614.

　　1977, "The Individual, the State, and Ethnic Communities in Political Theory," *World Politics* 29, 343–369.

Van Parijs, Philippe 2000, "Must Europe be Belgian? On Democratic Citizenship in Multilingual Polities," *The Demands of Citizenship*, Catriona McKinnon and Iain Hampsher-Monk (eds.), London: Continuum, pp. 235–253.

Vertovec, Steven 1996, "Multiculturalism, Culturalism and Public Incorporation," *Ethnic and Racial Studies* 19, 49–69.

Vestal, Allen D. and Foster, David L. 1956, "Implied Limitations on the Diversity Jurisdiction of Federal Courts," *Minnesota Law Review* 41, 1–41.

Vile, M. J. C. 1998, *Constitutionalism and the Separation of Powers*, Indianapolis, IN: Liberty Fund.

Vitta, Edoardo 1970, "The Conflict of Personal Laws: Part I," *Israel Law Review* 5, 170–202.

Volpp, Leti 1996, "Talking 'Culture': Gender, Race, Nation, and the Politics of Multiculturalism," *Columbia Law Review* 96, 1573–1617.

Waldron, Jeremy 1992, "Minority Cultures and the Cosmopolitan Alternative," *University of Michigan Journal of Law Reform* 25, 751–793.

Walford, Geoffrey 1995, "Faith-based Grant-maintained Schools: Selective International Policy Borrowing from the Netherlands," *Journal of Education Policy* 10, 245–257.

Walker, Brian 1997, "Plural Cultures, Contested Territories: a Critique of Kymlicka," *Canadian Journal of Political Science* 30, 211–234.

Walzer, Michael 1983, *Spheres of Justice: a Defense of Pluralism and Equality*, New York: Basic Books.

1989, "Citizenship," *Political Innovation and Conceptual Change*, Terence Ball, James Farr, and Russell L. Hanson (eds.), Cambridge: Cambridge University Press, pp. 211–219.

1990, "The Communitarian Critique of Liberalism," *Political Theory* 18, 6–23.

Washofsky, Mark 1981, "The Recalcitrant Husband: the Problem of Definition," *The Jewish Law Annual* 4, 144–166.

Watts, Ronald L. 1999, *Comparing Federal Systems*, 2nd edn., Montreal and Kingston: McGill-Queen's University Press.

Weber, Max 1978, *Economy and Society: an Outline of Interpretive Society*, Guenther Roth and Claus Wittich (eds.), Ephraim Fischoff et al. (trans.), 2 vols., Berkeley, CA: University of California Press.

Weiler, J. H. H. 1999, *The Constitution of Europe: "Do the New Clothes Have an Emperor?" and Other Essays of European Integration*, Cambridge: Cambridge University Press.

Weingast, Barry R. 1995, "The Economic Role of Political Institutions: Market Preserving Federalism and Economic Development," *The Journal of Law, Economics, and Organization* 11, 1–31.

Weinrib, Lorraine E. forthcoming, "'Do Justice to Us': Jews and the Constitution of Canada," *Not Written in Stone: Jews, Constitutions and Constitutionalism in Canada*, Michael Brown, Daniel Elazar, and Ira Robinson (eds.).

Weisbrod, Carol 1987–1988, "Family, Church and State: an Essay on Constitutionalism and Religious Authority," *Journal of Family Law* 26, 741–770.

Weithman, Paul J. (ed.) 1997, *Religion and Contemporary Liberalism*, Notre Dame, IN: University of Notre Dame Press, 1997.

Weitzman, Lenore 1985, *The Divorce Revolution: the Unexpected Social and Economic Consequences for Women and Children in America*, New York: Free Press.

Wendt, Alexander 1994, "Collective Identity Formation and the International State," *American Political Science Review* 88, 384–396.

West, Robin 1988, "Jurisprudence and Gender," *University of Chicago Law Review* 55, 1–72.

1990, "Equality Theory, Marital Rape, and the Promise of the Fourteenth Amendment," *Florida Law Review* 42, 45–79.

Wildavsky, Aaron B. 1979, *Speaking Truth to Power: the Art and Craft of Policy Analysis*, Boston, MA: Little and Brown.

Williams, Melissa S. 1998, *Voice, Trust and Memory: Marginalized Groups and the Failure of Liberal Representation*, Princeton, NJ: Princeton University Press.

Wing, Adrien Katherine (ed.) 1997, *Critical Race Feminism: a Reader*, New York: New York University Press.

Witte, John F. 2000, *The Market Approach to Education: an Analysis of America's First Voucher Program*, Princeton, NJ: Princeton University Press.

Yamamoto, Eric K. 1999, *Interracial Justice: Conflict and Reconciliation in Post-Civil Rights America*, New York: New York University Press.

Young, Iris Marion 1989, "Polity and Group Difference: a Critique of the Ideal of Universal Citizenship," *Ethics* 99, 250–274.

1990, *Justice and the Politics of Difference*, Princeton, NJ: Princeton University Press.

1997, *Intersecting Voices: Dilemmas of Gender, Political Philosophy, and Policy*, Princeton, NJ: Princeton University Press.

1999, "State, Civil Society, and Social Justice," in Shapiro and Hacker-Cordón, pp. 141–162.

Yuval-Davis, Nira 1997, *Gender and Nation*, London: Sage Publications.

Yuval-Davis, Nira and Anthias, Floya (eds.) 1989, *Woman–Nation–State*, London: Macmillan.

Zuhur, Sherifa 2001, "The Mixed Impact of Feminist Struggles in Egypt during the 1990s," *Middle East Review of International Affairs (MERIA)* 5, on-line <http://meria.biu.ac.il>.

CASE LAW AND LEGISLATION

UNITED STATES

Board of Education of Kiryas Joel v. Grumet, 512 US 687 (1994).

Bob Jones University v. United States, 461 US 574 (1983).

Braunfeld v. Brown, 366 US 599 (1961).

City of Boerne v. Flores, 521 US 507 (1997).

Employment Division, Department of Human Resources of Oregon v. Smith, 494 US 872 (1990).

In re *Gault*, 378 US 1 (1967).

Geduldig v. Aiello, 417 US 484 (1974).

Goldman v. Weinberger, 475 US 503 (1986).

Lemon v. Kurtzman, 411 US 192 (1973).

Lyng v. Northwestern Indian Cemetery Protective Association, 485 US 439 (1988).

Miller v. Albright, 523 US 420 (1998).

Mississippi Band of Choctaw Indians v. Holyfield, 490 US 30 (1989).

Mozert v. Hawkins County Board of Education, 827 F.2d 1058 (6th Cir. 1987), cert. denied, 484 US 1066 (1988).

Ohio Civil Rights Commission v. Dayton Christian Schools, 477 US 619 (1985).

Parkinson v. J. & S. Tool Company, 313 A.2d 609 (1974).

Perez v. Brownell, 356 US 44 (1958).

Reynolds v. United States, 98 US 145 (1878).

Santa Clara Pueblo v. Martinez, 436 US 49 (1978).

Sherbert v. Verner, 374 US 398 (1963).

Wisconsin v. Yoder, 406 US 205 (1972).

Indian Child Welfare Act of 1978 (ICWA), 25 USC §1901–1963 (1994).

Religious Freedom Restoration Act of 1993 (RFRA), 42 USC §2000bb (1994).

New York Domestic Relations Law, McKinney 2000.

American Uniform Marriage and Divorce Act (UMDA).

CANADA

Barry v. Garden River Ojibway Nation 14 [1997] 4 CNLR 28 (Ont. C.A.).

Bliss v. Attorney General of Canada [1979] 1 SCR 183.

Canada (Attorney General) v. *Lavell; Richard Isaac* v. *Ivonne Bédard* [1974] SCR
  1349.
Native Women's Association of Canada (NWAC) v. *Canada* [1994] 3 SCR 627.
R. v. *Morin* (1995) 101 CCC (3d) 124 (Sask. C.A.).
R. v. *Moses* (1992) 71 CCC (3d) 347 (YT Terr. Ct.).
An Act to Amend the Indian Act (Bill C-31), RSC 1985, c. 32 (1st Supp.).
Ontario Family Law Act, RSO 1990, c. F.3.
Divorce Act, RSC 1985, c. 3 (2nd Supp.).

INDIA

Mary Roy v. *State of Kerala*, AIR 1986 SC 1011.
Mohd. Ahmed Khan v. *Shah Bano Begum*, AIR 1985 SC 945.
S. Mahendran v. *Secretary, Travancore Devaswom Board*, AIR 1993 Ker. 42.
State of Bombay v. *Narasu Appa Mali*, AIR 1952 Bom. 84.
Code of Criminal Procedure Act, 1973.
Constitution of India 1950.
Dissolution of Muslim Marriage Act, 1939.
Hindu Adoption and Maintenance Act, 1956.
Hindu Marriage Act, 1955.
Hindu Minority and Guardianship Act, 1956.
Hindu Succession Act, 1956.
Indian Christian Marriage Act, 1872.
Indian Divorce Act, 1869.
Muslim Women's (Protection of Rights on Divorce) Act, 1986.
Parsi Marriage and Divorce Act, 1936.
Special Marriage Act, 1954.

INDONESIA

Supreme Court No. 435K/Kr/1979, *Yurisprudensi Indonesia*, vol. II, 1981, p. 28.
Supreme Court No. 338K/Pid/1991, *Varia Peradilan* 1997, p. 35.
National Marriage Act, 1974.
Religious Courts Act, 1989.

ISRAEL

CA 3077/90 *Plonit* v. *Ploni*, 49 (2) PD 578.
HC 1000/92 *Bavli* v. *Rabbinical High Court*, 48 (2) PD 221.
Adoption of Children Law, 1981, 35 LSI 360.
Capacity and Guardianship Law, 1962, 16 LSI 106.
Dayanim Law, 1955, 9 LSI 74.
Druze Religious Courts Law, 1963, 17 LSI 27.
Q'adis Law, 1961, 15 LSI 123.
Rabbinical Courts Jurisdiction (Marriage and Divorce) Law, 1953, 7 LSI 139.
Spouses (Property Relations) Law, 1973, 27 LSI 313.
Succession Law, 1965, 10 LSI 101.
Women's Equal Rights Law, 1951, 5 LSI 171.

KENYA

African Christina Marriage and Divorce Act (ACMDA) (Cap. 151).
Hindu Marriage and Divorce Act (HMDA) (Cap. 157).
Mohammeddan Marriage and Divorce Act (MMDA) (Cap. 156).

MALAYSIA

Mansjur v. *Kamariah* [1988] 3 MLJ xliv (Federal Territorial Appeal Board).
Rokiah v. *Mohd. Idris* [1989] 3 MLJ ix (Federal Territorial Appeal Board).
Islamic Family Law (Federal Territories) Act 1984.
Islamic Family Law (Federal Territories) (Amendment) Act 1994.

SOUTH AFRICA

Amod v. *Multilateral Motor Vehicle Accidents (MMVA) Fund*, 1999 4 SA 1319 (SCA).
Ryland v. *Edros* 1997 (1) BCLR 77.

UNITED NATIONS (HUMAN RIGHTS COMMITTEE)

Sandra Lovelace v. *Canada*, 36 UN GOAR Supp. (No. 40) Annex XVIII; UN Doc. A/36/40 (1981).

Index